Heartland of the
Imagination

Heartland of the Imagination

Conservative Values in American Literature from Poe to O'Connor to Haruf

JEFFREY J. FOLKS

McFarland & Company, Inc., Publishers
Jefferson, North Carolina, and London

ISBN 0-7864-5976-6
softcover : 50# alkaline paper ∞

LIBRARY OF CONGRESS CATALOGUING DATA ARE AVAILABLE

British Library cataloguing data are available

© 2012 Jeffrey J. Folks. All rights reserved

No part of this book may be reproduced or transmitted in any form or by any means, electronic or mechanical, including photocopying or recording, or by any information storage and retrieval system, without permission in writing from the publisher.

Front cover design by David K. Landis
(Shake It Loose Graphics)

Manufactured in the United States of America

*McFarland & Company, Inc., Publishers
Box 611, Jefferson, North Carolina 28640
www.mcfarlandpub.com*

To Nancy
"One man loved the pilgrim soul in you" — W.B. Yeats

Contents

Preface   1

Introduction   5

1. Poe and the Cogito   33
2. Poe and Lindsay, Literary Outcasts   51
3. Vachel Lindsay's Covenant with America   73
4. Agee and Dostoevsky: Two Writers Possessed   89
5. Flannery O'Connor's Conservatism: A Reading of *The Violent Bear It Away*   113
6. Naipaul's Turn in the American South   136
7. The Fiction of Kent Haruf   155

Epilogue: The Dialect of the Tribe   173
Works Cited   195
Index   201

Preface

Many years ago I arrived at that "singular and final" moment so powerfully evoked by Whittaker Chambers in his great autobiography, *Witness*: crossing from a life of confusion and indecision to one of earnest independence and belief. For many years now, my interest has been focused on conservative writers of the kind represented in this book. I have been particularly interested in writing that presents the heartland, broadly interpreted, as an alternative to the expanding secularism and materialism of modern Western culture. These conservative writers from the American South, the Midwest, and, in the case of V.S. Naipaul, the Caribbean, are keenly aware of the importance of preserving a civilization of individual responsibility, intellectual tolerance, and coherent values. In their varied portraits of traditional communities under attack by modernity, ranging from Flannery O'Connor's Georgia to Vachel Lindsay's Illinois to Kent Haruf's Colorado and beyond, these fiction writers are responding to the same menacing revolution in contemporary values and thought that has troubled conservative thinkers from Edmund Burke to Michael Oakeshott.

In this book I begin with Edgar Allan Poe because he was the most important precursor of the conservative imagination in American literature. In his harrowing portraits of perversity and evil, Poe was strongly influenced by the nation's conservative religious origins. Yet Poe was no puritan: in his narrative evocations of the economic possibilities and expansive ambitions of the young nation, Poe suggested the dynamic potential of American capitalism.

Not surprisingly, Poe served as a major influence on the career of Vachel Lindsay, a writer who shared Poe's vision of the potential of a conservative culture in the New World. As for Flannery O'Connor, a fundamentally Christian ethic of compassion and moderation informs her writing. Set against a universe of moral chaos is the strength and commitment of characters like Old Tarwater in *The Violent Bear It Away*. More so than has been realized by some of her recent critics, O'Connor explored the political conflicts playing out in the South and in America as a whole. A mature reading of her fiction, work produced in the midst of extraordinary crisis and change, must acknowledge her keen awareness of the political nature of man. Always cautious and restrained by temperament, Flannery O'Connor allied her writing with a conservative ethos of faith and humility.

V.S. Naipaul, with whom I deal in Chapter Six, challenges citizens of Western democracies to recognize the value embodied in their own traditions and to consider the limitations of those cultures in which individual rights and liberties may be far less secure. Naipaul finds an escape from such limitations by way of the "universal civilization" that emerged as a result of the spread of classical–Christian civilization and that has now been institutionalized, often in a secularized form, throughout much of the developing world. This civilization corresponds in large measure to the bourgeois culture of democratic capitalism that Michael Novak has brilliantly analyzed in *The Spirit of Democratic Capitalism*.

As suggested earlier in the case of Naipaul, identification with the imaginative heartland extends well beyond writing from the geographical heartland of the United States, nor does every resident writer of the heartland embrace conservatism. A striking example is the contrast between James Agee and Fyodor Dostoyevsky. Although Dostoyevsky's "heartland" was, of course, quite different from that of the American writers whom I consider in this book, his defense of orthodoxy suggests a moral perspective similar to those faced by American and European conservatives. By contrast, James Agee, whose parents hailed from the Midwest and the South, adopted the radically secular and materialistic ethos of modernism, and in doing so he set himself against the inherited traditions of his family and region. The final writer whom I consider in this book, Kent Haruf, represents a return to sanity. He is keenly aware of the potential damage to life resulting from a faithless and cynical modern culture. Indeed, among all of the writers dealt with in this book,

Preface

Haruf seems to reflect most explicitly upon the need for prudence and caution in relation to what he views as a deeply confused public culture.

As human beings within the classical–Christian tradition have done for millennia, conservative writers of the Americas have labored to study, interpret, and transmit a redemptive body of knowledge and belief. In doing so, they have bequeathed a narrative record of remarkable intellectual journeys, and in reflecting upon these journeys we may gain insight and inspiration. Among these journeys was that of the late Lewis P. Simpson, the scholar who first guided me toward the study of American literature as the beneficiary of an inherited tradition of values and beliefs. The place of the heartland within Western civilization as a whole and the role of religious experience within that civilization were matters that were never far from Simpson's mind. Through a career spanning a half century and including now classic books such as *The Man of Letters in New England and the South* and *The Dispossessed Garden*, Simpson brought an untiring moral seriousness to the task of criticism. His work opened up avenues of thought for generations of critics to explore further. In the last of his books, *The Fable of the Southern Writer*, Simpson wrote that with the rapidly changing culture of our young nation, "each American has had the generational experience of being displaced in time" (232)—a phenomenon that he viewed as both destructive and yet somehow essentially "American." Having been born in a time and place little removed from the western frontier and having lived long enough to witness the attacks of September 11, Simpson must surely have experienced this sense of displacement himself. Yet in the work of a great artist or critic, Simpson realized, there is enduring wisdom that transcends change. As his understanding of the place of America within the broader civilization of the West matured, aided in part by his careful reading of the work of his colleague for a time at Louisiana State University, Eric Voegelin, Simpson explored the traditions of belief that for millennia had helped to check that sense of displacement. In my own study of American culture, now spanning forty years, I have gained from Simpson's profound reading of America's place within classical–Christian civilization and, to the best of my ability, attempted to emulate his splendid example.

PREFACE

The singular and final moment that I mentioned at the beginning of this Preface altered my approach to reading, and it led me to publish, among other places, in the conservative journal *Modern Age*. I will be forever grateful to Dr. George A. Panichas, its former editor, for his encouragement and advice at a pivotal moment in my career. I am grateful as well to the many colleagues and students at Doshisha University with whom I first discussed some of the ideas in this book. Likewise, Doshisha made possible the presentation of versions of several chapters at national and international conferences.

As in all I have undertaken, my greatest debt here is to my wife, Nancy, who has listened to everything before it was set down, read it in several revisions after it was written, and, I fear, can only anticipate more of the same now that this writing has appeared in book form and other work has begun. For her wise counsel and enduring love, I am indeed grateful.

* * *

I am grateful to the editors of *Modern Age* and *Southern Literary Journal* for permission to reprint essays that first appeared in their pages. These essays include:

"Poe and the Cogito," © 2009 by *The Southern Literary Journal* and the University of North Carolina at Chapel Hill Department of English. Reprinted with permission. All rights reserved.

"Vachel Lindsay's Covenant with America," *Modern Age* 50.3 (2008): 320–30.

"The Kindness of Strangers: The Fiction of Kent Haruf," *Modern Age* 50.2 (2009): 118–27.

Introduction

"Men are free when they are in a living homeland, not when they are straying and breaking away." For a writer who seemingly spent most of his adult life "straying and breaking away," it is a remarkable admission, but perhaps D.H. Lawrence knew better than most whereof he spoke. His life was one of stateless exile, displaced from Britain and wandering for decades from southern Europe to Australia and Mexico and many places in between, yet Lawrence's career seems to have been the harbinger of a form of cultural nostalgia that would dominate much of Western writing in the following decades. It was this same sense of longing for an authentic, purposeful, vital homeland that underlay T.S. Eliot's insistence on the importance of tradition, the imperative of writing "with a feeling that the whole of the literature of Europe from Homer and within it the whole of the literature of his own country has a simultaneous existence and composes a simultaneous order" (72). The same longing for a homeland — a heartland, in all but name — pervaded the criticism of George Orwell, C.S. Lewis, F.R. Leavis, and Cleanth Brooks, each of very different critical temperament but in fundamental agreement, one would imagine, with Lawrence's codicil to the above statement: "Men are free when they are obeying some deep, inward voice of religious belief" (126).

To say that this impulse was nostalgic is not to diminish its importance nor to suggest that it was inauthentic. Those who are exiled from their true home must of necessity experience a strong sense of nostalgia, not, however, for a fantasized past but for the great prize that they know to have been lost: the reality of a meaningful and ordered existence devoted to a purposeful end. This sense of loss registers the decline of a

Introduction

coherent civilization — in the case of the West, the classical–Christian civilization of Europe — that formed the basis of a stable and ordered rationality and ethics. Though little of contemporary criticism seems capable of grasping the crucial importance of civilization in this sense, for millennia mankind has universally understood the importance of a shared, stable belief system grounded in aspiration toward excellence and virtue. Yet only quite recently, in the course of a few decades, have our intelligentsia become convinced that such a belief system is oppressive and that only in an ethos of radical personal autonomy in which there exists no shared ideals or aspirations or its polar opposite — faith in authoritarian systems of collectivism and egalitarianism — can liberation be found. Clearly, under such an illusion no one can dwell within a stable belief system or obey the dictates of any sort of humane rationality. One can only do as Lawrence himself did: wander in search of a longed-for homeland or, worse yet, abandon the search entirely and wallow in the smug assurance that no such homeland exists.

One could produce many books dealing with those who are floundering in that assurance, and much could be learned about the damage and confusion that their cynicism has engendered. Elsewhere, in a number of books and articles, I have written about the damage of just such a "culture of repudiation," but in this book I wish to focus on the conservative tradition itself as an alternative to those seemingly intractable forces of cynicism and doubt. For reasons that I will investigate in the following chapters, the concepts of refuge and homeland that have become increasingly appealing to a growing number of conservative writers and filmmakers. The idea of a sanctuary from the world of foreboding and danger, along with the myth of the hero who gains strength from withdrawal and who lives on to struggle in an uncompromising way for his values — these ideals are familiar not only in the conservative literature of the Americas but in the literature of other lands as well.

Numerous writers from the U.S. and Britain, and from nations beyond the Anglo-American circle, have sought refuge in what they identify as their own particular conservative heartland. Wordsworth, Coleridge, Poe, Hawthorne, C.S. Lewis, T.S. Eliot, Flannery O'Con-

Introduction

nor — the list of those seeking shelter from modernity and associating this shelter with some form of escape, whether geographical or cultural, is indeed impressive, so much so that the conception of writing as a journey to a spiritual or cultural heartland might be said to be the central preoccupation of letters in the past two centuries. For dozens of major figures, the heartland is an adopted if not literal home. Just one example will suffice for now. William Faulkner's cultural roots were far more cosmopolitan than his identification with his "little postage stamp of native soil" might suggest, but in adopting the persona of the localized north Mississippi writer, he was attaching his work to a conservative ethos that would concentrate his energies upon certain subjects and certain modes of thought, and to a great extent limit his emphasis on others. Like other great modernists of the twentieth century, Faulkner, at the beginning, was essentially a late romantic, but what was unique in his case was that over the course of his career the romantic elements, such as a belief in millennial perfectionism, were filtered through a realm of local and regional experience that was anything but romantic. It was inevitable that an increasing tension should appear in Faulkner's writing between the abstract simplicity of his romantic intellectual birthright and a complex realism arising from his actual experience. Because of the fact that in his case this local experience was so recently molded by the experience of the frontier and because of the awareness of war and occupation in his own region, the tension in Faulkner's work was unlike that of any other major modernist.

In the tension between the romantic ethos and the actual experience of a culture on the periphery of his civilization, Faulkner's career might be said to have resembled that of James Joyce. Certainly, Joyce's fiction reflected his own local background of conflict, occupation, extremism, and war, as well as an economic deprivation akin to that of the American frontier. But even in this Faulkner's temperament was quite different from that of Joyce, who ultimately seems to have embraced the romantic creed and turned his back on the experience of his local region. With Stephen Dedalus, Joyce fled history into the abstract world of the imagination and with a sweeping romantic declaration repudiated the experiential world. With Faulkner, the journey was just the opposite. Faulkner surrendered the artist's privileged position in favor of the truth of local experience and the reality of ordinary people. Although Faulkner continued to waver throughout his lifetime, there exists a clear distinction between Faulkner and the other major modernists. He was the most closely tied to his local experience, and that was his salvation.

One of the peculiarities of Faulkner's writing is that his complex employment of modernist technique was, almost exclusively, used to explore a consciousness that was essentially rural and agrarian. At the center of Faulkner's imagination is not the expatriate society of Hemingway, the urban society of Fitzgerald, or the tortured personal ambivalence of Wolfe: ultimately, despite the confusion of his early works and the complex interplay of different social classes and cultural perspectives, Faulkner's moral imagination can be seen as grounded in the classical–Christian civilization and, more particularly, in the Protestant middle-class culture that has thrived during the last three centuries in Western Europe and the United States. Faulkner was a fierce defender of the values of individual responsibility, personal honor, and self-respect. No matter how sophisticated his technique or widespread his reading and knowledge, for most readers Faulkner could never be mistaken for a writer who was working outside his regional culture, even if he could be understood as a good bit more than that.

In terms of a majority of the writers considered in this book, the idea of a place of refuge is associated with various distinctive regions of America, whether these be the South, the West, or the Midwest. These regional cultures, sometimes misrepresented as provincial, in fact constitute an American heartland that has faithfully preserved the traditions and ideals of the nation's founders. As Frederick Jackson Turner noted over a century ago, "if there is a sectionalism in the [United States], the sectionalism is Eastern. The old West, united to the new South, would produce, not a new sectionalism, but a new Americanism" (186). One thing that each of the regional cultures of the heartland has in common is deep rootedness in reformed Protestantism: the essential faith in the role of each individual in the mission of divine providence. Whether in the rhetoric of America's great political leaders, from George Washington to Abraham Lincoln to Ronald Reagan, or in the work of its theologians,

Introduction

philosophers, historians, or poets, the country's sustaining belief has always been rooted in the assurance of God's plan for a hopeful, purposive future. And while the conservative culture of the heartland continues to hold fast to this belief, there can be little doubt that coastal culture as represented by the elite universities, mainstream media, and federal political class has grown increasingly dismissive of this sustaining faith. Among modern writers, one need only contrast the moral emphasis in the work of heartland figures such as Thornton Wilder, Robert Penn Warren, Wright Morris, Saul Bellow, Flannery O'Connor, N. Scott Momaday, and William Stafford with the urban skepticism of John Steinbeck, Henry Miller, Norman Mailer, Allen Ginsberg, James Baldwin, and Adrienne Rich. The cultural divide continues in the twenty-first century, and a large number of contemporary names could be added to the lists on both sides of the cultural phenomenon that Gertrude Himmelfarb has termed "the Fourth Great Awakening." In the work of writers and public figures such as Leszek Kołakowski, Christopher Lasch, Richard Neuhaus, Leo Strauss, Isaiah Berlin, Daniel Patrick Moynihan, Václav Havel, and Pope John Paul II — admittedly a rather diverse group of thinkers — there seems ample ground for Himmelfarb's prediction of a great "moral awakening" (*One Nation, Two Cultures* 143) not only in the American heartland but throughout Western civilization.

I would like to think that my longstanding interest in the work of Elias Canetti, evident in this as in my previous books, also reflects a search for traditional structures of thought that might be brought to the interpretation of literature and culture. Underlying the scientific veneer of Canetti's great study of crowd behavior, *Crowds and Power*, there rests a passionate need to come to terms with the searing events of twentieth-century European history: two devastating world wars, a ruinous economic depression, the rise of fascism and communism, and the unprecedented horror of the Holocaust. All of these events touched Canetti's life directly and drove him to complete the body of work for which he was awarded the Nobel Prize in 1981. Born in Ruse, Bulgaria, on the banks of the Danube, educated in Vienna and Berlin, and residing for much of his adult life in London, Canetti was by no means a provincial writer living in a far-flung rural heartland. Nonetheless, his critique of fascist and communist totalitarianism and other horrors of our times is grounded in a cautious, conservative temperament. As he warns, the tyrant's "most fantastic triumphs have taken place in our own time, among people who set great store by the idea of humanity" (*Crowds* 468): that is, among the radical intellectuals who inhabit the cosmopolitan centers of Europe, Asia, and America. Quite tellingly, Canetti's forceful critique of fascism and communism manifests a moral revulsion identical in its origins, if not always in its conclusions, with that evident in much of conservative Anglo-American literature.

Likewise, the identification of Gertrude Himmelfarb's critique and that of her husband, Irving Kristol, with a contemporary Great Awakening within American heartland culture might seem a bit of a stretch, given that both Himmelfarb and Kristol have been lifelong denizens of the coastal region — Brooklyn and City University of New York no less, in her case — but that very incongruity demonstrates the extent and appeal within American culture of the conservative ethos. As I demonstrate in the case of Edgar Allan Poe, conservative writers may be drawn to the more traditional, less cosmopolitan regions and subcultures of America even if, as with Poe, the writer did not literally reside in the heartland. In the case of Poe, how could he have done so? The trans-Appalachian regions of the South and Midwest were only beginning to be settled in the years when Poe came of age. Despite the rapid growth that was to follow after 1840, at the time of Poe's birth the greater Mississippi valley had a population of only one million. The very term "heartland" did not come into use until a half-century after Poe's death, and even then it conveyed the dual meaning of heartland as geographical region and heartland as moral culture.

An understanding of conservatism is further complicated by the fact that an affinity for traditional values is hardly limited to American writers, in part because the origins of conservative American culture can be traced to a larger civilization that flourished in Europe, and particularly in Britain, prior to English settlement in North America and that has continued there to this day. It is also the case that American conservatism, since it has emerged as an independent cultural force, has exerted its own distinctive influence on global civilization outside the United

Introduction

States. As Himmelfarb put it in *The Roads to Modernity*: "Having derived a good deal of its own Enlightenment from the mother country, the United States is now repaying Britain by perpetuating the spirit of her Enlightenment" (232). Even the myth of heartland refuge replicates a foundational myth of European civilization — a conception of redemptive flight adapted from millennia of classical–Christian narratives stretching back to the accounts of Moses, Odysseus, Aeneas, and Dante and involving, more recently, the Puritan flight from Europe, a foundational myth of our young nation. As Flannery O'Connor wrote in a letter to Ted Spivey: "I think that what [God] began when Moses and the children of Israel left Egypt continues today in the Church and is meant to continue that way" (*Habit* 337). Perhaps this defense of an inherited civilization by way of flight from cultural innovation and religious apostasy involves something even more fundamental: the necessity of continuity itself, that much underrated virtue, as the basis of rationality and order within *any* civilization. In *The Closing of the American Mind*, Allan Bloom identified the human need to live within a definite culture, pointing out that "a man needs a place and opinions by which to orient himself.... The problem of getting along with outsiders is secondary to, and sometimes in conflict with, having an inside, a people, a culture, a way of life. A very great narrowness is not incompatible with the health of an individual or a people, whereas with great openness it is hard to avoid decomposition" (37).

I would argue that among conservative writers this need of "a place and opinions" is a preeminent matter. The fiction of Eudora Welty, a prominent writer who might well have been included among those discussed in this book, has often been approached by critics who stress the importance of her admission that "place" is "the lesser angel" in her imagination ("character" being the "greater" angel). However useful this mode of criticism, it has not always been concerned to ask just *why* a sense of place should be crucial or what Welty's admission of its importance reveals about her moral imagination. In Welty's case, the importance of place has to do with a concurrent sense of the vulnerability of existence. In this sense, place takes on the character of a refuge that her characters embrace or reject, to their advantage or regret. Those who reject the shelter of familiarity, continuity, and normality place themselves at hazard of violence of all sort, both at their own hands and at the hands of others. They are stepping outside protective codes of rationality and ethics, and, in doing so, they risk moral confusion, alienation, and even madness.

Isaiah Berlin, Leszek Kołakowski, Kenneth Minogue, and a number of other thinkers will be employed in this book to consider why it is that a heartland ethos should be so important to the writers whom I choose to consider. Bloom was not the only recent critic to claim that the conception of life as a moral quest, suggesting a defense of the moral imagination and if needed a redemptive flight from moral enslavement or corruption, may be located deep within the human psyche as a necessary structure of survival. As Russell Kirk wrote, "transcending the differences of culture and history and race and national frontiers, something that we may call the conservative impulse or the conservative yearning, does exist among all peoples. Without this instinct, any society would fall to pieces" (20). Kirk's traditional conservatism — conserving a particular civilization against unwarranted change, conserving a particular place or set of customs against overdevelopment or innovation — and Bloom's more psychologically grounded notion of the mental "need" for continuity of culture and environment are merely two examples drawn from a large body of conservative philosophical reflection stretching back to Edmund Burke and continuing through Michael Oakeshott and Leszek Kołakowski. Among the critics and philosophers in this conservative tradition are George Orwell, Raymond Aron, Sidney Hook, Jacques Maritain, Allen Tate, and Cleanth Brooks. The many creative writers who might be associated with this tradition of culture include William Wordsworth, Jane Austen, Charles Dickens, Henry James, Fyodor Dostoyevsky, Joseph Conrad, Robert Frost, T.S. Eliot, William Faulkner, C.S. Lewis, Czeslaw Milosz, Saul Bellow, Aleksander Solzhenitsyn, Philip Larkin, and V.S. Naipaul.

As one can see from the above lists, the conservative tradition, as I conceive it, is broad and eclectic. It is, however, no accident that conservative writers generally emerge from and choose to remain among a particular sort of moral culture and perhaps, if given the choice, within a particular sort of physical setting. One finds Edgar Allan Poe, whose

Introduction

editorial and publishing work necessitated his living in proximity to New York City, inhabiting a humble cottage in what was then the rural setting of Fordham, and in this cottage, occupied with his dying wife, Virginia, and his mother-in-law (also his aunt), Mrs. Maria Clemm, Poe, despite his impoverishment, conjured up a chimera of happiness, even of ideality. In the same way, returning from the New York metropolitan area to her mother's farm outside Milledgeville, Georgia, first as a consequence of medical necessity but then embraced freely, Flannery O'Connor, one of America's most important conservative writers, found that the return to what she viewed as normality had spared her a lifetime of false starts. Similarly, V.S. Naipaul made his way from Trinidad to Oxford and London, eventually settling in the rural western counties of England in which there exist remnants, at least, of a coherent agrarian tradition.

From the perspective of the heartland, whether literal or imagined, the cosmopolitan center often seems a place of delusion and enslavement. No writer in English expressed the need for flight from urban degradation more vividly than did John Bunyan, and it is hardly coincidental that *Pilgrim's Progress*, along with the Bible, should have been the overwhelming bestseller of America's first century of nationhood. The moral allegory of Bunyan's writing was perfectly in tune with the Protestant religious temper of the conservative heartland. His hero's flight from the City of Destruction into a daunting wilderness in search of religious freedom and moral purity expressed the aspirations of America's Puritan founders as well as those of a large segment of the nineteenth-century population inspired by the second Great Awakening. In fact, Pilgrim's virtues mirror the typical qualities of Anglo-Saxon morality as defined by F.A. Hayek: "Independence and self-reliance, individual initiative and local responsibility, the successful reliance on voluntary activity, noninterference with one's neighbor and tolerance of the different and queer, respect for custom and tradition, and a healthy suspicion of power and authority" (235). These same virtues are universally celebrated as the ideals of conservative culture.

In contrast, the millennialist ambitions of the urban intelligentsia seem an assault upon the life-affirming traditions cherished in the heartland. In pursuit of their goals, again and again the intelligentsia have

INTRODUCTION

resorted to methods that involve censorship, manipulation, and violence. Stalinism and Nazism both began as socialist movements that promised justice and equality, but they soon enforced the most restrictive standards of correctness intended to safeguard the rule of despots. It is worth recalling that it was among conservative traditionalists — men such as Dietrich Bonhoeffer and Aleksandr Solzhenitsyn — that the staunchest and most courageous opposition to both Hitler and Stalin were to be found. By contrast, as M. Stanton Evans has demonstrated in his insightful history of the McCarthy era, it was the liberal intelligentsia that was willing to compromise with communist authoritarianism and in many cases to actively advance its interests. As Evans writes of these elitists, "To many already afflicted with anomie and dark misgivings, the economic/political crisis of the age looked like the coup de grace for traditional views and customs. The supposedly ironclad theories of Marx and Lenin and alleged wonders of Soviet planning were thought to have the answers no longer provided by the older culture" (64). Since the conservative writer had not given up on the "older culture," he had little use for the theories of Lenin or Marx, nor for those of other corrosive and adversarial theorists who would come later. The heartland was simply not so credulous as to believe that a distant central authority, based on a speculative and abstract logic of egalitarianism, remote from and ignorant of the actual lives of the citizenry, could be trusted to deliver the promised utopia. Rather, it would seem likely that all that can come of Marxism is poverty and enslavement, and such has been the result in every case where it has been tried.

* * *

"Refuge" is an English word derived from *refugere* ("to escape") and *fugere* ("to flee"). But to escape from what; to flee from whom? In the context of the past two hundred years in the West, the answer can be suggested by considering a few of the classic oppositions of culture: those between city and country, between innovation and tradition, between Marxism and capitalism, and between atheism and religious faith. Although their individual tendencies and needs have varied widely, Western writers seeking refuge in the heartland — that place of security and solace, more often imaginary than real — have looked to nature for solace, have found themselves defending property rights and tradition, and have held to or adopted religious modes of belief. In most cases, their chosen status as refugees has been motivated by the knowledge that these same proclivities have been endangered by the force of secularization and modernity.

Few writers have so eloquently pleaded the case for the damage of modernity and the need for resistance as has V.S. Naipaul. As a novelist, a critic, and the author of a number of incisive travel narratives, Naipaul has explored the contemporary sense of an age "surfeited with news, culturally far more confused [than the "bourgeois" era of the past], threatening again to be as full of tribal or folk movement as during the centuries of the Roman Empire" (*New York Review of Books* 4 March 1999; qtd. in French 239). In response to this confused era of decline into tribalism, an era in which salvational ideologies have resorted to the most barbaric means of "rescuing" the oppressed, Naipaul looks to what he sometimes calls the "universal civilization," an ethical civilization grounded in classical–Christian civilization but supple enough to gain adherents on a global scale. This adaptable civilization, based on general ethical and legal principles rather than narrow dogma, promotes the fundamental Western virtues of "do unto others," "the pursuit of happiness," and respect for the individual. As Naipaul wrote in the *New York Review of Books* (31 January 1991): "So much is contained in it: the ideal of the individual, responsibility, choice, the life of the intellect, the idea of vocation and perfectibility and achievement" (qtd. in French 448).

Although some might argue with the notion of a triumphal classical–Christian civilization displacing other, more "narrow" cultures, Naipaul challenges us to recognize the value embodied in the former civilization and to consider realistically the limitations of those non–Western cultures in which individual rights and liberties may be constrained by authoritarian rule, tribal oppression, clericalism, or public corruption. It is perhaps curious that Naipaul finds the only escape from such limitations — limitations often associated with tribal or religious fanaticism — in a "universal civilization" that emerged in large part as a result of the dominance of the classical civilization of Greece and Rome and the Judeo-Christian tradition within Western Europe and North America. Certainly this tradition involves its own instances of fanaticism, yet Naipaul's vision is focused not on the indisputable failings of the Western past but on the much broader, "awakened" global civilization that has emerged from it. It is important to pay close attention to the inclusive nature of Naipaul's ideas and to understand that the revitalized civilization he sees derived from Western thought may just as well blossom in Shanghai or Mumbai as in London or New York. As Naipaul points out, that powerful idea of "the pursuit of happiness," an idea rooted in the rule of law, personal freedom, and respect for property rights, has a profound appeal to human beings everywhere. Originating within the classical–Christian tradition of Western thought, the pursuit of happiness is an idea that is now embedded in the legal codes and political institutions of many nations.

This virtuous society is inextricably bound to an optimistic ethos of free-market capitalism which is, in turn, integrally connected to a traditional conception of the nuclear family. It is hardly surprising that property rights and the nuclear family should be two of the most important elements of conservative identity, though perhaps the centrality and relatedness of these elements have not been as widely understood as they ought to be. In *The Spirit of Democratic Capitalism*, Michael Novak has demonstrated that family attachment is, in fact, the primary engine of economic development within democratic capitalist societies. As Novak writes: "Insofar as democratic capitalism depends for its economic vitality upon deferred gratification, savings, and long-term investment, no motive for such behavior is the equivalent of regard for the future welfare of one's own progeny" (163). Given this fact, the alteration of the contours of family life that come with a loosening of the definition of family structure and an increased dependence of families on government support can be expected to diminish the prosperity and well-being of society. More important, dependence entails an assault on human liberties. As Kenneth Minogue points out, "the poor and the dependent ... are the lever by which governments accumulate power over everyone, dependent and independent alike" (*Politics* 117). To which one must add, public health, environment, education, and correctness of opinion now serve

Introduction

as further "levers" to support the expansion of government powers and limitations of human liberty.

In the case of nearly every writer considered in this book, "refuge" implies a flight from the repressive centralization of government associated with a bureaucratic culture hostile to the family. The need to defend the traditional family and to defend liberty has become all the more pronounced since the rise of socialist states in Europe and the Americas following the first World War. Thus, one prominent conservative author, William Faulkner, dramatizes the conflict between the unsettling force of modernity and the traditionalism of his region. The central thrust of works such as *Go Down, Moses, Light in August, Absalom, Absalom!*, and *Requiem for a Nun* may be said to be the need to make sense of a rapidly changing modernity in the terms that Faulkner inherited from the religious, ethical, and social traditions of his civilization. Moreover, the danger to inherited belief systems, as Faulkner intuited, lay not just in the militarism of the Axis powers or in Soviet communism but also in the statist ambitions of liberal administrations in America itself. Faulkner's writing from the 1930s makes explicit the depths of his concern. In voicing this concern, Faulkner set himself against the prevailing political fashions of the day, but he also recognized that the origins of contemporary statism lay in a long tradition of radical intellectualism. Faulkner's rural persona, his conservative distrust of government centralization and planning, his localism and patriotism, his deep passion for the outdoors, and his inherited sense of the sanctity of family are all set against the abstract idealism, universalism, and utopianism of the liberal intelligentsia. Both in terms of their moral imagination and the conduct of their personal affairs, there is probably no more pronounced contrast than that between Faulkner (1897–1962) and Bertolt Brecht (1898–1956), a writer who was nearly an exact contemporary but whose "harsh, hard, heartless, cynical, part-gangster, part-sports-hearty" intellectualism (Johnson 175) must be viewed as diametrically opposed to the essentially traditionalist tenor of Faulkner's writing. It is inconceivable that either Brecht or his admiring audiences could ever appreciate the ethical perspective of a writer whose major protagonists include the ultra-traditional survivalist Isaac McCaslin or the bumbling, backwoodsy Christian fun-

Introduction

damentalist Byron Bunch. In the contrast between these writers one grasps the clash of cultures that has fueled the rise of modern conservatism.

Clearly related to the defense of individual liberty is the fact that conservatives tend to define themselves as common men and women, ordinary citizens, and mainstream Americans in contrast to the economic, social, and cultural elitism of coastal culture. On the other side of the Atlantic, George Orwell was very much a defender of this sense of the right of common men and women to lead their lives free of the control of the cultural elite. As he wrote in a review of Cyril Connolly's novel, *The Rock Pool*: "The fact to which we have got to cling, as to a lifebelt, is that it is possible to be a normal decent person and yet to be fully alive" (qtd. in Podhoretz 57). Conservative suspicion of the intelligentsia exists for the quite proper reason that the cultural innovation advocated by the elite, projected via an ever more aggressive attack on traditional belief structures, threatens the necessary continuity of life still cherished by conservatives. As Ludwig Wittgenstein, a philosopher imbued with deeply conservative instincts, once wrote: it is more important to pursue "the understanding that consists in seeing connections" (qtd. in Monk 308) than to open up radically new directions of abstract understanding. In retrospect, Wittgenstein's philosophy may be seen to have entailed a rejection of cultural innovation. As he wrote in proposition number 344 in *On Certainty*, "My *life* consists in my being content to accept many things" (44e). It is precisely the wisdom of "accept[ing] many things" that is at issue in the contemporary cultural divide: on the right, the wisdom of faith and family seems self-apparent, while on the left one hears only the reflexive mantra of "Question Authority."

Those who seek refuge in the heartland tend to be motivated by a life-affirming religious impulse that is associated with acceptance of this kind. As Roger Scruton puts it, "The essence of the religious life [is] not progress and experiment, but the journey back to the place that protects us" (*Gentle Regrets* 237). Though quite varied in their denominational affiliations, what these traditionalists seek, first and foremost, is the survival of their religious and ethical values — the vital connection with the past that the ruling cultural elite seems most determined to deny them —

Introduction

and at the heart of these values lies the Judeo-Christian belief in the goodness of creation. This simple but immensely powerful principle implies any number of corollaries: the sanctity of life, a purposeful and hopeful conception of history, the principle of human dominion and stewardship of the earth, and the positive virtue of self-reliance and work. Along with these beliefs, given the assurance of the goodness of original creation and the teleological shape of history, there exists a strong sense of the virtue of continuity and a skepticism regarding change. As George Panichas writes: "Continuity, as *sacra historia*, recognizes a hierarchic structure, affirms universals, dramatizes ascent and aspiration, sanctifies causal relationships" (5). The conception of the goodness of creation also suggests a number of points of resistance to modernist and postmodernist culture: rejection of cultural relativism, skepticism concerning multiculturalism and feminism, aversion to welfare socialism, dissent from nihilism and anarchism in any form, and revulsion at assaults on religious freedom in the name of civil liberties.

It is naïve to imagine that these overriding cultural divisions are not reflected in our literature and media. It is perhaps only because literature is most often mediated by the elite culture that the interests of the conservative majority receive so little support in our academic criticism even as, in the literature and film itself, conservatism finds expression not only in a vast culture of explicitly Christian writing — for example, in the mega-bestseller *The Purpose-Driven Life* by Rick Warren or in Mel Gibson's highly successful film *The Passion of the Christ* — but also in more mainstream works such as the classic films of Alfred Hitchcock ("the last Catholic director," as he has been called) or the Nobel Prize–winning fiction of V.S. Naipaul. Gazing upon the prevailing secular culture, the conservative writer cannot help but view it as "grotesque." The secular culture that is granted implicit assent within the national media and within academe is generally hostile to religious faith and, in fact, to the bases for moral order of any kind. As Irving Kristol put it, "The ethos of our current counterculture is ... the ethos of a carnival. It is cynical, nihilistic, and exploitative; it is candidly sensationalistic and materialistic" (146). The carnivalistic quality of modern culture has even been made to seem a virtue by a series of postmodern critics reaching back for their inspiration to Mikhail Bakhtin, but among conservative writers it is seen for what it is: an instrument of assault on the essential sustaining point of faith, a belief in the goodness of life.

* * *

It is not simply "escape" that our conservative refugees are seeking. More often, their goal is a cultural stronghold from which to defend an inherited civilization until such time as it might be rekindled and restored. Their destination ought not be viewed as a survivalist bastion, or the clandestine abode of a saving remnant — though there are certainly some who have thought of it in these terms — but rather as a temporary shelter where civilization might be preserved and passed down. In the memory of each of the writers discussed in this book is the knowledge that classical–Christian civilization has been threatened before and that time and again it has been rescued. For American writers, the preeminent example of this redemptive flight was the removal of a small band of Puritan saints from England to the Netherlands, and from there, for some at least, to a perilous wilderness on the North American continent. As Clinton Rossiter stressed, the Puritan origin has shaped the nation's moral imagination as "American democracy has been and remains a highly moral adventure" (*The Roots of American Order* 3rd ed.; qtd. in Kirk 78). Yet America is not by any means the only nation to embrace this conception of its founding as an act of religious or ethical preservation. The archetypal event of this sort and the model for all Western conceptions of its own as a moral adventure was the biblical flight of the Hebrew people from Egypt. This mythic conception of the defense of one's civilization is repeated again and again in the course of our history, from the flight of Aeneas from Troy, preserving the original civilization that would serve as the basis of Roman identity, to the bracing words of Churchill's "beaches and hills" oratory at the moment of gravest danger during World War II. Flight is a moral act and is morally active: it is a principled retreat after which one may regroup and renew the struggle.

One must flee to an imagined realm of safety, and of sanity, because among the faithful there is the recognition of the moral superiority of the heartland in relation to a declining and apostate national culture.

Introduction

Within the national culture, materialism, secularism, and hedonism prevail, displacing the more virtuous society conceived by the Founders. As Himmelfarb wrote in surveying the effects of the revolutionary spirit of the 1960s, the counterculture "liberated a good many people from those values — virtues, as they were once called — that had a stabilizing, socialized, and moralizing effect on society" (*One Nation, Two Cultures* 18). It has often been remarked that the fundamental aims of the Constitution of the United States — to "establish Justice, insure domestic Tranquility, provide for the common defence, promote the general Welfare, and secure the Blessings of Liberty to ourselves and our posterity" — are the reflection of an ethical civilization that prized order, moderation, liberty, and self-sufficiency above all. These same virtues continue to be prized within conservative culture, if not within the nation as a whole. The ethical thrust of the Constitution was precisely the opposite of that implied by statism: to protect the welfare of the citizenry against the tyrannous expansion of government power. The Framers considered their work, above all, to be moral in nature, for they were attempting to protect human liberty from the encroachment of absolutism as well as from the anarchy resulting from the rivalry of factions. They also considered theirs to be a religious endeavor, for they were devising a system of government that corresponded to an understanding of what they knew to be a divinely created human nature. That nature, as the Founders perceived, manifested an unquenchable thirst for liberty and a godlike quality of ambition and creativity. The Constitution that they produced was "worldly" in its recognition of the rights of private property, personal liberty, and free enterprise, but it was at the same time inspired by the knowledge that the new nation was the product of an ancient religious civilization.

Certainly, the ends of justice and liberty enshrined in the Constitution must be contrasted with the quite different sense of liberty, equality, and fraternity celebrated in the documents of the French Revolution. Nobody ever analyzed the opposing sense of rights underlying these different revolutions more clearly than Edmund Burke. In his *Reflections on the Revolution in France*, he distinguished the "*real* rights of men," which he specified and defended adamantly, with the "false claims of right" advanced by the social revolutionaries in France. The real rights centered on the "advantages" of civil society—justice, opportunity and profit, inherited property, free enterprise, and freedom from confiscatory taxation. Inimical to these real rights are those false rights "which are absolutely repugnant to [civil society]" (441), among which is the presumed right of a man to be "judge in his own cause" and with this the fraudulent right to pursue free will, personal justice, or equality "by any means necessary," as one would say today. This mean, divisive, and anarchic assertion of false rights emanated from a radical denial of the fact that human nature, including the "destructive passions" that government must guard against, is the product of divine creation. Civil society does not rest on a contract that can be broken but on a recognition of the proper aspirations and needs of human beings everywhere and on the right of human beings to proper government.

The origins of American political thought are too complex to be discussed here in any detail, but it is fair to say that the cautious, sensible, worldly culture underlying the thinking of Burke, Hume, Smith, and Locke, among others, played a decisive role in the conception of the American system of government. Central to this tradition of thought was the realization that real rights must be protected not only from tyrannous authority but from the anarchistic force of false rights, including the claim of equality. In doing so, government protects the God-given right to exert one's abilities and to train, nourish, and otherwise promote the abilities of one's progeny to the best of one's ability. As the work of the Constitution demonstrates, the Founders understood that real rights must always be defended by a strong system of checks and balances. Even then, they feared that this system would not be enough, given the allure of false rights and the incitements of demagogues.

One does not look to creative literature for an explication of constitutional law or history, but for the conservative imagination the American Constitution and the common law tradition provide a basis for conceptualizing rationality and ethics. The emphasis on justice and personal dignity in Poe's stories connects his writing with a larger civilization, the same classical–Christian heritage to which the Framers referred in their deliberations. Many decades later, Naipaul's conception of the universal civilization reflected a profound understanding of the necessity of

Introduction

shared tradition and of the virtues of the Western tradition in particular.

* * *

The mythic conception of refuge within either an imagined or literal heartland assumes, of course, that there exists a particular civilization that one intends to preserve and about which one feels passionately enough to risk one's interest, if not one's life, in the attempt. As a preservation of civilization, refuge points toward a return that will reintroduce conservative values to the nation as a whole. In terms of the opposition between modernity and tradition, what is preserved is an inherited body of knowledge and belief whose continuity, as opposed to the innovative and unsettling qualities of modern culture, is seen as redemptive in and of itself. It is in this vein, for example, that James Bowman speaks of the "honor culture" that has fallen into disrepute in the West with the rise of a more rationalistic, secularized, relativistic culture. In the course of his extraordinary "history" of honor, Bowman comes to see that the honor culture, as part of a broader civilization of faith and purpose, may be necessary to the survival of the West — that, "in fact, the culture of our governing elites is woefully, even fatally, inadequate to the demands that will eventually be placed upon it without some return to a sense of honor in the old-fashioned sense" (290).

In this book I begin with Edgar Allan Poe, not because he was a citizen of the "heartland" in a literal sense but because he was the most important precursor of the heartland imagination in American literature. Even as he spent most of his adult life in the northern cities of New York and Philadelphia, Poe's literary imagination, as well as the audience for which he was writing, may be located outside of the cosmopolitan centers. His fiction portrayed life in the South and West as a model of freedom and opportunity, if not always of perfection, just as it often revealed the urban centers as locales of crime, poverty, and despair. In several of his works, including *The Journal of Julius Rodman*, his fictionalized travel memoir predicated on a Lewis and Clark–style journey through the American West, the grandeur and potential of the heartland were fully on display. The possibility of refuge within a conservative rural culture is also suggested in a number of Poe's more romantic and idealized stories, including "Eleonora" and "Landor's Cottage," as well as several of the stories set in the mid–Atlantic region and the Carolinas, but it is attested perhaps even more emphatically in Poe's correspondence regarding his hopes for a publishing venture predicated on his long-planned "quality" magazine, *The Stylus*. For most of his career, a lifetime of dependence on intermittent editorial work and poorly paying freelancing (he sold "The Raven," for example, for fifteen dollars), Poe contemplated the magazine project that might reward him with wealth and fame. He attempted to bring the project to fruition first by way of an unsuccessful bid to purchase the subscription lists of the *Southern Literary Messenger*, then by the sale of private subscriptions to acquaintance in the South and West, and finally by securing the financial backing of Edward H.N. Patterson, a newspaper publisher from Oquawka, Iowa.

Unfortunately, Poe died before ever setting forth on his journey to St. Louis, where Patterson had proposed meeting on October 15, 1849. *The Stylus* was to have been the venue in which Poe would have published the best that the young nation could produce. It might also have sealed Poe's affiliation with the South and West, and his alienation from the cosmopolitan centers of the Northeast, bringing into alliance with the heartland a writer, editor, and critic of great imaginative power. Unfortunately, with his untimely death before the venture could even commence, Poe's later literary works focused not on the potential of the great heartland of America but on the hopelessness of existence in the increasingly urbanized culture of the East. In "The Man of the Crowd" and the letters and reviews associated with the "Longfellow War," the impersonal cynicism of the liberal urban culture is revealed. (In yet another series of tales, those focusing on the aristocratic political culture of Europe, Poe conveys an even greater sense of malevolence derived not merely from an apostate American secular culture but from the hateful tyranny of European absolutism. Among these stories are "The Masque of the Red Death," "The Pit and the Pendulum," "The Purloined Letter," and "Hop-Frog.")

Poe's contemporaries recognized that he was writing for a mass audience in the American heartland, not for an elite segment of readers in

Introduction

the cosmopolitan centers. Whatever his humbug concerning antipathy toward "the mob" or his aspiration to write for a select body of discerning readers, Poe's actual success, both during his brief lifetime and especially in the century and a half following his death, has always been tied to a unique ability to give voice to the acute sense of moral peril of ordinary human beings. Like Alfred Hitchcock, an artist who by his own admission owed something to Poe's example, Poe employed the horror tale to express his ceaseless awareness of human frailty and his need for a framework of order founded on a religious sensibility. Hitchcock's *The Birds*, of course, is not really "about" crazed birds, any more than *Psycho* or *Vertigo* is about schizophrenia. All of Hitchcock's major films, in fact, center on a subject utterly familiar to Poe and to the conservative imagination, more generally: the forlorn abyss of loss and mortality into which each human being falls at birth and which he can only escape through the strength and solace of religious faith. The moral vertigo that emerges as the central feature of Hitchcock's great films is merely the reaction of the traditionalist sensibility to the rise within Western civilization of the materialist ethos, with all of its accompanying selfishness, alienation, and cynicism. These conservative films are "resolved," if that is the word, through the apprehension or death of those malevolent figures of crime that bring bewilderment into the normal world of faith and trust. Similarly, Poe's tales are resolved through all sorts of narrative manipulation, from deus ex machina appearances and unlikely intellectual deductions to miraculous examples of triumph and rebirth (as well as horrific scenes of annihilation and death), but they all rely on the premise of an underlying condition of peril familiar to those conservative readers who have never lost their sense of human necessity derived from their recognition of the fallen condition of mankind.

One might speculate further as to why Poe's writing appealed more strongly to the common man of the heartland than to the elite coastal reader. I would argue that for the conservative imagination Poe's stories of criminality, sadism, and aggrieved honor may be taken as cautionary tales not so far removed from Bunyan's religious allegories. For the reader determined to make moral sense of his world and to discover order and purpose in it, Poe's writing contains not a hint of irony or self-parody.

Poe is alerting the reader to the fearsome dangers of life based, presumably, on his own unfortunate choices. Having regained his faith and seen the error of his ways, he is writing to warn others of his mistakes of overblown pride and conceit.

It would be difficult, in fact, to maintain that Poe was not influenced by the nation's Calvinist ethos, nor can one deny that Poe was acutely interested in the economic possibilities and expansive ambitions of the young nation. His military background and sympathies, had he lived, would probably have rendered him a forceful advocate for the doctrine of Manifest Destiny, the proposition mandating the expansion of American civilization across the entire North American continent. One might even speculate that, had Poe remained at West Point to graduate with his class of 1834, he might have joined his near contemporary Robert E. Lee (who *did* graduate — the year before Poe's arrival) in the Mexican-American War and the Civil War. Given his successful experience as a noncommissioned officer and his unquestionable intellectual ability, Poe might well have become one of the leading military men of his generation — but, of course, then he would never have published the literary masterpieces for which he is known.

* * *

Not surprisingly, Vachel Lindsay identified Poe as the single greatest influence on his early writing, if not on his entire career, this despite some significant differences of belief and artistic method. What Lindsay detected in Poe, I suspect, was a brilliant predecessor with the same urgent desire to communicate his vision of the fulfillment of a reformed Protestant culture in the New World. Although Lindsay's critical comments on Poe are not extensive and appear mostly in the course of his youthful letters, Poe was a major influence on Lindsay and perhaps contributed to Lindsay's early success with a popular audience — as well as to his eventual dismissal by elite readers and critics. There is perhaps no other writer of significance who so closely shared the ethos of America's religious conservatives — those who later became known as the Religious Right — as Vachel Lindsay. At the end of his life, Lindsay suffered merciless rejection and ridicule at the hands of the cultural elite, treatment

Introduction

that contributed to his early suicide, but Lindsay never compromised his beliefs or altered his ambition to become the preeminent spokesman for the heartland.

As noted earlier, the identification with the kind of moral and religious tradition that can be termed "heartland" is not limited to the geographical heartland of the United States, nor does every resident heartland writer exemplify those moral and religious virtues. A striking example of these facts is the contrast that I draw between James Agee and Fyodor Dostoyevsky. The son of a southern father and Midwestern mother, Agee's family heritage and upbringing would seem to locate him squarely within American heartland culture, yet few intellectuals have rejected the heritage of their parents so completely as did Agee. Dostoyevsky, on the other hand, began his writing career in rebellion but quickly turned to a defense of the native traditions of his homeland. Although Dostoyevsky's "heartland" was, of course, quite different from that of the American writers whom I consider in this book, his defense of traditional Western civilization against modernity suggests that he confronted challenges to his faith and traditions that were not so very different from those faced by Americans and by other Europeans. Remarkably, Dostoyevsky can be seen to be anticipating in considerable detail, and forcefully rejecting, the corrosive arguments posed by Agee and other modernists. The "debate" between Agee and Dostoyevsky is a fascinating example of the expanding gulf that separates liberals and conservatives.

In an era of increasing cultural division — the "culture wars" of the eighties and nineties, followed by the bitter cultural and political divisions of the new century — it is not surprising that the fiction of Kent Haruf should have gained a large audience of enthusiastic readers. In this cultural environment, one suspects that Haruf's fiction serves as a voice for a large segment of conservative but politically quiescent readers. The moral certainties that underlie Haruf's fiction, focused as it is on family, responsibility, and faith, accord perfectly with the values of this "silent majority," as it was once called. This majority, in turn, rather than being merely a political movement of passing significance, must be seen for what it is: nothing less than the modern-day manifestation of the foundational identity of the United States. The values of personal responsi-

INTRODUCTION

bility and moral clarity implicit in Haruf's writing are, after all, traceable to the reformed Protestant teachings of America's Founders. Haruf's image of virtuous men and women inhabiting a moral wilderness and making it whole embodies the ethos embodied in the lives of the Puritan settlers. In the words of Bronowski and Mazlish, it is "a regimen which included getting up very early, working very hard, and being always concerned with good morals and good reading." This, along with "the virtues of thrift and abstinence" (94), are evident and implicitly celebrated in all of Haruf's exemplary protagonists.

As with all of the writers considered in this book, Haruf writes of refuge because he is keenly aware of the potential damage to life resulting from the corrupting influence of a secularized and self-indulgent modern culture. Indeed, among all of the writers dealt with in this book, Haruf seems to reflect most explicitly upon the need of prudence and caution. In the face of vast moral confusion, soulless materialism, and unprecedented concentration of power in state-sponsored bureaucracies, individuals must recover the clarity and conviction necessary to discriminate between what is life-affirming and what is destructive, and they must do so to a great extent outside the auspices of the general culture and the official intellectual climate of the present. Yet resistance of this sort is not to be construed as a prideful and romantic indulgence, a rejection of the world because the world does not cater to our every wish (something akin to the arrogance of Percy Shelley's "Ode to Liberty," in which, having "spurned the chains of its dismay," his soul finds itself "sublime and strong," like "a young eagle.... Hovering in verse o'er its accustomed prey" 229). The conservative temperament is not a fantastic flight on eagle's wings intent on revolution, nor is it a monastic withdrawal from mundane participation in the circle of families, friends, and communities. It is, quite simply, a sensible retreat from alienated modernity back toward a civilization that one knows to be purposeful and true. For the writers of the heartland, refuge affords a place of security, reflection, and renewal. Their lives as writers partake of a continuous devotion that is essentially religious in nature, no matter how different their doctrine and creed. From Poe and Lindsay to O'Connor, Naipaul, and Haruf, the heartland imagination speaks of refuge from the intrusion of unwanted experiment

Introduction

and of freedom from bureaucratic control. As human beings within the classical–Christian tradition have done for millennia, the writers of the heartland have labored to study, interpret, and pass down a redemptive body of knowledge and belief. In doing so, they have bequeathed a record of remarkable spiritual and intellectual journeys, and in reading of these journeys we may gain insight and inspiration from their burdens, their labors, and their triumphs.

In the Epilogue to this book, I expand the discussion of American culture beyond literature and essay. In this section, entitled "The Dialect of the Tribe," the title of course taken from T.S. Eliot, I consider the sense in which American culture and the culture of the Western democracies generally have become more "tribal." It was V.S. Naipaul who first alerted me to the possibility that even in an age of unprecedented affluence, serious fault lines have begun to appear within the once coherent civilization of the West. In Naipaul's sense of the word, the West has begun to regress from a civilization of faith and of law toward a less articulate, less ordered state in which personal withdrawal, cult-like patterns of belief, and anarchic rebelliousness have become commonplace. These forms of irrationality and rebellion are part of a broader tendency within Western civilization which Kenneth Minogue has analyzed as the "antagonist" culture, and which Roger Scruton has defined as the "culture of repudiation." As these cultural forces work their way from philosophy and literature down through the general culture, including the popular culture of television, film, music, and the Internet, the effect is to encourage the manifestation of alienation in tangible forms within the lives of ordinary human beings. Men and women who were once protected within stable belief systems are now liberated, if not forced, to construct their own personal systems of ethics and rationality. Unfortunately, these personal systems lack both the coherence and the compelling sense of truth that characterized classical–Christian civilization of the past. The result is that most free spirits of our time have been cast into a demoralized cynicism, convinced as they are that neither traditional faith nor their own ad hoc moral systems have the authority to compel belief.

In everyday life, it is not difficult to pinpoint the effects of this retreat from traditional belief. The assaults of Dylan Klebold and Eric

Introduction

Harris at Columbine High School appear to have been motivated by the uncontrollable anger of these two young men against society at large and in particular against the Christian youth of their school. It is important to understand, however, that the Columbine massacre was not an isolated cultural event. Every moment of the day and night, through its popular music and other media, the general culture replays identical feelings of alienation and resentment, often in terms that are entirely as murderous as were the actions of Klebold and Harris.

At the heart of this anger is a narcissistic rebellion against traditional authority of all kinds. Within the antagonist culture, the common institutions of society — family, church, school, and workplace — are viewed in hostile terms, or as irrelevant at best. To employ a phrase that has been lent currency by every pop guru from John Lennon to Julian Assange, "freedom and openness" has become an obsessive mantra within the culture of repudiation. Unfortunately, few within the general culture understand quite what they mean by the phrase nor where it is leading them. Unlimited freedom points not to happiness but to anarchic domination; the ultimate outcome is the tyranny of the strong over the weak. Likewise, unlimited openness leads not to greater understanding and connection but to suspicion and compartmentalism. In sum, the ethos of freedom and openness cannot stand the test of actual experience. As William Faulkner wrote in *Go Down, Moses*, "[N]o man is ever free and probably could not bear it if he were" (281).

Faulkner's words, however, are not enough to stop contemporary culture from undertaking various attempts at ultimate liberation. In the course of doing so, much of great cultural importance has been jettisoned, including faith in the nuclear family. The damage resulting from this dismissal in incalculable, for it is not only or primarily men and women who are victims of broken homes but the children whom those homes were supposed to protect. Likewise, the damage emanating from the loss of coherent traditions of religious belief is immeasurable. In the absence of a shared tradition of faith, society tends to revert to a default setting of dismissing moral discriminations altogether. In a culture in which each person operates more or less on the basis of an à la carte system of personal preferences, the "correct" position of society as a whole is invari-

Introduction

ably an avoidance of moral distinctions. In the absence of consensus, ethics reverts to the lowest common denominator, as it must if it is to offend no one.

In "The Dialect of the Tribe," I offer an analysis of the ethical discourse that has accompanied and enabled modern tribalism. With the help of the writing of Isaiah Berlin, among others, I trace the loss of shared traditions of belief to the Romantic tradition and to a number of neo–Romantic writers. Central to this tradition, and to its modern variations, is the emergence of the unbounded ego — not as a reviled manifestation of human pride but as a crucial aspect of the cultural superman. The narcissism on display within popular culture, from the antics of Mick Jagger to the virtual self-created worlds of online gamers, is so pervasive as to need little documentation. The effects of modern tribalism, however, call out for discussion and analysis.

In this book I have traced the relation of a number of important writers and artists to a conservative tradition of thought and belief that heavily influenced America's founding and that continued to influence if not dominate American moral discourse today. The classical–Christian tradition, upon which America's Founders relied as the basis for their conception of law, social organization, and rationality itself, continues to serve as the foundation of American thought today. One of the important functions of conservative artists such as Naipaul and Haruf is to underscore the continuing significance of the West's traditional belief system, even as that system adapts and evolves in the face of challenges brought about by such factors as advancing technology and global demographics. In their artistic works, the conservative writers whom I have chosen to analyze in this book have discovered valuable new ways of defending and reinvigorating a belief system that has served Western civilization for centuries and that has had a decisive influence on emerging societies from China to India. In doing so, they have devoted their artistic talents to a task of crucial importance for the continued well-being of the Western democracies and of the earth's population in general.

- 1 -

Poe and the Cogito

With his famous theorem, cogito, ergo sum, René Descartes initiated a modern conception of individual consciousness that signaled the divorcement of mind from a physical world that was now comprehended only by way of a method of doubt. In its dualistic conception of existence, Descartes' theory split the individual mind from the world of nature and society, resulting in a growing sense of uncertainty and isolation. In the decades following Descartes' death in 1650, European and American philosophers attempted to come to terms with the difficulties posed by Descartes' famous theorem and with the extreme reliance on rational analysis that the theorem implied. Among these philosophers, Pascal, Spinoza, Rousseau, Franklin, and Jefferson arrived at differing conclusions, but whether they experienced the cogito as liberating or enslaving, each was profoundly affected by the challenge to conventional truths that it entailed.

Edgar Allan Poe's philosophical leanings, while hardly systematic and shifting throughout his career, reflect a context of epistemological doubt of the sort that Descartes set as the starting point of his inquiry. Poe follows Descartes in pursuing a basis of certainty in the face of this condition of doubt, and he seeks for that certainty in the same place: that is, in the clarity and conviction of the human mind itself. Yet the problem for Poe is that this approach failed to provide the conclusive proof of existence and order of the sort that Descartes claimed by way of the ontological proof. The further Poe delved into the contradictions of the human mind, the more evidence he found not of a transcendent force of unity and arrangement as suggested by the existence of human reason itself but of selfishness, disorder, and criminality.

Nonetheless, Poe, who lived two centuries after the French philosopher, spent a great deal of his efforts working out the implications of Descartes' cogito. In his stories of the unbridled and isolated ego, Poe presses Descartes' point to its logical end: the annihilation that follows the proposition that the noncommunicative, self-sufficient ego may operate independently of the physical senses. Given the isolation of self from world implicit in Descartes' thinking, the self is both impotent to effect change in the objective world and is also beyond the restraining influence of that world outside itself. As the self becomes convinced of its total separation from physical reality, the imaginative world, as in "William Wilson," is transformed into a mere hall of mirrors for the self-reflecting ego; or, alternately, objective reality becomes enslaved to the monarchical ego, as in "The Gold-Bug." Whether in the guise of the narrator of "The Black Cat," of Monsieur Dupin in the detective stories, or of the insanely controlling figure of Prince Prospero in "The Masque of the Red Death," Poe explored the implications of Descartes' theorem, but having exposed its flaws, Poe discovered few resources for salvaging the relationship of the ego to outside reality.

A recognition of the implications of Descartes' distinction between essence and existence is to be found everywhere in Poe's writing. From "Descent into the Maelstrom" to "M.S. Lost in a Bottle," from "The Pit and the Pendulum" to "The Fall of the House of Usher," the material universe inhabited by Poe's characters is shifting, chaotic, and treacherous, and the narrator's knowledge of this world is consequently unreliable in ways that summon up the central philosophical dilemmas investigated by Descartes: the dream hypothesis (the inability to prove a distinction between waking and dreaming states) and the demon hypothesis (the possibility that existence is unknowingly controlled by a demonic power). A suggestion of both conundrums is evident in the passage in "William Wilson" in which the narrator, during his fifth year at Dr. Bransby's school, enters the bedroom of his rival with the intention of carrying out a malicious prank of one sort or another. What he discovers in the visage of his sleeping rival, instead, inspires instantaneous horror—a horror that derives from observing that his antagonist in the sleeping state appears utterly different from the waking imitator who torments him.

1. Poe and the Cogito

As Poe writes, "I gazed;—while my brain reeled with a multitude of incoherent thoughts. Not thus he appeared—assuredly not thus—in the vivacity of his waking hours" (*Poetry and Tales* 347). He discovers, in other words, perhaps for the first but hardly for the last time in his iniquitous career, that the radical order of disembodied thought that serves as the foundation of his identity may be fallible. His midnight encounter with the second William Wilson discloses the existence of an entirely distinct epistemological reality from that of his perception of his tormentor in the waking state. The "truth" of our condition, Poe suggests, may not be quite so apparent to our confident intellect as we might suppose. Rather, our dependence on objective reality, our embeddedness within language, and our primal enslavement to fear and desire may constitute a "dream-state" that, while incontestably more real than our individuality, is almost too horrifying to consider. At the slightest hint of this distinction, we flee with William Wilson back into the fraudulent security of believing that the waking-state of reason and self-interest is the actual condition of life.

Descartes' argument for the certainty of mathematical truth and, by extension, the certainty of the existence of God, among the most influential arguments of modern philosophy, clearly influenced Poe, whether directly or indirectly, but ultimately this argument from Mind only led Poe further into doubt. As Tom Sorell explains, Descartes' central argument is, firstly, that "the human mind was constituted by God to enjoy perfect certainty about material things when conceiving them mathematically"; secondly, that "God had the power to create whatever we could conceive with certainty"; and, thirdly, that "God was too benevolent to let the human mind fall into error when it conceived with certainty the mathematical nature of matter" (3–4). Such reasoning bears resemblance to Poe's argument concerning the relationship of Mind to God in his final book *Eureka*, yet the complete separation of mind and body that occurs in *Eureka* is, in fact, an abandonment of being altogether, not the triumphant wedding of God and human reason that one discovers in Descartes. As Leszek Kołakowski insists, following the intuitions of a number of anti-rationalists including Peirce and Wittgenstein, reason can never explain the existence of the self, and the great mystery that Poe runs up against in *Eureka* is just that: the primary necessity of considering the self's position in the midst of a world of pain and death. As P.M.S. Hacker writes, characterizing Wittgenstein's position, the fact "that I have a toothache does not mean that my mind has a toothache" (23): the pain is not the mind's to suffer but that of one's entire life within an inexplicable universe. The mind cannot exist apart from the body existing in the world. "In place of the descriptivist, cognitivist, conception," writes Hacker, "Wittgenstein proposes a completely different picture—an expressivist, naturalist one" (36).

In Poe's writing, there is a glimpse of this Wittgensteinian epiphany, for having grasped the cognitivist conception of the relationship of Mind and God, Poe presses this conception to a logical reductio ad absurdum. For Descartes, it is the mathematical understanding of the workings of the cosmos, in particular, that stands out as the one bastion of certainty in a human world that is otherwise fractured and unreliable. In *Eureka*, Poe builds upon the perception of mathematical certainty that he has worked with earlier in his career, as in "The Purloined Letter," in which the poet and mathematician are merged in the protagonist, and in numerous other stories including "The Pit and the Pendulum" or "A Descent into the Maelström," in which a careful observation of geometrical shapes and natural forces by the mechanistic, "engineer-like" sensibility appears to redeem the protagonist from the surrounding chaos. But in *Eureka*, these earlier intuitions concerning the certainty of mathematics are subverted and replaced by a theory of cosmic order that is at once seemingly redemptive and hopelessly nihilistic.

What Poe attempts in this final book, it would seem, is to move beyond the limited virtues of mathematical reading, just as Descartes did, and to employ them to suggest that the mathematical structure of the universe reveals the necessary existence of God. Like Descartes, Poe appears to suggest that the mind's ability to perceive an existing order of certainty is, in and of itself, a proof of transcendent order. This radically cognitive ability to "see through" the structure of the universe even points to the existence of deity, though not necessarily to a benign one, and beyond that to the likelihood of the mind's independent existence from the body after death. Yet this conclusion was not satisfactory in the

1. Poe and the Cogito

case of a writer as tortured as was Poe. Poe's grand proposition in *Eureka*—that "in the Original Unity of the First Thing lies the Secondary Cause of All Things, with the Germ of their Inevitable Annihilation" (*Poetry and Tales* 1261)—amounts to a fatalistic admission of defeat, a poetic cri de coeur rather than philosophical system-building. Rather than a progressive effort of any sort, it is, as Poe perhaps too eagerly informs us, a repudiation of the "conclusions" and "sagacity of many of the greatest and most justly reverenced of men" (*Poetry and Tales* 1261).

Poe was entirely conscious of Descartes' bases for doubt in the dream hypothesis, the demon hypothesis, and the general unreliability of the senses. What exacerbated the condition of doubt in Poe's case, however, was that unlike Descartes, he was unable to secure a basis for belief in human reason. Descartes' ontological argument, which is grounded in the absolute security of the human comprehension of God—the conviction that the act of cognition itself provides evidence of certainty, akin to that of mathematical knowledge—involved human perceptions that were necessarily clear and convincing. All of this was lost on Poe, since Poe had been thrust into a world in which the reliability of the senses, the objective reality of the physical world, and also the reliability of reason seem to have been discredited. Poe is unable to deploy the ontological argument for the existence of God because he lacks compelling evidence for the clarity and reliability of cognition, and beyond this, for the simple reason that Poe, like many of his contemporaries, including Hegel, had lost confidence in Descartes' circular "proof" of God's existence. In his case, Poe seems almost to have fallen back into a pre–Cartesian mode of thought. While Descartes could say, "I think therefore I am," Poe might be understood to say, "I think, but my thoughts are as likely to be inspired by demons or comprised of dreams, illusory sensations, or altered states of perception of precisely the sort that Descartes set out to conquer in the *Discourse*." In stories such as "The Tell-Tale Heart" or "A Cask of Amontillado," Poe presents a world that is treacherously unreliable.

Unlike Descartes, Poe does not resort to the rationalistic force of the cogito to resolve these problems since he rejects the Enlightenment faith in Progress that emerged among Descartes' successors as a corollary to a certitude in mathematical truth. At the same time, Poe appears to have been completely incapable of the redemptive pre–Cartesian posture of "shutting his eyes in the face of doubt," to use Wittgenstein's expression from *Philosophical Investigations* (224). He is trapped, in other words, between an overwhelming sense of the sort of existential doubt that drove Descartes to formulate his theorem and an inability to accept any sort of proof that might assuage his anxiety. While in *Eureka* Poe ultimately conceived of a form of immortality, with the entire cosmos of matter existing within the cognition of the perceiving intelligence, he does so only following a stage of annihilation, though even this annihilation may be said to take place simultaneously with the act of perception by an immortal Mind. Yet Poe's overly elaborate formulation of cosmic "order" is hardly redemptive, since it is practically a travesty of Descartes' analytical method, which systematically works "to decompose complex problems into problems as simple as possible" (Sutcliffe 17).

Despite the aspect of genius projected in many of his protagonists, Poe does not appear to believe that human reason can serve as a criterion for truth and thus as a bulwark against skepticism based on the perceived unreliability of experience, and recent philosophical studies have identified precisely why this should be so. What Cartesian analysis has left out, as Michael Polanyi suggests in his investigation of tacit knowledge, is nothing less than a broad range of crucial but unarticulated understandings upon which our most essential human relationships are based. For Polanyi, as for Poe, the Cartesian reliance on reason as a basis for faith was an absurdity. What Polanyi discovered, however, and what Poe failed to grasp fully, was that our ability to function on the basis of a cohesive and meaningful understanding of our condition rested not on what human reason understood explicitly but on a more essential, and far more copious, range of tacit knowledge. As Walter B. Mead points out, poetic and musical forms of expression are necessary means of "conveying, or making explicit, those experiences more heavily dependent upon the tacit dimension of knowledge" (307). This truth, to which Poe indistinctly alluded throughout his career, but never articulated, was grasped by artists and theologians alike in the ages before Descartes; it is only now beginning to be reaffirmed by philosophers such as Polanyi

1. Poe and the Cogito

and Kołakowski. From a historical perspective, Poe's career should be positioned in that uniquely difficult era in which confidence in Cartesian rationality had broken down but in which there existed no clear consensus concerning the nature of its limitations. Poe was essentially an untutored pioneer in the critique of Cartesian philosophy and in the investigation of forms of imaginative and intuitive understanding that are only now beginning to be elucidated.

From this awkward position, Poe is forced to confront a chaotic and unknowable condition of existence and to do so having discarded Descartes' progressive faith in reason and science. Descartes' belief in the innate truth of mathematical ideas, for example, is not supported but undermined in Poe's depiction of a number of mathematically inclined madmen or criminals. While the predictive power of mathematics may remain unchallenged, the notion that it can serve as the basis for a life-affirming and productive epistemological structure is absent. Poe's leading mathematicians, among others the demon mistress Ligeia, the malevolent Minister D_____, and the psychopathic loner William Legrand, seem fanatical and unfeeling by virtue of the fact that they have divorced themselves from the world of the senses. They live within a lonely, abstract world in which the power of intellect has been placed at the service of unbridled ego. The mental life of these protagonists resembles that of Descartes and his followers who, as Steven B. Smith writes, aspired to the place of *un vrai homme* guided by "the notion that life is an adventure in self-making" (23). This stress upon "authenticity," crucial in the Cartesian tradition, is undermined in Poe's fiction in which its overly confident representatives turn out to be enslaved rather than liberated by ego. Poe's central personae, from Legrand to Prospero to Usher, and even the mad poet-narrator of *Eureka*, are travesties of the self-made man, a fact that would suggest Poe's severe doubts regarding Cartesian optimism.

The difficulty for Poe was, quite simply, finding a compelling alternative to Cartesian rationalism. In the absence of faith in traditional institutions and beliefs, as Kenneth Minogue writes, "the recurrent modern nightmare" is "that society is always on the edge of unraveling into an anarchic collection of violent and selfish individuals" (*Alien Powers*

24). Poe rejected Descartes' use of mathematics as a truth criterion, but having done so, he seems to have retained only an egoless world that nonetheless lacks the external, objective structure of which the absolute ego has absolved him. The result, as figured in Poe's many images of the void, is a universe that is now emptied both of human will and of objective structures of belief, a world of random phenomenological occurrences that are perceived by the ego but not shaped by or even linked to it in any way. This is the world of "The Man of the Crowd," a sphere in which the story's protagonist exists only insofar as he is immersed in the crowd but also a sphere in which the fixated narrator seems to exist only in his capacity to compile a mental inventory of the old man's "criminality." As the narrator announces at the beginning, "There are some secrets which do not permit themselves to be told" (*Poetry and Tales* 388). The universe, especially the psychological realm, is opaque to even as keen an observer as the narrator. As he informs us, nightfall deepens his "interest" in the "scene" of squalid, alcoholic, criminal dissipation. In the end, it is not only the man of the crowd who seems "the worst heart of the world" (*Poetry and Tales* 396): in its obsessive "interest" in crime, the rationalistic ordering (by way of comprehending, not controlling) of an anarchic social and natural world seems even more terrible than that of the tyrannical ego of some of Poe's earlier stories.

Like that in "The Man of the Crowd," Poe's narrators are always impotent in the face of the injustice they so clearly register. What Poe's personae typically lack is the animating purpose and empathetic feeling to accompany their much vaunted intellect. Too often they seem brilliant thought-generating machines, endlessly emitting theories on all matters but utterly devoid of purpose or feeling. This was precisely Wittgenstein's criticism of the Cartesian tradition — that, despite its mechanical facility of reasoning, it could never arrive at a conception of being. In a famous passage from *Philosophical Investigations*, Wittgenstein engages in a dialogue with himself concerning the central difficulty of Cartesian ethics, the problem of doubt arising from the epistemological uncertainty of one's relationship to other human intelligences. "I can be as certain of someone else's sensations as of any fact," Wittgenstein's interlocutor declares. "But," he is asked, "if you are certain, isn't it that you are shut-

1. Poe and the Cogito

ting your eyes in the face of doubt?" "They are shut," he declares (Philosophical Investigations 224; qtd. in Hacker 44).

Poe's detective stories, which present the reader with protagonists severely isolated from society and functioning, largely, through the intellect, illustrate the problem of dualism identified by this critique of the cogito. Unlike the Wittgenstein persona, Poe's detective hero, M. Auguste Dupin, seems too keenly aware of the pervasive malaise of doubt separating one mind from another, too intelligent to "shut his eyes" to doubt, though not intelligent enough to discover Wittgenstein's solution of simply shutting his eyes anyway. Except for the shadowy and acquiescent figure of the narrator, who is simply Dupin's passive sycophantic expositor, Dupin is alienated from every human being. He is an impoverished young man of aristocratic birth who has "ceased to bestir himself in the world" (*Poetry and Tales* 400). As the narrator stresses in his rambling preamble to "The Murders in the Rue Morgue," those who possess inordinate powers of analysis experience "the liveliest enjoyment" (*Poetry and Tales* 397) in their exercise of intelligence, not in a relationship to other persons. These analytical powers of mind, which appear to ordinary human beings to be "preternatural," are the source of the greatest pleasure for Dupin.

The exception to this rule is, of course, Dupin's relationship to the Minister D_____, his near equal in intelligence and imagination in "The Purloined Letter." From this relationship, the utmost pleasure is derived because of the satisfaction of competing and besting a worthy opponent in a competition of the highest significance: a combative joust or duel "where mind struggles with mind" for mortal stakes. Like the game of draughts, which requires the player to enter and prey off the mind of the opponent, the form of analysis employed by the detective hero involves an identification with and subsequent occupation and domination of the mind of the opponent. In this respect, it carries Cartesian dualism to its ultimate end in which the domineering power of a single isolated intellect has been unleashed in the absence of empathy. Thus, at the end, in his complete triumph over his opponent, Dupin admits that he "should like very well to know the precise character of [the Minister D_____'s] thoughts, when, being defied by her whom the Prefect terms 'a certain personage,' he is reduced to opening the letter which I left for him in the cardrack" (*Poetry and Tales* 697–98). He would, in other words, enjoy savoring to the fullest the Minister's realization of his own downfall, hardly a noble sentiment in Dupin.

"The Purloined Letter" ends, however, not so much with Dupin's actual triumph over the Minister D____, a triumph which is postponed indefinitely by virtue of the as yet undiscovered jest, but with an elaborately self-lacerating examination that casts out the ego from his own personality. As we see in Dupin's comment that the Minister has harmed him in the past and in his behavior toward the royal female personage, there can be little doubt that the Minister D____ does represent an unrestrained force for mischief: not a "rational" form of control but an instinctual will to dominate and abuse others. The queenly personage that we see in so many of Poe's stories demarcates Poe's painful separation from the maternal figure but also his loyalty and protective feeling toward that figure. If the Minister is the double of Dupin, the relationship of the Minister D____ to this lady enacts an aggressive and unforgiving side of a single persona. Though Poe never says as much, one senses that the letter through which the Minister has gained power may, if not literally, in some layer of Dupin's psyche, at least, have originated with Dupin himself, and that it is Dupin's civilizing and courteous passion that has been purloined and employed by the Minister not only as a means of gaining the upper hand in court politics but, more importantly, of obstructing desire, an intention hinted at in the etymology of the word "purloined." To purloin in Old French is "to put off, delay," or in its Latin root to put "at a distance." In this sense, of course, there are two "purloined" letters in the story: the queen's stolen epistle and Dupin's substitute for it.

At this point Poe attempts a peculiar and seemingly unconvincing linkage but one that was in fact central to metaphysical speculation during his lifetime. Like Hegel, who perceived that "the whole universe is an enormous sentient whole," and one in which "we are able to understand what each part of it is doing, provided that we have a sufficiently clear degree of metaphysical insight" (Berlin, *Freedom and Its Betrayal* 81), Poe perceives in the animate nature of "things"—the quality of Mind

1. Poe and the Cogito

operating within both animate beings and inanimate objects — a connection of physical reality with the isolated ego. Both the ego and the inorganic world's sentience participate in the same Mind that flows through everything. As Leszek Kołakowski points out in *Metaphysical Horror*, contemporary scientists of matter are attempting to establish a similar linkage: they "are now trying to rediscover mind in matter ... to reanimate the corpse of the universe and arrange its disjecta membra into a living whole" (75). In this reconceptualization of the "Whole-in-each-part," quantum physics has returned full circle to intuitions that were present in some of the earliest human thinking on divinity and the nature of the cosmos.

A crucial aspect of this unity must be the certainly that a principle of justice underlies and pervades existence at every level, and certainly, in stories like "The Purloined Letter" or his last tale, "Hop-Frog," Poe's crucial motive is the desire of the protagonist to avenge a wrong. Indeed, it is not saying too much to claim that the dominant passion of Poe's life was a compulsion to gain justice and to reassert a proper balance of freedom and restraint in a world of the unbalanced ego — a world tyrannized by the domineering ego or a world in which the ego has been subsumed by experience. In Poe's stories, however, justice often takes the form of an attempt to gain retribution rather than reinstate balance: to punish injustice and to regain what is rightfully one's own, whether that be one's honor or a rightful social or economic rank in society. Poe understood that, in the absence of a system that will bring about swift and certain punishment for criminal activity (to say nothing of that activity which is legal but morally criminal), victims of abuse are filled with rage, and this barely controlled anger is fatal to those who accumulate it, as it is to those around them.

As with the authoritarian nature of the mental powers of a Dupin, however, the problem with vengeance is that it never really reestablishes a balance of ego and superego. The satisfaction of revenge unleashes a smug pleasure as the former victim experiences his triumph over his former oppressor, yet the annihilation of the repressive antagonist gives rise at the same moment to the emergence of a new source of oppression in the figure of the formerly repressed ego. With the failure of vengeance to bring about justice, Poe is led to conceptualize a response to the cogito that resembles the terms in which the ego has appeared in traditional religious texts. Poe's final twist on this relationship of self and world is to imagine, as he does at the conclusion of *Eureka*, that the ego, having been subsumed in an order of Mind outside of itself, is then able to subsume within itself the totality of Mind in the outside universe that has subsumed the ego itself. As Poe writes in the final words of *Eureka*: "Think that the sense of individual identity will be gradually merged in the general consciousness — that Man, for example, ceasing imperceptibly to feel himself Man, will at length attain that awfully triumphant epoch when he shall recognize his existence as that of Jehovah. In the meantime bear in mind that all is Life-Life-Life within Life — the less within the greater, and all within the Spirit Divine" (*Poetry and Tales* 1358–59). This seems almost a form of self-cannibalism, allowing the ego to be annihilated by the Mind of which it is not merely a part but the whole. With the ego annihilated by the world, the world is then annihilated by the ego. But this paradoxical conception, with the ego nested Babushka-like within the cosmos which is at the same time nested within Mind, would seem to be Poe's final word on the subject. In this never-ending contestation, Poe seems never to have grasped the miraculous nature of human cognition, not in the Cartesian sense as the reliable proof of stable objective reality but as a miraculous fact to be grasped as such. As Kołakowski points out, the very strangeness of the process by which mind perceives and orders reality outside itself — and the remarkable nature of the ability from which the process proceeds — suggests "the Platonic-Augustinian theory of anamnesis" (*Metaphysical Horror* 78). In its cognitive ability to perceive the nature of the external world and to conceptualize its own nature and relationship to existence, the human mind reveals its participation or remembrance of participation in an order of Mind outside itself. As Kołakowski notes, "The very act of cognition, as Plato would have it, presupposes an affinity, or even a kinship, between my mind and the mind of the world" (*Metaphysical Horror* 76).

It is true that, at certain points in his writing, Poe seems to imply precisely that. In the context of a tradition of religious and metaphysical

1. Poe and the Cogito

thought stretching from Vedic texts to modern-day physics, Poe's intuition of universal sentience and of the human mind's containment of the cosmos seems more a restatement of familiar truths than a Eureka-like discovery. The difficulty, however, is that Poe looked to the universe of matter — the unlikely fiction of sentience within houses, stones, corpses — not to the miraculous quality of vital being itself, as the solution to his Cartesian dilemma. Whereas Descartes perceived certainty in mental processes, as in the clarity and assurance with which the human mind grasps mathematical or metaphysical concepts, Poe required a greater confirmation of order, one which at times he seemed to have glimpsed in the structural patterns of temporal, spatial, and psychological realms. Poe, for example, discerned an identical pattern of ebb and flow in the natural, cosmological, and psychological worlds; he discerned the same vortex pattern in the maelstrom, the whirlwind, the solar system, and numerous other phenomena; and he identified an identical structure of musical patterns in instruments, voices, emotional moods, and patterns of light and color. And so the separation of the ego from reality is "solved," but only by the doubtful claim of the universal sentience of matter: in this schema, the ego is neither the dominant monarchical ego nor the separate isolated ego. Instead, it is the participant in an order of matter that encompasses the entire cosmos.

The problem with this happy solution, other than its fundamental lack of proof, is that it suggests a deterministic universe more horrible in its own way than the Cartesian division that it addresses. In this conception, the ego participates in the larger world of phenomena whether it wishes to or not, and it participates presumably in the same way and with the same quality of consciousness as any other animate or inanimate form of being. It is possible to imagine that Roderick Usher gains a sense of solace from the ancient identification of the Usher male progeny with the physical structure that they inhabit, as well as with that other "house" of Usher — the abstract conception of patriarchal family as an enduring, established entity. But even if this be the case, it should also be clear, as his recital of "The Haunted Palace" makes apparent, that the identification of isolated ego with the house in both senses implies not a merging of "Life with Life" but a death sentence. As soon as the ego has accepted the comforting assurance that its merging with universal sentience (the physical house) or with temporal order (the patriarchal house) has secured release from all existential threats, it opens the way for the sort of swift destruction symbolized by Madeline's return from the tomb — a return like that of Ligeia's that one is tempted to read as the vengeance of Wittgensteinian being on Roderick's retreat into a dead house, dead ancestors, and dead art. Having buried the anxieties of space and time that threatened the ego and thus released the ego from the continuing necessity of struggle, Roderick is truly defenseless, and he soon collapses to the floor, coupled in death with the very anxieties that he wished to expel. The ego, in Poe's conception, appears interchangeable with various forms of animate and inanimate matter, swept along like so many of Poe's narrators by the irresistible force of Mind. Abandoning the ego to this irresistible stream "solves" the psychological problem of isolation as well as the ethical problem of the ego's relationship to other beings, but it does so at the expense of the loss of being. Poe seems to arrive again and again at the dilemma that he never solved. Posited as an absolute, the ego inevitably turns tyrannical; lacking authority, the ego is crushed in the larger operation of Mind that Poe finds it necessary to posit as a response to Descartes' cogito.

One of several avenues of escape that Poe explored was that of aestheticism. Poe's critical works at times affirm the position that beauty and truth are separate realms, and that the artist is the servant of beauty alone, removed in this sense from the pressures of an anarchic world. As Poe asserts in his brief essay, "On Imagination," "Beauty ... is at once [the] sole object and ... inevitable test" (*Fall* 497) of the imagination. Yet such a position, the denial by the aesthete that the world of affairs impinges on his concerns as an artist, is itself evidence of Poe's desperate awareness of the extent to which the world of affairs did impinge on the artist, especially in the uncertain times of immature national literary identity in which he labored. Poe might have done well to consider how futile it is for the artist to wall himself off from existence or to censor his own perception. Czeslaw Milosz suggests at various points in his writing the great difficulty of remaining a single person, and certainly in the many personae contained within one person and in the many relation-

1. Poe and the Cogito

ships that one takes on in one's life there exists a healthy force of destruction that breaks down the separateness and self-reliance of the ego. Or, as Christopher Lasch had it, "The best defenses against the terrors of existence are the homely comforts of love, work, and family life, which connect us to a world that is independent of our wishes yet responsive to our needs" (248). Yet perhaps it is precisely this point that Poe's creative work is making even as he resists it in his more self-conscious aesthetic theorizing. From the unstable particles that comprise the walls of the house of Usher to the chaotic make-up of Usher's mind itself, Poe's universe is a fearful place because of the ego's isolation and defensive claim of unity.

It is important to note that Poe's assertion of aestheticism takes place in a world that, absent the controlling force of practical reasoning or moral custom, is less, not more, ordered. Aestheticism does not represent escape from being into art but a further stage in the dissolution of being. The further Poe ventures into the controlling intellect — whether that of the artist, the theorist, the detective hero, or compulsive criminal — the more he finds himself removed from the stable order that can only emanate from the conditional nature of being itself. One of the implications of Poe's difficulties in regard to the cogito is, in fact, the necessity of resorting to authoritarian sources of order in the face of the anarchy unleashed by the artist's abandonment of responsibility for the actual world of human affairs. Repeatedly, Poe's protagonists resort to absolutist tendencies in an effort to bring order to the chaos of the very world that they have forsaken. In one version of the absolutist narrative, as figured in "The Gold-Bug," but also in the Dupin stories, "Landor's Cottage," "The Domain of Arnheim," and other works, the protagonist retreats from the urban chaos to a suburban or rural sanctuary, or into an anonymous refuge within but apart from the urban swell, in which he can live a superior existence beyond the vulnerability of the crowd. Within his retreat from the world, the protagonist can salvage his pride and not compromise his principles to a mercenary and faithless world.

The problem with this defensive maneuver is that the protagonist's retreat, like Sullivan's Island in "The Gold-Bug" or the castellated abbey in "The Masque of the Red Death," always remains within contact of the experiential world. The element of control that Legrand seeks on Sullivan's Island is mitigated by the memory of family misfortunes that Legrand still carries within himself, and these memories and resentments, not the brilliant rationality that he projects, largely determine his actions in the story. Likewise, the danger of disease that Prospero and his troop seek to escape is carried with them and, indeed, multiplied by virtue of their enclosing themselves within a seemingly airtight edifice. Escape from the threatening world of experience does not make that realm any less anarchic: rather, it ensures that, left to its own devices, it will gather force and pursue the refugee. In this respect, the very idea of refuge within Poe's writing is intertwined with his response to a Cartesian conception of rationality as the source of certainty and assurance. The protagonist's yearning for a stable, unassailable order within his private life is an important reflection of his lack of confidence in relation to the objective world of economic and psychological survival. In Poe's case, this uncertainty was focused on the world of publishing and authorship, on his relationship to his guardian, John Allan, and on the transience of life itself, especially that of the beloved women in his immediate circle.

While Poe's conclusion in *Eureka* that the cosmos as a whole exists within Mind is rejected by many readers, as a philosophy that echoes the late Enlightenment thought of Hume and Berkeley it might be regarded as no more fantastic than the revolutionary political ethos upon which America itself was largely based: the belief that the American nation was the product of Mind as revealed in the principles of the Declaration, the Constitution, and the Bill of Rights. The revolutionary nature of this view is suggested by Lewis P. Simpson when he points out in "The Antebellum South as a Symbol of Mind" that "The American republic ... was devised and willed into historical existence by a group of men of letters ... who assumed mind to be the world historical model of society" (127). As Simpson goes on to explain, the belief that society is the creation of mind was diametrically opposed to all previous conceptions of the state; it was "a historic reversal of the ancient relationship of society to mind," one that was based on the conception of an "ideal society" or on the "authority of a society existing in time" (127). While Simpson's sweeping assertion obscures the complex political discussions,

1. Poe and the Cogito

debates, and compromises underlying the creation of America's founding documents and fails to take into account the significant reservations entertained by many among the Founders, his essential argument concerning the role of "Mind" in America's creation points to an important aspect of American identity. From the very founding of the nation, despite the warnings of some among the Founders themselves, intellectuals have been attempting to promote an ideal society fashioned by utopian conceptions of a future civilization in which are guaranteed ever-greater rights and freedoms. To some extent, at least, our distinctive identity as a nation is premised upon this bold and idealistic attempt to re-create society as a product of Mind. In the manner in which it traced the consequences of positing an order of existence based purely on cognition, Poe's fiction may be read as cautionary tales addressing this radical aspect of American culture.

Herein lies a further irony in that Poe died the year after the publication of the Communist Manifesto. It is not far-fetched to argue that Marx's misguided search for a perfect society may be seen as a continuation of avenues of rationality that Poe explored in *Eureka*. The Manifesto's inflexible, idealizing, and inhuman quality, with its fiction of an inevitable progression toward a worker's paradise, emerged out of the same intellectual climate that influenced Poe. While it may be that Poe and Marx are quite opposed in their aristocratic and proletarian tendencies, they are similar in their exploration of radical modes of romantic and utopian thinking. Yet Poe reacted far more subtly and with far greater skepticism to the claims of political, social, and technological progress that pervaded Victorian thinking. The idea that the condition of workers could be dramatically improved as the result of a proletarian revolution which has seized all property in the name of the State would have struck Poe not only as absurd but as demonic.

With his great sensitivity to the damage of authoritarianism of all sorts, Poe, had he lived, would have seen through the monstrous hoax of communism. He had, after all, already dramatized his unease with the conception of national identity founded on the basis of disembodied Mind, a conception that Hegel would flesh out in his theories of universal Mind pervading the historical realm. As Poe seems to have intuited, contemporary claims of perfectibility introduced a transcendent motif of progress that led inextricably back to the alienation of human existence from being itself. As in Poe's *Eureka*, the Babushka-theory of Mind and cosmos subsuming one another involves a deathly severing of individual ego from historically continuous and coherent belief systems. As Kołakowski insists, "a community, in order to be real, must include past and even hypothetical future generations, and to live [sic] in a spiritual space in which the past is actual" (*Metaphysical Horror* 105).

In the end, however, Poe's flight from the damage of the cogito led him further away from this sort of coherence because, though he sensed the potential destructiveness of a purely abstract rationality, he was unable to conceive of compelling alternatives. In the end, Poe's imagination engaged in a flight from the metaphysical horror of Descartes' fraudulent solutions into the greater horror of blankness, annihilation, and the void. In his own way, Poe attempted a metaphysical solution to the failure of a metaphysical solution, an impasse that would only be broken with Wittgenstein's brilliant analysis of "Knowledge [that] is in the end based on acknowledgement" (*On Certainty* 49e). Wittgenstein recognized that mathematical and nonmathematical assertions of all kinds are not only reasonable but essential: "My life consists in my being content to accept many things" (*On Certainty* 44e). One can only wonder at how little Poe accepted, and how large were his doubts, even to the point of taking from him his life, in Wittgenstein's sense of the word. What remained of life for Poe was miserable and terrifying, and in the end there was no refuge and no solution.

- 2 -

Poe and Lindsay, Literary Outcasts

Vachel Lindsay dates the beginning of his literary career precisely to the evening when, at age thirteen, his mother, Catherine Frazee Lindsay, introduced him to the writing of Edgar Allan Poe. Lindsay, in fact, recalls the exact moment when his mother handed him the volume of Poe. The young Lindsay sat up all night reading, and afterward he insisted that "Ulalume" was not only his favorite among Poe's works but perhaps his favorite poem in all of literature. Lindsay continued his love affair with Poe's work throughout high school, and for the remainder of his life he maintained his belief that Poe was the foremost American poet and the one for whom he felt the greatest affinity. Writing to Witter Bynner, Lindsay stated that Poe was "Another stung creature — who knew not Peace" but who possessed the gift "to produce the eminently original thing." Mixing his metaphors to an absurd extent, Lindsay declared that his "carnal passion" was the desire "to carve a jewel like Ulalume or Ligeia" (*Letters* 52).

It is not difficult to understand why Lindsay valued Poe so highly. In Poe, Lindsay had discovered, or believed that he had discovered, an author whose sensibilities mirrored his own. Like Lindsay, Poe was a romantic with a strong strain of moral disapproval for, even revulsion at, the coarser aspects of American culture. Both writers aspired toward an aesthetic order of purity that would lift them out of their commonplace existence: Poe by way of an aesthetic theory that ostensibly removed art from contact with the practical world of ethics, law, and commerce; Lindsay, at first, by way of a similar aestheticism, as evidenced by his enthusiasm for Ruskin and for the arts and crafts movement, then by way of a program employing aesthetic activities in the service of civic uplift and moral revitalization. In both writers the aesthetic emphasis was matched by the influence (in Poe's case, largely unacknowledged) of a conception of order rooted in reformed Protestant ideals of chastity, self-regulation, and personal aspiration. Immersed in a nineteenth- and early-twentieth-century culture of religious revivalism, temperance, civic reform, and Chautauqua-style efforts at cultural and moral uplift, Poe and Lindsay responded with literary programs that attempted to reform and re-educate the public taste.

As the means of disseminating a program of moral reform, Lindsay forged poetic forms that would appeal to a mass audience, just as Poe, despite his aristocratic pretensions, wrote from the assumption that literature must address the general reader in an effort to shape the taste of a young democratic society. In an astute remark, Lindsay noted that Poe's democratic nature was revealed not in spite of his striving for perfection but *because* of it: "Your true democrat is Poe as much as Longfellow" (qtd. in Ruggles 102). Through works such as "The Raven" and "The Gold-Bug," Poe had gained fame and reputation, and Lindsay aspired to match this popular success. As it turned out, Lindsay's success came rather easily, if not especially early, and he obtained a degree of celebrity that he soon came to regret. A few of his poems, most conspicuously "The Congo" and "General William Booth Enters Heaven," achieved fame while Lindsay was still in his early thirties, and Lindsay soon became a well-known public figure, reciting these popular works to large audiences time and again. Lindsay referred to these works, which relied on obvious rhythmic and oral qualities, as the "Higher Vaudeville." Several of Lindsay's poems in this vein appear to have been influenced by "The Bells," one of Poe's purely musical poems, but none so obviously as "The Santa Fé Trail," in which Lindsay wrote: "Hark to the *faint*-horn, *quaint*-horn, *saint*-horn," on and on in similar fashion.

As T.R. Hummer points out, one of the ironies of Lindsay's career is that his work was first championed by imagists and modernists such as Amy Lowell and W.B. Yeats, not by a popular audience, but this support was short-lived. Soon enough John Gould Fletcher, a proxy for modernist opinion, attacked Lindsay's work, comparing it to that of Kipling, in whose writing Fletcher found a similar "free-and-easy facility, preference for ragtime rhythms, tone of vulgar optimism and desire to preach" (qtd. in Ruggles 283). To this list of Lindsay's cultural sins one must add the fact of his nativism: he believed implicitly in American exceptionalism and in the historic mission of American democracy. Lindsay's thematic interests were, in fact, the opposite of expatriate modernists such as Fletcher or Ezra Pound — a fact that Pound perceived immediately upon the publication of Lindsay's early work in *Poetry*. Unlike those disaffected expatriates eager to critique American prosperity and power ("fanatical exponents of Balkan and Eastern European ideals," Lindsay called them [qtd. in Ruggles 310–11]), Lindsay embraced the values of heartland America and of its middle class, and he looked beyond the less appealing aspects of American democracy to the potential for a nation that would employ its wealth and power to spread democracy around the world.

Lindsay's intention had always been to write for the masses, and underlying this intention was a persistent need for approval. "What he was really seeking was love," writes Eleanor Ruggles (97), and there is considerable evidence that the source of his emotional emptiness can be found in his relationship to his parents, especially to his mother. As with Poe, who above all things "needed unmitigated love and unqualified approval" (Hutchisson 54), it was a psychic abyss that could never be filled, not by any amount of success in his vocation as poet or performer nor by any actual human relationship. When late in life Lindsay did finally marry a woman who seemed his destined soul-mate, the marriage was soon poisoned by Lindsay's sense of his own inadequacy and by a perverse sense that his marital happiness entailed the unforgivable violation of his young wife's sanctity. Beneath the failure of his marriage was the specter of a deep-seated lack of self-esteem.

Lindsay's letters reveal his own sense of his life as the pursuit of a sense of self-worth that lay always just beyond his grasp. It was a pursuit marked by euphoric moments of success ("I have just recited ["The Congo"] for the big fat-sides Lincoln Banquet here—audience of 1000 in the Arsenal and boomed it to the very back of the building" [*Letters*

88]) and, increasingly, of failure, including the humiliating dismissal of his philosophically most revealing work, *The Golden Book of Springfield*, by critics and the reading public. Lindsay's decline, beginning in the late 1910s as his reputation as a serious artist gave way to fame as a Chautauqua-style entertainer, was entirely as pathetic as the misery of Poe's final years. Coincident with his emotional and physical collapse in early 1923, Lindsay began to feel, as he wrote to his close friends Stephen and Rose Graham, that "The whole world is in a conspiracy to see for a high price my stalest fancies and kill off all my new ones" (*Letters* 269). Lindsay was fully aware of his dismissal by serious critics, and over time he grew increasingly fearful, even paranoid, concerning his betrayal at the hands of even his closest friends. As he wrote to Harriet Monroe, his long-time supporter at *Poetry Magazine*, in December 1920: "Please be good to me Harriet. I am very lonely. Life is not what it appears" (*Letters* 215).

Considering the icy reception accorded *The Golden Book of Springfield*, which had appeared the month before, Lindsay had good reason to feel that "life is not what it appears." Having given his "whole strength" to the book, Lindsay was mystified as to why "it remains a dull mystery even to my best friends" (*Letters* 242). Worse was to come, with the deaths of his parents (with whom he had an intensely emotional, if conflicted, relationship), his frustration with the failure of subsequent books, and his mental and physical collapse while on lecture tour in 1923. In the end, Lindsay was exhausted, overwhelmed by despair, and driven to madness. In March 1931, he telegraphed his wife from Asheville, North Carolina, where, as elsewhere, he had refused to recite "The Congo": "This school put on the thumbscrews till I was ready to scream because they could not sweat the Congo out of me. Two more such persecutions and I am a goner for sure" (*Letters* 452).

In terms of his rejection and misunderstanding, Lindsay viewed Poe as a kindred spirit, one who had suffered a similar degree of abuse and for similar reasons. Lindsay's poem "The Wizard in the Street" (subtitled "Concerning Edgar Allan Poe") is a passionate eulogy structured on the theme of rejection. In this poem Lindsay reveals much about his lifelong identification with Poe, for in Poe he finds a serious artist who has been misunderstood and dismissed by the critical establishment

2. Poe and Lindsay, Literary Outcasts

because of his unwillingness to compromise the depths of his aesthetic and spiritual concerns in the context of the crass materialism of the literary marketplace. Bleeding his heart, so to speak, into poetic work that either gained little notice or gained notice for the wrong reasons, Poe was striving for nothing less than immortality. His goal was the creation of lasting art within the impossible context of a young America that was not prepared to reward serious effort. To accomplish his purpose, it was first necessary to bring about a cultural reformation. As Lindsay describes his own situation as an artist struggling within a "blatant, well-fed place" (*Poetry* I: 94), he sees America little changed from the time of Poe, for the word "blatant," which appears many times in Lindsay's writing and letters, suggests a state of heedless materialism that is the worst environment for the artist. As he relates the tragic example of Poe, the "wizard" found dying in the street, Lindsay ponders the unwillingness of the public to take his own work seriously. From an early age Lindsay must have suspected that his own fate would mirror that of Poe.

One of many intriguing biographical connections between Poe and Lindsay is the way in which Lindsay's decline into paranoia — his insane belief that his father-in-law, among others, was plotting his assassination — replicates the irrationality of Poe's final months of life, including his avowal to the Philadelphia engraver John Sartain in July 1849 that he had been imprisoned by his enemies and pursued by assassins (Hutchisson 241). Poe and Lindsay shared a deep-seated defensiveness concerning their social backgrounds and literary reputations that often led them to alienate potential supporters and to spoil whatever opportunities had been kindled by their talents. This defensiveness caused both writers to expend their energies on seemingly petty disputes. The "War of the Literati," as it was called, pitted Poe against a powerful clique of New York writers and publishers, and it culminated in his ill-considered libel suit against Thomas Dunn English, formerly his friend and ally. Weakened by the feud and with his reputation seriously damaged, Poe failed to heed the advice of those few who still had his best interests at heart, such as William Gilmore Simms, who "advised Poe to stop wasting his energy on petty disputes" (Hutchisson 200). In a similar way, after finding that Lindsay was considering a lawsuit against composer John

Alden Carpenter, Harriet Monroe urged him to focus on his poetry, not on such inconsequential disputes: "Why waste your time and nerves over such futile controversies?" (qtd. in Ruggles 377).

For good or ill, Lindsay seems to have inherited much of his mother's zealous, contentious temperament. As in the case of Poe's mother, Eliza (even though she died in his infancy), Lindsay's mother exerted a lasting influence over her son. As Lindsay noted, "every line I ever wrote, was her opinions and ideas rewritten" (*Letters* 263). In Poe's case, this maternal attachment was accompanied by a lifelong sense of loss; in Lindsay, the dependence on his mother resulted in a conflicted sense of security and resentment, and may have precipitated a psychological and physical collapse not long after his mother's death. As with Poe, Lindsay comes most to life in those poems and letters in which he writes of his mother, yet one of the paradoxes in both cases is precisely the fact that the attachment carries with it an intense prohibition against further exploration. The very fact that Lindsay and Poe were so closely coupled with, almost absorbed into, their mothers' identities—so that in many of his sketches the Poe persona was indistinguishable from the figure of his mother—requires the writer to disguise its nature and avoid delving too deeply. The hesitancy to write about their mothers was an indication of the sacred nature of the connection, yet it also impelled them constantly if obliquely to explore this maternal tie.

Connected in a complex way to the maternal attachment was the obligation of male chivalry. Overwhelming evidence exists concerning Poe's intensely held conviction regarding the purity of women. In the late summer of 1849, months before his death, Elmira Royster, whom Poe was courting in Richmond, reported the strong objection that Poe took to "a visiting female friend [who] said something coarse" (Silverman 426). Similarly, in "The Purloined Letter," Dupin's motive for retrieving the incriminating letter, other than the considerable reward of fifty thousand francs, may be discovered in his code of chivalry. He is, after all, "a partisan of the lady concerned," the royal personage who will now have the Minister D_____ in her power rather than the other way around (Poe, *Tales* 697), but far more is suggested in the unraveling of the psychic relation of Dupin to the Minister D_____ in the story's final paragraphs.

Dupin especially resents the lack of principle in the powerful official who is otherwise so much like Dupin himself. The pleasure of confounding the Minister rests not only in this resentment or the motive of revenge: at a deeper level, it reflects Dupin's rage at that bestial element of human nature manifest in the Minister as an individual and suggested by the words from Crébillon's *Atrée* that Dupin copies onto the blank sheet. In classical tradition the entire heritage of evil originates, after all, with Thyestes's seduction of Atreus's wife, possibly the sort of evil turn that the Minister "at Vienna once, did" Dupin (698). Similarly, the sadistic fury to which Hop-Frog rises in Poe's tale of the same name, the last story he ever wrote, is precipitated not by his own abuse at court but by the King's effrontery at insulting his beloved Trippetta, like himself a dwarf who has been abducted from her home, when she attempts to defend Hop-Frog against further insult. Immediately after Trippetta is shoved about and has wine thrown in her face, Hop-Frog hatches his *last jest*— the immolation of the King and his hateful court and his escape with Trippetta to the refuge of their own country.

In many respects, despite his midwestern upbringing, Lindsay was as much a southern gentleman as Poe. Lindsay speaks in many poems of protecting women from exploitation, including that of his own corrupting passion ("The Trap," "To the Maiden, Honest and Fine"); according women respect for their virtue, wisdom, and purity ("The Hearth Eternal," "My Lady in Her White Silk Shawl," "How a Little Girl Danced"); reverencing the maternal qualities of women ("Our Mother Pocahontas"); and restricting passion to a chaste, monogamous marriage ("The Perfect Marriage," "To Eve, Man's Dream of Wifehood as Described by Milton"). In "The Trap," Lindsay offers a portrait of the woman of the streets, a character that was a fixture of social reform writing in the late nineteenth and early twentieth century. Like Crane and Dreiser before him, Lindsay's poem captures the pathos of one young woman's "slow, foul death"— the experience serving as a warning to others, and to their mothers who "failed to advise, implore" their daughters (*Poetry* I: 138–39). In many of these poems, as well as in numerous drawings intended to accompany the poems with illustrations of virginal young lovers, ruling goddess figures, and female angels — as well as those negative figures of coquettes and sorceresses — it is the woman's "queen-like" qualities of order and control that Lindsay most admires.

Andrew Lytle once speculated that the southern conception of female purity played a practical role in the functioning of agrarian society. In an essay entitled "The Subject of Southern Fiction," Lytle noted that the underlying rationale for an insistence on chastity within an agrarian society was not a matter of "chivalric romanticism" but "of family integrity, with the very practical aim of keeping the bloodlines sure and the inheritance meaningful" (61). Before the invention of machinery that greatly lessened the need for a dependable supply of labor at critical times of the year, the agrarian venture was a corporate endeavor of the family, requiring the presence of an extended clan with unquestionable loyalty to the family unit. For the family bond to remain secure, blood ties must be incontestable. The insistence not only on the fact of chastity in the female but on what might seem its excessive display and celebration performed an essential role in maintaining the loyalties of an extended family in relation to the corporate endeavor of farming. Whether or not we accept the particular terms of Lytle's analysis in the cases of Poe and Lindsay, a similar connection between chastity and the redeeming role that women play in society, albeit expressed in more idealized terms, is evident in their works. As Lindsay writes in "To Reformers in Despair," the future of mankind depends on women as guardians of the hearth: the future utopia can be "Devout like early Rome with hearths like hers/Hearths that will recreate the breed called man" (*Poetry* I: 140). Given their influence on the family, Lindsey surmised, women are more powerful than legislatures, armies, and great industrialists.

In Lindsay's mind, reformed Protestant religion granted a "higher" place to women within society and within the institution of marriage, and in return — as with Poe's conviction that women must be protected from physical harm at the same time that their moral strength afforded the male a necessary protection from his own weaker self— required of them a degree of perfection that was almost unearthly. To fail to see this was to dismiss the "worship of women who are good and beautiful" (Lindsay, "Whitman" 4). It was in just this light that Lindsay imagined Elizabeth Mann Wills, one of a number of "inspiration girls" (in this

2. Poe and Lindsay, Literary Outcasts

case a very young inspiration girl who had been one of his students at Gulf Park Junior College) whom he courted in a passionate but impossibly old-fashioned manner. As Lindsay described Elizabeth in a letter in which he also proposed marriage, "You are virgin modesty and quietness, and meditation and individual conversation, and the village mood I have always worshipped and have always declared was the quiet pool in the heart of America" (*Letters* 287). One of the cornerstones of Reformation practice and belief, the sanctity of marriage was an integral part of the faith that, in fact, had had a transformative impact on Western civilization. Lindsay's assertion to Elizabeth that "you are certainly my only hope to be loyal to my best self" (*Letters* 287) was, in this sense, nothing more than the recitation of a commonplace of Protestant culture. Given the sinful, backsliding nature of the male, only devotion to the chaste female could restore him to his higher self. Much the same ethos informed what was perhaps Lindsay's favorite film, *The Romance of the Redwoods*, starring Mary Pickford, an actress whom Lindsay praised highly in his *New Republic* review entitled "Queen of My People" (7 July 1917).

As Lindsay continues in his letter to Elizabeth, it is particularly in the South that one finds what he calls "Democratic Chivalry," and "that is the reason the South is my country" (*Letters* 299). Lindsay's romantic feelings are further clarified in a subsequent letter to Miss Wills written en route to Spokane, Washington, on July 7, 1924. In this lengthy, rapturous epistle, Lindsay reveals the "most sacred literary secret of my whole life" (*Letters* 314): the fact that, at the age of nine, while reading *Paradise Lost*, he came upon a passage that related Milton's vision of marital love based on Milton's conception of Adam and Eve's relationship before the Fall. Now at age forty-four, Lindsay informs Elizabeth that he has spent his entire life searching for the mate described in Milton's poem, and, in the expectation of finding such a mate, he has retained his virginity in the face of "the terrible assaults of all the modern world on such a life" (*Letters* 314). As he goes on to tell her, this prelapsarian conception of marriage is far from that of the "puritan Milton" caricatured in the popular imagination. The true Miltonic vision merges chastity with an unspeakably ardent passion, resulting in a "wild and innocent love"

(*Poetry* I: 238), and it is this combination of virginal purity and voluptuous desire that Lindsay has sought and believes he has found in his relationship with Elizabeth.

Lindsay is keenly aware of the difference in their ages (forty-four and eighteen) and of the likelihood that Elizabeth will seek a mate closer to her own age, but he urges her to hold out for the love of a poet. Unlike the callow youth of twenty-six whom he imagines dancing (with a hip flask in his back pocket) with Elizabeth, the poet offers a future that combines worship, desire, and intellectual communion. He dangles before her eyes the prospect of a literary partnership in which she will ultimately rule a "literary Empire." It may seem a curious basis on which to propose marriage, especially to a young woman of eighteen, and yet in the context of Lindsay's devout background, it is not curious at all. What he offers his beloved is the literary equivalent of the Protestant ethic: a life of strict self-control combined with high ambition and purpose, and at the heart of this vision is the quest for public recognition that will serve as testimony of God's favor. What Lindsay urges is that Elizabeth conform to a conception of marriage as understood within reformed Protestantism and that she resist the new atheistical culture that Lindsay associates with modern dances, alcohol, jazz — the postwar culture of the urban northeast.

Even this proposal was a falling off from the zealous ambition of Lindsay's youth, in which he aimed to be a Galahad of the Road — a tramp in pursuit of the Gospel of Beauty who must necessarily fore go all hopes of earthly love. The Galahad figure, the chaste knight preoccupied with his quest and too busy to consider a domestic attachment, was the male counterpart of the chaste female. As in "The Mouse That Gnawed the Oak-Tree Down," a poem that reflects Lindsay's sense of his own patient pursuit of his mission, "He [the mouse] kept so busy with his teeth/He had no time to take a wife" (*Poetry* I: 221). Whether it is a matter of being "too busy" or, as Lindsay seems to suggest in his letters from the same period, a fear of failure in courtship as a result of awkwardness and self-consciousness, Lindsay was convinced that his mission must take precedence over his romantic pursuits. As he wrote in an early poem, "The Beggar's Valentine," "love can never be mine;/Passion, hunger and pain,/These are the only wine/Of the pilgrim bound to the road" (*Poetry* I: 8).

Clearly, Lindsay's reticence toward romantic love was bound up with his sense of artistic and spiritual mission. At a very early age he understood that there was no room for romantic love in the life of a saint, and sainthood was his avowed ambition. At the same time, his failure as a lover was connected with his admitted lack of social graces. In the company of young women, even if he had wished to enter into courtship (which he did, to no avail, several times), he possessed more than enough clumsiness to drive all prospects away. After a few serious attempts, he sensed that it was hopeless and resigned himself to bachelorhood, at least until the death of his mother left him completely alone. This is not to say that Lindsay ever conquered his physical desires. From an early age Lindsay was aware of the "black desire" within his nature: "Lust like the pulse of the tiger—/The hunger of hawk for dove," as he wrote in "Why I Fled from Duty." Fleeing from duty "lest I do her harm" (*Poetry* I: 110), Lindsay's persona preserves in a volatile lifetime tension both "white body" and "black desire," the preservation of chastity in the face of lustful desire.

Significantly, a similar dynamic underlies Lindsay's favorite poem by Poe, "Ulalume." On the anniversary of the death of "the lost Ulalume," the poem's narrator finds himself tempted by a desire of a worldly nature as suggested by the appearance of Venus, the morning star. "Warmer than Dian," or Artemis, Venus conjures up a "Lethean peace"— the peace of displacing the memory of Ulalume by the warmer presence of Venus, "With love in her luminous eyes." Cautioned by Psyche of the dangerous nature of his desires, the narrator ignores his soul's warning and follows the star until he is stopped short at Ulalume's tomb. Now with his heart "ashen and sober," the desolate narrator finds himself in a foul and haunted region from which it is unlikely that he will ever escape. Composed months after the death of his wife, Virginia, "Ulalume" might well be read as Poe's effort to rein in those desires for intimacy that have surfaced too soon after Virginia's death. More broadly speaking, however, the poem expresses an inhibition of worldly desire characteristic of Poe's entire life. Poe's sense that physical passion was degrading finds expression in "For Annie," in which the poet, now in a death-like state of rest, speaks of having been freed from the "Torture of thirst/For the napthaline river/Of passion accurst." That fiery river, Phlegethon, runs through Hades and torments those souls who have failed to restrain their desires.

The opposition of the characters of Ligeia and Lady Rowena Trevanion in Poe's crucial story "Ligeia" involves a similar contrast between a worshipful chastity and the suggestion of an impure or at least more mundane relationship, and in the end this tension is resolved in much the same way as in "Ulalume." The relation with Ligeia is suggested by the narrator's fascination with her large, luminous eyes. In their mutual exploration of unfathomable mysteries, Ligeia is an intellectual and spiritual guide: "Her presence, her readings alone, rendered vividly luminous the many mysteries of the transcendentalism in which we were immersed" (*Poetry and Tales* 266). By contrast, "the fair-haired and blue-eyed Lady Rowena" possesses no such spiritual traits — her fair hair and blue eyes are enough to suggest her inferiority in this regard to the darkly exotic and black-eyed Ligeia — but the fact that she has been all but sold to the narrator by her "haughty family" lowers her to an even greater extent. The deathly bridal chamber that is prepared for her, right up to the "pall-like canopy" and "ebony bed," would seem to express Poe's psychic suppression of physical desire and compel the "successful" transubstantiation of Ligeia's soul into Rowena's body.

Though involving an unconvincing turnabout at the end, "Eleonora" explores a similar tension of authorized chastity and illicit eroticism. The narrator's initial relation to Eleonora, like Virginia Clemm, his maternal first cousin, is one of Edenic innocence ("Hand in hand about this valley, for fifteen years, roamed I with Eleonora before Love entered within our hearts"). As if in punishment, soon after their innocence has been tainted by the admission of physical desire Eleonora falls ill and exacts a pledge of eternal chastity from the narrator. Yet in the conclusion of the story the narrator falls in love with and weds Ermengarde, after which Eleonora's spirit visits him and, "for reasons which shall be made known to thee in Heaven" (*Poetry and Tales* 473), absolves him of his vow of chastity. Those reasons remain hidden to the reader of the story, but perhaps the narrator's violation of his vow is mitigated by the essential similarity of Eleonora and Ermengarde — aside from the similarity of their names, both are "ethereal" and unworldly despite the fact that the one is an "artless and innocent" denizen of nature, the other a maiden whom he meets at a "stately court" (*Poetry and Tales* 470, 473).

The crucial point, however, is that the quality of unearthly beauty that Poe images in these female figurations is by definition supernal, unworldly, ideal. It is, in fact, impossible to express Poe's conception of Beauty in modern terms, in all of which it has been degraded to the level of the decorative, the mundane, or even the lascivious. Most importantly, Poe's conception of ideal Beauty is tied inextricably to a conception of order in the universe that is essentially moral and religious in nature. The crucial claim of the purity of the female — a purity defended by male chivalry, by the lady's retreat from the public sphere, and if necessary by death — is the essential accompaniment of and counterpart to a demanding code of male striving and self-sacrifice. Female purity is the most compelling earthly reflection of the divine light, and as such it is the guarantor of all male identity. All aspects of Victorian society that may be termed "moral" rested on this lynchpin of perfection.

Thus, for both Poe and Lindsay, female purity was tied inextricably to a comprehensive vision of reform of human society. As with Poe, Lindsay provided an artistic embodiment of cultural ideals that can be traced to the Protestant Reformation and more especially to the theology of John Calvin. Although Poe was not a religious writer per se, he was a visionary whose writing reflects the influence of a Calvinist upbringing. As Kenneth Silverman notes, John Allan, Poe's guardian, was "born to a pious seafaring family in the seaport of Irvine, Scotland" (11–12). The thrifty, demanding, relentless, and independent qualities of Allan's character, his "gloomy, Calvinistic outlook on life" (Hutchisson 20), reflect the influence of a vigorous Calvinist upbringing. (As Silverman points out, John Allan's "favorite words and phrases were 'fortitude,' 'correctness,' 'undeviating firmness,' 'perseverance,' 'good habits,' [and] 'prudence'" and his unwavering advice to young men was "never fail to your Duty to your Creator first, to your Employer next" [12].) As a youth, Poe reacted harshly against Allan's unyielding Calvinism: his early dissipation, his gambling and drinking, his lack of interest in business, and his extreme devotion to beauty, all seem directed against the narrow values of his moralistic father, and yet his guardian's Calvinism exerted a decisive influence on Poe's moral outlook. One of the ironies of Poe's life is that, in essentials, the unorthodox Poe adhered far more strictly to the religious ideals of reformed Protestantism than did his moralistic guardian, who, while given to dissipation, gambling and womanizing, excoriated the weakness that he saw in his dependent ward.

Despite his ambivalent attitude toward formal religion, Poe had always sought a unified explanation for the chaotic universe around him, and his yearning for faith was reawakened late in life by Marie Louise (Loui) Shew, a devout Episcopalian and trained nurse who extended the hand of charity toward Poe and his dying wife, Virginia. In Loui's company, Poe attended Episcopalian services during the Christmas holiday, 1847 (although he became so agitated during the service that he was forced to leave: evidence, perhaps, not of a lack of sympathy with religion but of overexcitement in its presence). Toward the end of his life, as the uncertainty of his health (including the perhaps questionable diagnosis of heart disease) convinced him that he was dying, Poe explored avenues of addressing the unresolved tensions of his life, including his excessive dependence on alcohol. On August 27, 1849, as Silverman informs us, Poe "took a public pledge against alcohol by joining a Richmond branch of the Sons of Temperance" (427), and he was urged by the editors of the Richmond temperance journal to write in support of the cause of temperance — just as Lindsay was to campaign for the Anti-Saloon League fifty years later.

In reality, Poe's thinking on religion was uncertain and confused, a mélange of Gnostic and orthodox ideas influenced as well by classical and romantic conceptions. Nonetheless, a careful reading of the Mabbott edition of his collected works, with its exhaustive annotation of biblical and church allusions, attests the extent of Poe's knowledge of biblical texts. As James M. Hutchisson points out, in stories such as "The Masque of the Red Death" Poe makes widespread use of Christian imagery, numerology, and phraseology (139). The effect of Poe's early religious training is evident in the ease and frequency with which he employs biblical references and images, and more importantly, in the way in which his works support a conservative conception of human corruption. But for the ambiguous relationship to crime that his heroes often betray, Poe's interest in the detective hero might be considered the encoding of a desire to "get at" the problem of universal corruption, punish its guilt, and force its reformation.

Poe's sense that death is shadowed by the ominous presence of an uncertain afterlife, one that Poe at times represents as annihilation and other times as a triumphal paradise of union with the divine, is another traditional Christian element in his work. In "For Annie," in which Poe evokes his metaphorical paradise after death in the arms of his beloved Nancy Richmond, the terms which he finds to describe this paradise are partly drawn from Christian tradition. The solace that he finds in Annie's arms is likened to "a water that quenches all thirst," a reference to John 4:14. Annie herself is "the queen of the angels," that is, the Virgin Mary. At the end of his life, in the poem "Eldorado," Poe speaks of an aging "gallant knight" who still seeks Eldorado and is instructed by a "pilgrim shadow" to continue bravely on his quest, "Down the Valley of the Shadow,/...If you seek for Eldorado." In the very last lines of poetry that he is known to have composed, Poe alluded to Psalm 23:4, the Lord's Prayer.

Unfortunately for Poe and for Lindsay, the fervent spirituality of their writing ran counter to the prevailing dynamic of American culture toward reliance on secular and materialist philosophies. The public that hounded Lindsay to recite "The Congo" had little interest in his program of social and spiritual reform. Much like Poe, Lindsay wrote out of a romantic sensibility that decried the evil of society, particularly the society of cities with their focus on commerce and industry, and that looked to nature and to spiritual/mental pursuits as a form of refuge. Just as in such stories as "The Man of the Crowd" and "The Murders in the Rue Morgue," Poe represents the city as unhealthy, violent, and neurotic, Lindsay connects urban society with illness and destruction. Just as Poe, in "Landor's Cottage," depicts an idyllic pastoral retreat from the horrors of urban life, Lindsay envisions the New Springfield, his idealized vision a redeemed human society, as an agrarian utopia populated by young men and women whose robust virtue resembles the "perfection of natural ... grace" that Poe found in Annie, the gray-eyed, unworldly figure of virtue and grace (based on Mrs. Nancy Richmond) of "Landor's Cottage" and "For Annie." Lindsay's poem "Factory Windows Are Always Broken" is one his best-known recitals of the misery of urban industry, and brief poems like "Another Word on the Scientific Aspiration" attack a scientific or mechanistic view that would reduce the mystery of the butterfly and other creatures to "machinery" or "see through" nature with x-rays.

One could cite a number of Poe's poems and stories, from his early "Sonnet — To Science" to his elaborate hoaxes of scientific inquiry in "Loss of Breath," "Mesmeric Revelation," "The Balloon-Hoax," "Some Words with a Mummy," and "The Facts in the Case of M. Valdemar," in which he works from a similar skepticism regarding the secular culture's overconfidence in science and technology. What connects all of these works is the author's rejection of the claims of scientific and medical authorities to offer a "solution" to mankind's essential condition of loss. In his hoax stories, Poe was not merely composing an entertaining parody of scientific experimentation: he was attacking the fundamental basis of a materialist ethos that had guided Western philosophy from Galileo and Machiavelli to Hobbes, Smith, and Hume. Much like his near contemporary, the philosopher Hegel, Poe would challenge the materialist philosophies by undermining the distinction between consciousness and the objective world, repeatedly asserting the identity of consciousness and object through his doctrine of the universal sentience of all matter.

By the end of his life, an awareness of the opposition between a northern elite and a heartland democracy was firmly established in Poe's thinking. The "Longfellow War," in which Poe attacked Longfellow's poetry and charged him with plagiarism, reveals Poe's gnawing resentment of the wealth and influence of the North and particularly of Boston. As Hutchisson writes, "Poe despised the literary coteries in Boston and believed that American literature suffered from a New England bias" (182–83). Considering his conflicts with the publishing establishment in New York and his disdain for Boston Transcendentalists, it is not surprising that in the last years of his life Poe staked his future on a scheme to publish *The Stylus* on the strength of subscriptions from the small

2. Poe and Lindsay, Literary Outcasts

towns and rural areas of the South and West, or that he planned a journey to St. Louis to inaugurate the magazine's publication in partnership with Edward H.N. Patterson. Under the plan the magazine was to be officially published in New York and St. Louis, though actually printed in Patterson's shop in Oquawka, Illinois, outside the western metropolis that was then the fourth largest city in America and by many considered the prospective center of American commerce and civilization. At some point in the venture, Poe must have entertained Lindsay's dream of an America governed from a heartland capitol.

In a similar way, the author's sense of an opposition of rural innocence and urban cynicism underlies Lindsay's important poem, "Bryan, Bryan, Bryan, Bryan." Bryan — "the one American Poet who could sing outdoors"— evokes a panoply of Western images: lively creatures of all sorts, fertile agriculture, exuberant moods and manners, as well as the hopes of a silver standard that would promote economic development. Bryan's opponent was "that respectable McKinley," the "slave" of Mark Hanna of Ohio, himself the big-city boss and "friend of Pierpont Morgan" beholden to Eastern money, commerce, and industry. In an uncanny way, Lindsay's explosive response to Professor Augustus Smith of Boston University, who had requested permission to set Lindsay's poem "Foreign Missions in Battle Array" to music, replicates Poe's hotheaded attack on northern cultural hegemony during his infamous performance at the Boston Lyceum on October 16, 1845. Lindsay accused Smith of attempting to "steal my song," and he connected this inclination with what he perceived as a pervasive cultural dominance of the northeast: "So much the worse for Boston," he wrote Smith. "May the ghost of Amy Lowell dance on your grave" (qtd. in Ruggles 377).

Poe's fantasy of capturing a growing heartland audience was part of a larger conception of regeneration that pervaded his life and writing and that appear with renewed force in his final book, *Eureka*. At the very center of Poe's cosmogony is the revelation that godhead and mind are one: God and all of creation exist within the human mind, which is thus assured of immortality even as the mortal flesh dies away. As Hutchisson writes, Poe's cosmic discovery in *Eureka* was "a confirmation, through scientific demonstration, of his belief in an other world of repeated dyings and rebirths" (219). The great mystery that Poe comes up against in *Eureka* is, of course, nothing less than the self's tenuous existence amid a world of pain and death. In the end, Poe's devastating sense of the transience of organic life forced him to surrender the physical and to embrace a position of philosophical idealism, a recognition of the collapse of the physical world in the face of the mystery of its own being.

Writing within the same philosophical tradition as Poe, Lindsay professed Gnostic conceptions of everyday life transformed by spirit, of a life "caught up into the unseen not so much that we may be saints of heaven, but rather kings of Chaos; that we may create new worlds that will praise us, rather than praise the Power that made us" (qtd. in Ruggles 108). To convey his vision of a redeemed immanent world, Lindsay drew on familiar symbols of rebirth and life eternal: the powerful sun, the cyclic moon, the returning flowers of spring, the ghostly revisitation, and the butterfly emerging from the cocoon. Underlying all of Lindsay's thinking about salvation was his lifelong Christian faith with its central belief in Christ's crucifixion and resurrection.

The image of the butterfly is especially suited to suggest the stage of rebirth that Lindsay envisages since it evokes a peaceful "aesthetic" reformation resulting from the rebirth of individual souls rather than a militant one dependent on political force. In "The Soul of a Butterfly," Lindsay pictures the dead corpse of the earth consumed by worms. Standing outside the walls of the ruined Jerusalem and facing north, not so much toward Europe as toward America (in the direction, that is, of a future reawakening of Protestant Reformation that might emulate or even surpass previous periods of revivalism in American history), Lindsay's persona listens as a voice cries, "The earth will live again." He watches as the earth, covered by a gray cloud and heavy mist, bursts into "bud and bloom" and flashes "with gold and red." Rising from the dead earth is "the soul of a giant butterfly," a creature of "wondrous grace" (*Poetry* I: 50). As in many of Poe's works on the same theme, most famously "The Fall of the House of Usher," Lindsay's poem concludes with a startling scene in which the narrator, constrained by the force of the transformative event, witnesses the awe-inspiring scene of rebirth. What Lindsay foresees in this rebirth is an America that has been transformed into an evangelical theocracy. As he writes in "The Town of American Visions," the New Springfield will be filled with "angel-bands in infinite array." These angel bands will dance on the earth, free of their despair, "And white streets flame in righteous peace at last" (*Poetry* I: 272), an evocative expression of the potential for goodness that Lindsay envisioned.

Clearly, Poe and Lindsay are connected by the similarity of the philosophical and religious traditions upon which they draw in their writing. Another reason for Lindsay's fascination with Poe was the knowledge that, both by temperament and family ancestry, he himself was to some extent a southerner, and Poe, along with Mark Twain and Sidney Lanier (both of whom Lindsay particularly admired), was, of course, among the South's leading writers. In the poem "Alexander Campbell," Lindsay records how his Scotch-Irish paternal ancestors migrated from Pennsylvania to the South, across the Appalachian Mountains into Kentucky, and from Kentucky westward into the Midwest — an ancestral journey that was part of a broader migration that to no small extent helps to explain the cultural affiliation of the South and West in American culture. In the wake of the Civil War and Reconstruction, this affiliation was not always so apparent, especially to those of southern heritage such as Lindsay's father. Lindsay once wrote to R.W. Gilder, "If there were ever two things my father wanted me to do they were to hate Lincoln and the Republican Party" (*Letters* 29), a remark that reveals the father's position in unequivocal terms. For Lindsay himself, matriculating in the Springfield public schools, "the Lincoln patriotism triumphed over the political opinions of a Southern-feeling household" (*Letters* 29), even though in deference to his father Lindsay retained a lifelong attachment to the South.

It was in the South that Lindsay chose to begin his tramping, an adventurous avocation that would eventually carry him across large portions of the mid–East, Midwest, Plains, and the West. In March 1906, at age twenty-six, Lindsay and his friend Edward Broderick, traveled to Jacksonville, Florida, from New York. From northern Florida, Lindsay and Broderick walked to Orlando. Lindsay then traveled alone, by foot, rail, and wagon through portions of Georgia, North Carolina, Tennessee, and Kentucky, where he concluded his first tramping adventure with a month-long visit with his aunt, Eudora Lindsay South. Lindsay's account of his encounter with the common people of the South comprises the first half of *A Handy Guide for Beggars*, published in 1916, in which he asserts his "high opinion of the fine people of the South" (67). Staying in a variety of log cabins, farmhouses, missions, and town residences, Lindsay attempted, not always successfully, to live by his "third rule" of the road ("Have nothing to do with money and carry no baggage" [*Handy Guide* viii]), as well as his other seven rules ensuring self-sufficiency and independence. As one might expect, Lindsay's idealistic faith in mankind was at times sorely tested, but in the end his faith in ordinary humanity was confirmed and rewarded. He returned from the tramp with enough notes to complete a readable book detailing his experiences.

Later, as his work met with critical rejection in the East, Lindsay turned even further to the South and West as the primary audience both for his published work and his lecturing, most of it organized between 1919 and 1923 by Professor A.J. Armstrong, chair of the English Department at Baylor University. In April 1919, following his first visit to Baylor, Lindsay wrote to Armstrong: "My visit to Texas has showed my soul the New South, which is different from the South of Southern cousins my own age I grew up with, and far indeed from the South that burns negroes alive, which I assure you existed very vividly in my mind" (*Letters* 179). By the following year, Lindsay actually decided to restrict his lecturing to the West and South, advising Armstrong that "I am entirely through with the East *as a public person*" (*Letters* 205). Years later, after he had taught for two years at Gulf Park Junior College in Gulfport, Mississippi, he hoped to "grow up with the new South" among the families of the female graduates he had taught (*Letters* 326), a wish that was connected with his ardent but unsuccessful courtship of Elizabeth Mann Wills.

Early in life, while teaching a Y.M.C.A. course in New York, Lindsay had found that he could not bring his students to appreciate the greatness of Poe's "Ulalume," even though the same audience was enthralled with lesser work by Kipling (*Letters* 29). In an uncanny way, this experience foreshadowed Lindsay's own dismissal from the canon several decades later, and as it turned out, Poe and Lindsay were dismissed for much the same reason. It was the story, as Marc Chenetier puts it, of "how a man of insight is fashioned into a freak and ultimately destroyed" (xxix). Simply put, Lindsay was rejected by most critics, editors, and readers in the East and by those who looked to the East for cultural identity because he was both provincial and old-fashioned, "faults" of which he was fully aware. "The man who is too much in harmony with his time is a compromiser," Lindsay had written following the rejection of his early poems by William Dean Howells and others (qtd. in Ruggles 75). Not only was he out of step with the drive toward modernization, he took seriously the cultural ideals of heartland America and sought to preserve and build upon them. No wonder he seemed a freak to Mencken and other "sophisticated" writers in the East: an evangelical Christian, a moralist, a teetotaler, a virgin and a prude, a traditionalist in versification, a supporter of traditional music and art over jazz and abstract forms, an avowed regionalist, and a patriot, Lindsay was utterly opposed to the direction of the urban-industrial society.

By understanding the basis on which Poe and Lindsay were dismissed from the literary canon, we can more clearly understand the cultural divide between a democratic heartland culture grounded in traditional conceptions of virtue and an elitist coastal culture dominated by a secular and materialist ethos. Since the death of Poe in 1849 and Lindsay in 1931, the divide has only widened, and in *One Nation, Two Cultures*, Gertrude Himmelfarb documents the extent to which the split between the dominant secular culture and the "dissident" traditionalist culture has continued to widen. Vachel Lindsay's lifelong regard for Poe and his sense of the similarity of their careers reveals a great deal about his own artistic purposes and his sense of the obstacles facing his work. In his perceptive assessment of the similarities of his career to that of Poe, Lindsay expressed a keen awareness of his opposition to and exclusion from an emerging urban-industrial culture with its own cultural perspective very different from his own. In his eulogistic treatment of his predecessor, Lindsay betrayed his awareness that both he and Poe had been fighting a lost cause — lost, at least, for the time being. In the ethos of modern urban America, there would be little room for the spirit of religious reform to which Lindsay dedicated his life, and, like Poe, his retreat to the heartland in search of a sympathetic hearing would also prove a disappointment. When Lindsay died on December 5, 1931, a frenzied suicide in the house in which he had been born and raised, he acknowledged the depth of his kinship with Edgar Allan Poe and with it, the defeat of his dream of spiritual reformation.

- 3 -

Vachel Lindsay's Covenant with America

On December 5, 1931, Nicholas Vachel Lindsay died in the upstairs bedroom that he had occupied as a child, having committed suicide by the horrific means of ingesting Lysol. In hindsight, the tragedy — and the slide into depression and paranoia that preceded it — were predictable, for in his career as heartland poet and polemicist Lindsay had set himself against the gathering forces of secularism and materialism in modern American society. Lindsay's quixotic mission, a cultural reformation that mirrored his beloved mother's evangelical faith, was nothing less than an attempt to reverse the course of modernity itself, and this as America was being transformed from a rural-agrarian into an urban-industrial society. At this most unpropitious moment, Lindsay entered almost single-handedly into his own personal culture war against the cynics and skeptics of his day, an effort that was perhaps heroic but certainly doomed. In the first decades of the twentieth century no one, not even the saintly prophet that Lindsay imagined himself to be, could have slowed the revolutionary social and technological changes taking place in America.

Lindsay's critique of modernity, though much influenced by the romantic tradition that included Blake, Shelley, and the German Romantics — Goethe, Schiller, and Heine — was distinctive in its emphasis on nativist and religious elements. Centered on what was called the "New Springfield," his idealistic scheme stressed civic revitalization based on what Springfield, Illinois, and other small towns might achieve if informed by a program of spiritual revival and cultural uplift. Like

Ronald Reagan, who emanated from precisely the same social and religious background, Lindsay envisioned a modern-day "city on a hill," its people redeemed by faith and dedicated to the global spread of democracy. Lindsay's was perhaps the last significant literary voice to reaffirm in an unqualified manner John Adams's providential faith in America as "the opening of a grand scene and design ... for the illumination of the ignorant and the emancipation of the slavish part of mankind all over the earth."

An early expression of this faith appears in the poem "Kansas," in which Lindsay recounted the idyllic weeks that he spent on the wheat harvest. These few blissful weeks on the Great Plains, where there was universal employment, great feasting and singing, healthy labor under the strong sun by day and sound sleep on beds of hay by night, served as a model for Lindsay's program of reform, for in these weeks, as he wrote in the poem, "tramps, one month, are men." Tramps become men because of their enlistment in a common effort focused on the production of the very staff of life; they become men because their labor plays a small but useful role in a civilization dedicated to human liberty, goodness, and advancement. Ill and physically exhausted, Lindsay himself left the work well before the summer ended, but he spent the rest of his life in pursuit of a similar, if more splendid, harvest: the redemption of an apostate society and its return to the purity, goodness, and faith that he recognized in the original covenant of America's founders. "I am haunted always by a vision of a splendid America," Lindsay wrote. "I have faith that America will come to her ripeness — in a hundred or a thousand years" (*Letters* 56). This faith in America was Lindsay's guiding principle throughout his lifetime, and despite the recurrent confusion, naïveté, and self-indulgent egotism that marred his writing, he remains an important spokesman for a conception of national identity that can be traced back to reformed Protestantism. Like Adams, Lindsay was inspired by an unshakable belief that Divine Providence had led his people to a land of freedom and opportunity.

As for all latter-day reformers, the central problem for Lindsay was the falling away of the public at large from the foundational ideals, both political and religious, to which he still fervently clung. Every line of his writing was devoted to the urging of a return to original principles: those principles of liberty, opportunity, and righteousness that underpin American civilization. In his defense of these ideals, Lindsay believed, he was contributing to the redemption of mankind both from the repressive caste system of old Europe and from the radically individualistic society emerging in America. While the blatant injustices of the European system of hereditary aristocracy were obvious, the destructive effects of modernity were not so apparent, especially to a public mesmerized by technological innovation. By the end of the nineteenth century, the American public had begun to view change as an end in itself, and in so doing had fallen prey to a dangerous form of idolatry. The fascination with what human ingenuity could accomplish had seduced public opinion away from a religious view of the world that instilled virtues of prudence and self-restraint.

The "Gospel of Beauty," as he called his version of applied Christian ethics, was Lindsay's key to the reformation of an apostate society. One of the fundamental values underlying this reform was that of humility, and for Lindsay the pathway to betterment was the "contrite heart" that would "take the death from us," as he expressed it in "Hymn to the Sun." A crucial element within all reformed churches, the culture of simplicity that Lindsay envisioned set him squarely against the voracious materialism that was, and remains, the cultural hallmark of an expanding secular culture. Like an earlier reformer, Cotton Mather, whose advice was to "stoop as you go through [the world], and you will miss many hard bumps," Lindsay sought to restrain the excesses of pride and self-gratification which he perceived in his countrymen. The way ahead, he knew, must always be informed by a keen awareness of the past and by a steadfast faith in the wisdom of tradition.

Admittedly, Lindsay was often naïve in the way he went about things, as when he plastered Springfield, Illinois, with privately printed "War Bulletins" that few cared to read, or when he traveled thousands of miles, walking and hitching rides as he attempted to trade poems for bread. Nonetheless, his optimism and innocence reflected essential virtues of American civilization. These qualities were rooted in the same unworldly faith that accompanied countless settlers on their journey west and that strengthened the resolve of emblematic leaders such as Abraham Lincoln and Theodore Roosevelt. Now, however, that resolve was in doubt, and Lindsay was convinced that the nation's essential covenant was under attack by the secularist forces of its own urban-industrial culture. Lindsay believed that rural and small-town America was still relatively free from this contagion, and the reform that he sought was associated with his belief that the heartland, the vast region stretching west from the Appalachian Mountains to the Pacific Range, embodied a more authentic America, truer to its cultural origins and founding principles, than that of the East or West Coasts. It is hardly coincidental that Lindsay's pantheon of heroes should comprise a cast of writers and public figures associated with the Midwest, West, and South, and that his roster of enemies should include Mark Hanna, the Ohio political boss who backed William McKinley against William Jennings Bryan in the presidential elections of 1896 and 1900. In place of the urban machine politics of the sort that elected McKinley, and that in subsequent years favored the American Republic with Coolidge, Taft, and Harding, he would have us admire the western populism of Lincoln, Bryan, and Theodore Roosevelt (a New Yorker but one with important biographical and ideological connections with the West). Lindsay's aesthetic tastes revealed a similar bias. Among American writers and politicians, his loyalties divide neatly along regional lines. In place of Emerson, Hawthorne, and Thoreau, he would have us read Twain, Sandburg, and Masters. Writing to Carl Sandburg in January 1917, Lindsay asserted that "the ideal American poet would have the tang of Mark Twain, the music of Poe, the sweep and mysticism of Whitman, and the platform power of Bryan" (*Letters* 143). (Elsewhere, however, he was far less sure of Whitman.)

To everyone who would listen, including the young critic and anthologist, Louis Untermeyer, Lindsay urged "the real open mind of America" as the standard of political and cultural success. This vision is expressed in one of Lindsay's finest poems, "Bryan, Bryan, Bryan, Bryan," composed in August 1919, almost a quarter century after the events it celebrates. The "open mind of America" suggests an expansionist economic policy that in Bryan's day centered on the idea of supplementing the gold standard with "free silver" and, thus, by vastly increasing the money supply, expanding economic opportunities for the common man. The open mind, however, implied much more than a shift in monetary policy: it urged a democratic over an elitist conception of American identity and with this an optimistic, culturally dynamic, and socially mobile conception of the nation's future. At the same time, paradoxically it might seem, this openness implied a staunch defense of the nation's moral inheritance and an interventionist foreign policy intended to export American values.

Tied to the presidential campaign of 1896, the events of the poem evoke Lindsay's youth — he was sixteen at the time Bryan visited Springfield — and, more important, the democratic ethos upon which his adult identity was founded. Lindsay reads into the 1896 campaign all of his youthful dreams, not only of political change but of artistic aspiration and even of courtship (his "best girl" is a "cool young citizen" wearing "in her hair a brave prairie rose"). Following Bryan's "Cross of Gold" speech, delivered like a thunderous incitement to reform, young Lindsay waits expectantly through the months leading up to the election, but, as with so much in Lindsay's life, election night brings defeat, not just for the candidate he has backed but for the entire universe of values to which he is inextricably tied. Lindsay's dream of a free, chaste, more hopeful America has been defeated by eastern money and eastern politics. Still, Lindsay predicts, Bryan's memory will linger long after McKinley and Hanna are forgotten. In the very act of writing his poem, Lindsay implies that the dream of the open mind of America, sung by "Homer Bryan" and celebrated by Lindsay himself, will endure for generations to come.

Lindsay's admiration of Bryan was predicated not merely on regional politics — the desire of the heartland for greater opportunity and autonomy — but, more importantly, on the fact that Bryan represented what Lindsay regarded as the providential mission of American democracy. In this conception, American values were linked to and, to a large extent, defined by the frontier and agrarian society of the recent past. As a spokesman for these values, Bryan was both a social conservative and a reformer with an idealistic view of what America might become, just the sort of man who would later serve as star witness for the prosecution at the Scopes "monkey trial" in 1925. Like Bryan and the heartland culture in which he and Bryan grew up, Lindsay was both an idealist and a religious conservative. A connection with the past, a wariness concerning change, and a predisposition to look to one's cultural inheritance for answers are fundamental aspects of this identity. The centrality of reform within Lindsay's thinking and his burning ambition to export American values were, in essence, part of an overriding mission to defend an inherited culture against the forces of radical change. In Lindsay's mind, reform implied a turning away from change.

Indeed, Lindsay's predilection was always to look to the past. His interest in ancient civilizations was catholic, and included a lifelong fascination with ancient Egypt and a strong attraction to Asia, particularly Japan. In all of his enthusiasms, however, Lindsay sought to define the present and the future in terms of enduring and universal aspects of human nature, and particularly in terms of those aspects that confirmed the values of his own civilization. The fondness for security, dignity, and order that he invokes in "Litany of the Heroes" reflects an almost Burkean predilection for established institutions and traditions. However revolutionary his talk of utopia might seem, upon closer examination it can be seen to be a refinement or continuation of a familiar cultural inheritance. Like most Americans of the heartland, Lindsay was a cautious reformer with an intense regard for the past.

One culture for which Lindsay had only disdain, however, was that of contemporary urban America. The virtues of the open mind could be discovered at almost any level of heartland society, but nowhere could they be found in the urban northeast. There Lindsay perceived the emergence of a new and destructive secular culture that he labeled "Babylon." Indeed, Lindsay was opposed to everything that the modern urban culture suggested: mechanization, advertising, commercialization, moral permissiveness, feminist emancipation, and, not least of all, jazz. Lindsay was furious when a selection of his work was published in Britain, without his prior knowledge, under the title *The Daniel Jazz and Other Poems*. As he stressed in his late poem, "The Jazz Age," jazz was the antithesis of everything he valued, whether that be agriculture, rural avocations such as fishing, classical–Christian culture (with special emphasis on classic British authors), or heartland writers such as Riley, Nye, or Twain.

3. Vachel Lindsay's Covenant with America

Lindsay attacked jazz in several poems, including "A Curse for the Saxophone" and "The Jazz of This Hotel," in which he pointed out that the "hot" jazz was in fact an urban art form that, at least to his ear, seemed callous and unfeeling.

In opposition to urban-industrial culture, Lindsay envisioned the re-emergence of an evangelical religious society centered in the American Midwest. Here would arise a procession of future forms of religious faith that would build their temples in the heartland. As he wrote to Erich Possett, "The church universal, as conceived by such papers as The Christian Century is my church. I believe it is far more vigorous, far more influential, far more a source of life and light than these two gentlemen [H.L. Mencken and Sinclair Lewis] will concede" (*Letters* 432). Almost everything that Lindsay attempted, in fact, was related in some way to the spiritual quest that began with his Campbellite ancestors, those disciples of Christ who on the American frontier split from the more ceremonial Presbyterian church to profess a reformed faith of even greater conformity to the origins of Christ's church. It was only seemingly anomalous that Lindsay, who never strayed far from the Campbellite faith, thought himself a prophet of some future, post–Christian civilization in which the faiths of all peoples would be linked within a single universal religious network. The unification of culture that he imagined was not the substitution of some vague universalist spirituality for his ancestral tradition: it was the blossoming of American democracy and evangelical faith on a global scale.

As evidence of his own sense of mission, Lindsay resigned all worldly prospects, including that of the medical career urged by his father, and set out on a series of tramping expeditions that carried him across much of the United States. Although she and her husband grew restive about Vachel's apparent lack of ambition and continuing financial dependence, his mother would certainly have approved of the way in which tramping suggested Christian outreach, and she would also have admired her son's uncompromising asceticism. Lindsay himself viewed tramping as a test of his faith in human goodness — the goodness of the common man within American democracy — but, as it turned out, the results of his survey of democratic man were decidedly mixed. As would happen throughout his life, Lindsay's idealism was betrayed by experience. His dream of America as a moral utopia simply could not hold up in the face of an increasingly commercialized and technocratic society. As Lindsay suggests in the poem, "The Bronco That Would Not Be Broken" (1914), the ideal of liberty to which he had devoted his life was under serious attack in the modern world — the world of centralized control that is represented in the poem by those who would constrain the energies of the bronco, even at the cost of killing it. As Lindsay understood all too well by the time he composed the poem, it is not just the material interests of society that are necessarily set against the tramp or the untamed bronco: it is also the force of a secularized culture that is inimical to tradition, particularly to those traditions of personal liberty and principled conduct that interfere with collectivist systems of production and social organization. The evocative quality of this poem results from the fact that in the untamed bronco of the prairie Lindsay discovered the perfect figure of his own emerging sense of disillusionment. The poem was Lindsay's poignant tribute to his own awkward pride and unruly provincialism, but it was also his acknowledgment of the price that he would have to pay at the hands of the tamers and killers of dreams. Like the bronco, Lindsay would die on the prairie exhausted by those who would restrain his religious idealism and bleed him for their own profit, but like the bronco Lindsay would "scorn" them and never stop dancing.

At the time he wrote "Bronco," before the outbreak of war in August 1914, the political implications of his program of reform must have seemed rather straightforward to the young Vachel Lindsay. As the world's only major power untainted by monarchy or titled aristocracy, the United States was duty-bound to spread the ideal of freedom around the world. By this, Lindsay meant not merely a democratic system of government that guaranteed basic rights and that extended opportunity to the masses, but also one that promoted the *moral* advancement of its people: in other words, democracy infused with the values of religious conservatism. The difficulty for Lindsay, as for all reformers of his kind, lay in the application of these high principles to the actual world. As a writer who came of age in the first decade of the twentieth century, he would face one test after

3. Vachel Lindsay's Covenant with America

another in his covenant with America. In his response to the first World War, the Bolshevik Revolution, the rise of fascism, the Roaring Twenties, and the early years of the Great Depression, Lindsay found his old-fashioned convictions challenged and derided from all sides. His moralistic notions of democratic mission, private virtue, and neighborly goodwill seemed quaintly inadequate, certainly inapt if not perverse, to most of his contemporaries, particularly so following the outbreak of war on a scale unknown in human history.

Lindsay was an ardent supporter of Woodrow Wilson — not a Campbellite but a southern Presbyterian, close enough — and of his plan for an international governing body, yet, after the horrific consequences of the European war became apparent, Lindsay was forced to reconsider his support for an interventionist foreign policy and to defend his position in the face of opposition from many of his friends. He fervently supported Wilson's plan for world democracy under an organization like the League of Nations, and to bring this about the use of military force had seemed necessary, but once the war began, and in particular as America moved closer to entering the conflict, Lindsay admitted his uncertainty. In a poem from summer 1917, entitled "The Bankrupt Peacemaker," Lindsay even referred to himself as the "Quitter Sublime" (*Poetry* I: 298) because of the agonizing indecision that he had endured over the previous three years.

As the war continued to grind on, Lindsay was filled with guilt because of his support for Wilson. At times, he even wished that he might enlist and be killed himself rather than have to witness the deaths of others for which he felt partially responsible. Writing to Eleanor Dougherty on April 4, 1917, he admitted: "My heart is very sad tonight about the war. I have not the heart to challenge Wilson. I voted for him and cannot regret it — yet Jane Addams' dauntless fight for peace goes home to my soul" (*Letters* 148). Addams, the co-founder of Hull House, had pressured Lindsay to oppose the war openly, but, though he wavered and admitted frequent reservations, Lindsay never broke with Wilson's position. As it was, Lindsay had little hope that the first World War would be the last major conflict of his lifetime, and in an uncanny way he predicted a second, much greater struggle — a global struggle to defend the international government that would be established after the first and that, if the human race survived it, might put an end to war forever.

It was not just the war, however, that tested Lindsay's faith in America's providential role in history. The emergence of a worldwide communist movement with its millenialist faith in revolutionary struggle, a movement that began to gain the allegiance of intellectuals in America as well as abroad, forced Lindsay to reconsider his own cultural inheritance. On the surface, at least, communist ideology appeared to coincide in certain respects with the program of moral and civic reform that his evangelical beliefs entailed, and for a brief time he viewed the Russian Revolution as a step toward world liberation, a process that would lead, as he fantastically supposed, from Socrates and the biblical Elijah through Christ, Rousseau, the leaders of the French Revolution, and Woodrow Wilson. Despite his championing of Kerensky's provisional revolutionary government in the months before the October Revolution, however, Lindsay soon recognized Marxism as the godless and materialist ideology that it was. During a visit to New York, he lectured the editors of *The Masses*, including Max Eastman, that they should "read Jefferson" and work within the Democratic Party, but, as he expressed it, "they were poisoned by Manhattanism and patronized us green boys from the West" (qtd. in Ruggles 232). Never again would Lindsay's complacent interpretation of history lead him to speak in the same breath of the prophet Elijah and Karl Marx.

Lindsay's faith in America was also tested at home, especially in the area of race relations. The August 1908 race riots in Springfield, which Lindsay witnessed firsthand, had a powerful and lasting effect on his attitudes toward blacks. In his letters, Lindsay condemned the white rioters, portraying them as recent immigrants to Springfield whose actions were unrepresentative of local society as a whole. Afterward he began to incorporate a growing concern with race into his writing and public speeches. As he acknowledged in a letter to Harriet Monroe, his best-known poem, "The Congo: A Study of the Negro Race," was, in part, the product of his reflections on the riots. In the future that Lindsay foresaw, African Americans would be assimilated within a national culture, and he

3. Vachel Lindsay's Covenant with America

intended his poem, which depicted the civilizing of African "savages" by Christian missionaries, as a blueprint for this process of assimilation. Perhaps only a young poet as pure of heart, not to say naïve, as Lindsay could have failed to foresee that the actual effect of "The Congo" on his audiences would be the very opposite of his intention, since it further lodged black identity within the stereotypes of primitivism and sensuality. As one who since childhood had haunted a room at Springfield's Leland Hotel where black workers gathered, who frequented black church services to satisfy his curiosity concerning black religious practices and sermon oratory, and who cherished Springfield's reputation as the home of the Great Emancipator, Lindsay was surprised and troubled by the response of W.E.B. DuBois who, writing in *The Crisis* in 1916, charged him with racism. Yet nothing he could have done would have placated DuBois, whose radical view of American society was opposed to Lindsay's in so many respects.

In offering his plan for the future of the black race, Lindsay was certainly paternalistic, but there is no doubt that, in his own way, he was also well-intentioned. Lindsay's open-mindedness concerning race was a long-standing fact of his character and one that distinguished him from many of his contemporaries. It was not happenstance that the Congo should have formed the subject of Lindsay's most famous poem, nor that the circumstance of the death of General William Booth in 1912 provided the subject of Lindsay's other celebrated early poem, "General William Booth Enters into Heaven": both were intimately connected to Lindsay's devotion to that fundamental principle of American civilization that guaranteed "the pursuit of happiness" to all. The Congo had always fascinated Lindsay, just as it had his entire generation following the celebrated meeting of Henry Morton Stanley and David Livingstone in 1871. The "track running through the jungle" in Lindsay's poem was in fact a verbal replication of the cover illustration of Stanley's *Darkest Africa*, while Livingstone's work as a medical missionary was just the sort of ambition that Lindsay's parents held up to him during his childhood. (It was, in fact, precisely the vocation that Lindsay's brother Paul and sister-in-law Olive undertook, not in Africa but in China.) Booth's missionary work on behalf of the poor was equally admired and familiar.

Lindsay himself had found employment campaigning for the Anti-Saloon League in 1909. In all of his major interests, including his fascination with Egyptian hieroglyphics and his curiosity concerning Asia, there was a tight personal logic — a logic that always pointed back to his family's role within the transmission of Western civilization from Europe to America, and from America to Africa and Asia.

Lindsay was never one to relinquish anything from the past, and this was especially true of anything pertaining to his relationship with his parents. Everything in his life came together in his yearning to preserve the little family that had struggled so hard to establish itself in the promised land of Springfield, the state capital and home of the martyred Lincoln. Lindsay was heir to an ancestral legacy of suffering and dispossession but also to the glorious inheritance of which he had been made aware by his mother, and Lindsay's admission that "every line I ever wrote, was her opinions and ideas rewritten" was hardly an overstatement. His plan of reform was not the run-of-the-mill fantasy of human perfectibility of the sort promulgated by generations of romantics, anarchists, and revolutionaries before him: it was the occasion for his stardom in a role that was a family obsession, the opportunity to fulfill at last the ancestral mission into the wilderness.

Unfortunately, as was often the case, Lindsay both underestimated the difficulties of this grandiose scheme and overestimated his own abilities. By returning classical-Christian civilization to its origins and by sharing the virtues of this reformed Protestant civilization with other peoples, Lindsay hoped to unify all nations within a single federation and all denominations within a single church or association of churches. The result, as he imagined it, would be the fulfillment of the millennial dream of permanent peace and universal happiness. In the poem "Incense," Lindsay described just such a future in which many new faiths would arise, all of them working in cooperation and housed in a world headquarters — a religious body analogous to the League of Nations. It should come as no surprise that the command center of this bright new global faith was to be located in Lindsay's home town of Springfield, Illinois, while the new and improved Ganges was, of course, the Mississippi River. As a result of their unity and conviction, these future belief systems

3. Vachel Lindsay's Covenant with America

would exert far greater influence than had the great religions of the past, and as the future religion's preeminent prophet and artist, Lindsay would be the messianic voice of the nation, and thus of the world. As the modern-day prophet of a redeeming vision of purity, order, and social harmony, Lindsay would be Alexander Campbell's successor — a rival and more, one might say, of the religious leader to whom his mother was so strongly attached.

With so much to offer, Lindsay expected that his plan of a heartland utopia would find ready acceptance by the public, yet it was this aspect of his work — not the frivolous performances that he disparagingly called the "Higher Vaudeville" — that readers largely disregarded. The reason, Lindsay believed, was that the denizens of the heartland failed to appreciate the value of their own civilization. The revolution had been betrayed from within as the young were seduced by the allure of a contemporary technological culture with its stunning invention of the automobile, the airplane, the radio, the telephone, and the moving picture. This was certainly part of the answer. How could an old-style Chautauqua performer, no matter how talented and enthusiastic, compete with Charlie Chaplin, Mary Pickford, or William S. Hart? How could the "poem games" that Lindsay dreamed up or the straight-laced prudery upon which he insisted gain a hearing in the Jazz Age? In the context of an explosion of new media, new affluence, and new personal freedom, how could Lindsay expect to obtain a hearing for his message? For an author of a highly traditionalist temper who turned forty in 1919, there was little chance of holding an audience unless that author exercised the exceptional shrewdness of a Robert Frost or possessed the philosophical depth of a Thomas Mann. Lindsay, slightly the junior of both of these men, displayed neither unusual sagacity nor philosophical acumen. What he did possess was faith in the religious teaching of his ancestors and optimism that his ancestral civilization would continue to prosper and expand. As he described it, his was the "west-going heart" filled with the conviction that America was the land of liberty, opportunity, and goodness. Yet as the gap widened between his devout traditionalism and the increasing cosmopolitanism of his contemporaries, Lindsay was simply worn down by the pressure of opposition.

Sadly, as he grew older, Lindsay's political thinking hardened into forms that were at times truly disturbing. By his early forties, Lindsay had come to see that the country was losing contact with its agrarian roots. The rural heartland was being overwhelmed by the wealth and influence of the urban northeast; the heartland people were losing faith in their heritage while new groups of Americans — newly arrived immigrants, many of them Jews — were importing what seemed an alien, anti-American culture. For a brief period, a dangerously reactionary tone entered Lindsay's writing. The anti–Semitic and jingoistic message was obvious in "I Like Nancy Boyd," in which he lauded the "patriot" Nancy Boyd, a young woman whose poem on the virtues of American housekeeping had appeared in the August 1922 issue of *Vanity Fair*. Praising Nancy for her love of country, Lindsay derided those hyphenated Americans, as he labeled them, who seemed to him grasping and foreign. This egregious passage, not the only such attack in Lindsay's writing from this period, was the opposite of the "open mind" that he had earlier espoused. It was as if he needed someone to blame for the personal and professional crises that he was facing. Clearly, it was a betrayal of the catholic appreciation of other cultures and religions that distinguished his writing in the two decades before his early forties and in the decade following.

A growing isolation from his contemporaries was one factor contributing to Lindsay's collapse in 1923. At such a point, it is not surprising that he should seek consolation from an attractive young woman of literary tastes who would venerate the accomplishments of the famous author he had become, if only on the basis of works that he now repudiated. Lindsay's marriage, at age forty-five, to twenty-three-year-old Elizabeth Conner was followed by an extended honeymoon in his beloved Glacier Park. It was an idyllic period of the sort that Lindsay had imagined in his earlier reflections on marriage and that he recorded in a number of poems, including those subtitled "The Forest-Ranger's Courtship." Lindsay had always visualized matrimony as taking place within a universe of spirit and beauty, and for a short time, at least, the union was filled with the intense blend of innocence and passion that Lindsay had first encountered in Milton's description of Adam and Eve before the Fall. Lindsay was incapable of accepting anything less, but with the

3. Vachel Lindsay's Covenant with America

arrival of two children and the mounting pressure of debts, the marriage descended into a ceaseless ordeal. Lindsay spent much of the seven years of his marriage separated from his wife as he struggled to earn a living from readings and brief teaching appointments, and in his isolation he grew increasingly suspicious of almost everyone around him. His suicide, the desperate and self-punishing act of a hopeless man, made sense only in that it reflected Lindsay's uncompromising nature. Lindsay had attempted to defend a grand ideal of goodness and purity in the face of pervasive cynicism, and when he became convinced that he had failed, he was driven mad.

Yet, at least Lindsay tried. Most of his contemporaries followed the cynical and self-serving course of standing aside as their civilization was brought into question. To many of these, Lindsay was an embarrassment, a writer who was so outré as to defend his country and his religious tradition at a time when it was entirely unfashionable to do so. Amy Lowell once referred disparagingly to Lindsay as "a middle Westerner of the middle class." In a similarly patronizing manner, the English poet Robert Graves, who entertained Lindsay and his mother in the company of T.E. Lawrence during Lindsay's speaking engagement at Oxford, characterized Lindsay as "an extremely simply man — Middle-Western clay with a golden streak," a graceful but dismissive allusion to the famous refrain from "The Congo," with the great river portrayed as a "golden track" running through the jungle. Graves noted that, though "everyone enjoyed the performance," it was "an exercise in elocution and mime — not a reading" (299). Neither Lowell, a Bostonian of the upper class, nor Graves, a public school graduate and Oxford-educated classicist, took Lindsay's poetry seriously, much less his underlying vision of a society steadfast in its adherence to traditional Christian virtues. Had they cared to listen, Lindsay's celebration of conservative values, including his dedication to personal rectitude and civic reform, would have left them not only dismissive but hostile, for they were representatives of precisely the sort of eastern and European elitism that he had always detested. It was elitism of this sort that was responsible, he believed, for much of the world's poverty and war, and only a world redeemed by faith and virtue would have any chance of a better future.

It is now over a century since Lindsay first proclaimed his "vision of a splendid America," yet it is unlikely that he would judge that the spiritual reformation that he envisioned has come to pass. Had he lived, Lindsay would be only more disillusioned by the failure of the League of Nations and subsequent bodies, the declining influence of religion in America outside the heartland and throughout much of the developed world, the growing power of a debased and venal media, and the expansion of consumerism to unprecedented levels. It would seem that nearly all that remains of Lindsay's efforts is the memory of a dedicated and impassioned writer who refused to compromise his values and who paid a terrible price for his commitment. Despite his frequent naïveté, miscalculations of effect, and makeshift philosophy, however, Lindsay was a writer whose depth of concern and unshakable fidelity to his nation's founding ideals should earn him respect and revaluation.

Moreover, Vachel Lindsay should continue to be read because, in the three-quarters of a century since his death, the American political landscape has come to be occupied to a significant degree by an conservative sensibility that resembles his own. The undeniable influence of modern-day evangelical faith on American politics is something with which mainstream intellectuals have not yet begun to come to terms. Like Graves and Lowell, those who do not share Lindsay's beliefs would rather deride what they do not understand, but American intellectuals do need to understand this sensibility because, as Lindsay predicted, it has come to ripeness, and it will remain a crucial factor in American society. The future that Vachel Lindsay prophesied is not going away, and it is incumbent upon readers to understand how deeply engrained within American civilization is the religious conservatism of which he was an important voice.

- 4 -

Agee and Dostoevsky: Two Writers Possessed

James Agee, whose selected works have now been dignified with inclusion in the Library of America series, has always been a writer whom the radical imagination has found appealing. Consistently antagonistic toward conventional belief, rebellious against tradition, unpatriotic, and a sworn enemy of restraint, Agee became a hero of the bohemian Left and even something of a cult figure before his premature death from a heart attack at age forty-five. Although Agee's body of work is not extensive, consisting of two rather brief novels (including the Pulitzer Prize–winning *A Death in the Family*, left incomplete at the author's death and edited by his publisher), *Let Us Now Praise Famous Men* (his chronicle of a season spent among the Alabama sharecroppers), a slender volume of youthful poems, and numerous essays, reviews, and film scripts, Agee's more important legacy, it could be argued, consists of his having served as the embodiment of the sort of fashionable cultural alienation that would become the hallmark of so many young people in the 1960s and subsequent decades and that, even today, holds powerful sway over the estranged imagination of the radical elite.

The appropriateness of comparing Agee with his great Russian predecessor, Fyodor Dostoevsky, might not seem obvious at first: not, that is, until one reflects on the centrality of the figure of the nihilistic revolutionary within Dostoevsky's fictional imagination. In the character of Stavrogin in *The Possessed*, Raskolnikov in *Crime and Punishment*, and Ivan Karamazov in *Brothers Karamazov*, Dostoevsky probed the combination of arrogant pride and abstract alienation that would underlie what has by now become a familiar persona in our literature: the faithless, self-absorbed, modishly cynical youth in perpetual rebellion against the perceived philistinism of his or her elders. The importance of comparing Agee and Dostoevsky lies precisely in the fact that it was Agee who would become for the late modernist and postmodernist generations in America the consummate representative of this figure of alienation. It was as if in the fictional rebels that Dostoevsky conjured up and so incisively critiqued, the Russian author was not Agee's predecessor but his contemporary or even his successor. In his acute diagnosis of cultural malaise, Dostoevsky perceived far more clearly than did his American successor the malevolent roots of Agee's self-destructive and self-indulgent impulses. Had he lived into the twentieth century and witnessed the fashionable nihilism of Agee and so many of his peers and followers, Dostoevsky would have abhorred what he saw, but he would hardly have been surprised. Every aspect of Agee's harmful and estranged imagination was already there, recorded for all to see, in the deathly nihilism of Dostoevsky's tortured protagonists.

Ironically, Agee's occasional references to Dostoevsky suggest more than a casual interest in the Russian writer's work. As Michael A. Lofaro and Hugh Davis note in *James Agee Rediscovered*, Agee had studied Dostoevsky, especially *The Possessed*, with I.A. Richards at Harvard (xxv), and, as Agee's notebooks reveal, Dostoevsky was among the authors whom Agee most admired and whom he even linked with Jesus Christ and William Blake, Agee's supreme exemplars (100, 298). Given Agee's admiration for the Russian author, it would be reasonable to expect to find similarities in their imaginative conception of life. It might appear, for example, that Agee's grasp of religious experience was of a similar nature to that of his predecessor. Certainly, Agee's career was much focused on that central concern of Dostoevsky, the clash between secular rationalism and religious belief, but the ways in which these terms were understood by Agee and Dostoevsky and the conclusions derived were, as it turned out, utterly opposed.

Among the most revealing discussions of Agee's religious sensibility is that in Agee's letter to Father Flye of August 10, 1939. Admitting his ambivalent response to the moral earnestness of *Goodbye, Mr. Chips* (the

4. Agee and Dostoevsky

movie and the book), Agee stresses the "purity" of his own religious temperament. The artist, he believes, must be fanatical in his defense of the "sacred," "merciless of mishandling" and "merciless toward the sincerely part-good." "In certain respects," he adds, "this mercilessness is non– or anti–Christian" (*Letters to Father Flye* 121). In what he viewed as a defense of the sacred, Agee actually felt it necessary to oppose nearly all forms of customary practice, inherited belief, or institutionalized authority. Agee's radically antinomian idealism led step-by-step toward alienation from, and indeed opposition to, all forms of conventional practice and traditional belief systems. In place of these conventional forms, Agee attempted to forge a personal ethics of radical purity and sincerity.

Agee's assertion of this "merciless" critique — the individual's right to dismiss inherited moral truths in favor of his own intuitions — would have been viewed by Dostoevsky with considerable misgiving. If anything, it resembles the rejection of the Christian inheritance by the Grand Inquisitor as narrated in Bk. V, Ch. 5, of *The Brothers Karamazov*, for the Inquisitor's tragic conflict, that "of having accepted the morality of Christ the Son and of acting in His name while no longer believing in God the Father" (Frank, *Mantle* 617), was very much Agee's central difficulty as well. Yet the fact, common to the Inquisitor and to Agee, that one harbors an uncompromising sense of compassion for mankind accompanied by anger at God for the injustice of man's condition does not lessen the damaging consequences of a rejection of the fundamental props of religious belief.[1] As Dostoevsky makes clear in the narration of Ivan Karamazov's meeting with the devil in Book XI, Chapter 9, of *Brothers Karamazov*, an ethics based only on one's personal inclinations — likes and dislikes that may shift from month to month and that may even be grounded in perversity and evil — is inadequate in the absence of an established, broadly accepted system of transcendent faith. As Dostoevsky put it in the notes for his planned 1881 *Diary of a Writer* (which remained unpublished due to his death in January 1881): "Conscience without God ... can deviate to the most immoral things. It is not enough to define morality as being true to one's convictions. One must also constantly raise the question: Are my convictions true?" (qtd. in Frank, *Mantle* 711).

This crucial difficulty never seems to have occurred to Agee. The puzzling fact about Agee's "defense" of the sacred is that, though he professed intense religious feelings, he at the same time denied the existence of an active, living God. In Agee's view, as he wrote Father Flye, God "delivers autonomy to all His creation and creatures and in compassion and ultimate confidence watches and awaits the result" (*Letters to Father Flye* 180). Agee's theology, in which there exists a complete separation of God from the world, was, of course, nothing new. Enlightenment thinkers from Rousseau and Voltaire to Franklin and Jefferson shared the same opinion, but in Agee's case such skepticism seems to have been particularly at odds with intensely demanding pietistic feelings and spiritual needs. For Agee, the salvational mythology of Christianity would seem to have been what was most required, yet it was this aspect of Christianity above all to which Agee objected. To be sure, Agee does speak frequently of Christ as one of his great heroes. At one point he even links his admiration of Dostoevsky and Christ, but it is important to understand the terms in which Agee conceives of Christ. Christ is a great and wise prophet, but one lacking divinity. Furthermore, as characterized in Agee's writing, Christ is largely an antagonistic figure — a figure of critique rather than redemption. The impossible, infinitely demanding terms of Christ's teaching, as Agee conceives it, function as a sort of lever in support of Agee's critique of conventional society. Christ stands *with* Agee as yet another fanatical, uncompromising figure of repudiation, dismissing the world's mediocrity and compromise. The Christ that Agee imagines is not a figure who comforts humankind but one who has been sent to annihilate the imperfect world and replace it with a new order of terrifying purity. As he made clear in a notebook entry comparing Christ with Chaplin and Blake, Agee saw Christ not as a redeemer of ordinary mankind but as an uncompromising scourge, demanding "withdrawal from the world" and "the destruction of the world as is" (*James Agee Rediscovered* 132).

Dostoevsky's sense of man's relationship to a living God, a religious orientation that V.V. Zenkovsky terms "Christian naturalism" (131), is just the opposite of Agee's sense of a remote and "second-rate" God. Even Dostoevsky's admission of doubt, as in his celebrated 1847 letter to Mme. Fonvizina, points in a different direction than does Agee's unbe-

4. Agee and Dostoevsky

lief. Admitting that he was "a child of the century, a child of disbelief and doubt," Dostoevsky nonetheless insists that he has fashioned a *Credo* that has transformed his life and art: "to believe that nothing is more beautiful, profound, sympathetic, reasonable, manly, and more perfect than Christ" (qtd. in Frank, *Ordeal* 160). The proposition that at one point Dostoevsky associates in *The Possessed* (other English translations are titled *The Devils* and *Demons*) with Nikolai Stavrogin but that Stavrogin has repudiated—"that if someone proved to you mathematically that the truth is outside Christ, you would better agree to stay with Christ than with the truth" (*Demons* 249)—was drawn almost word for word from an earlier letter and later expanded into a fully articulated ethical and aesthetic theory. These were theories that Dostoevsky was forced to defend against the attacks of liberal critics, just as tradition has had to be defended in our own time. Following the publication of *The Idiot*, which was attacked for the "fantasticality" of its characters, Dostoevsky wrote to his close friend Maikov that his art rested on a belief in "fantastic realism," which was "a totally different conception of reality and realism than our novelists and critics. My idealism—is more real than their realism" (qtd. in Frank, *Miraculous Years* 308).

More so than any of Dostoevsky's novels, perhaps, *The Possessed* seems prescient in its portrayal of a spiritual confusion of the sort that Agee's writing epitomized. In this novel, in particular, Dostoevsky focused on the fate of a demoralized society in which ethical and religious traditions had been rejected and supplanted by a confused welter of ideological fashion, half-hearted rebellion, and mere personal whim. Lacking an overriding purpose, members of this privileged but decadent society engage in destructive acts of spite, malice, and self-contempt, and at the very heart of this corrupt and defeated culture is the seething rage of those who know themselves to be separated from God. With the loss of the sacred, as the Polish philosopher Leszek Kołakowski has demonstrated, comes inevitably the collapse of moral distinctions at all levels, and with this collapse there arises a culture ruled not by stable, inherited conceptions of value but by mere force, whether this be the force of charismatic personality or the force of raw power. As Kołakowski writes: "The omnipresent Nietzschean or Sartrian chimera which proclaims that man can liberate himself totally, from everything, can free himself of tradition and of all pre-existing sense, and that all sense can be decreed by arbitrary whim, far from unfurling before us the prospect of divine self-creation, leaves us suspended in darkness" ("Revenge of the Sacred" 72).

Stavrogin is the foremost representative of this distinctively modern mode of alienation, one that is not merely heedless of the value of human life but that is set against the dignity of the individual human being. What Stavrogin is rebelling against is not just the particular religious tradition that Dostoevsky associated with the character of Father Zosima in *Brothers Karamazov* or, in the end, with Stefan Trofimovich in *The Possessed*: he is rejecting the possibility of belief altogether. As Frank points out, Stavrogin is intellectually committed to a proto–Nietzschean experiment of attempting "to pass beyond the limits of morality" (*Miraculous Years* 489), but at its very heart the experiment contains the fatal flaw of egotism. Lacking genuine humility, Stavrogin finds that he is incapable of self-regulation or genuine self-development. The fundamental insight of Christian repentance, the fact that human nature requires a structure of authority capable of controlling those powerful self-destructive impulses within human beings themselves, is rejected by Stavrogin, just as it was by Agee. One suspects that Dostoevsky, had he lived to witness Agee's sad career, would have lumped Agee with those Westernized liberals — Turgenev, Herzen, and the rest — who had abandoned both God and country. As Dostoevsky wrote to his friend Maikov describing the liberals of his time: "Instead of the loftiest, divine beauty, which they spit on, they are so disgustingly selfish, so shamelessly irritable, flippantly proud, that it's simply incomprehensible what they're hoping for and who will follow them" (qtd. in Frank, *Miraculous Years* 218). As Isaiah Berlin wrote in *The Roots of Romanticism*, a recently published book based on the 1965 A.W. Mellon Lectures in the Fine Arts presented at the National Gallery of Art in Washington, D.C., a fundamental aspect of Western civilization is the conception that "there is a body of facts to which we must submit" (119) and about which we can learn through inherited knowledge as well as through the endeavors of our contemporaries. What makes Stavrogin such a frightening and dis-

4. Agee and Dostoevsky

ruptive character is precisely the totality of his rejection of Western rationality in this sense. It is not that he is a reformer who intends the improvement of existing institutions and circumstances, nor even a revolutionary in the sense of one who wishes to replace a corrupt social reality with something more progressive. Stavrogin is a nihilist, a confirmed devotee of death and one who is possessed by an almost erotic sense of the seductiveness of violence.

The apprehension of this deathly seduction lies at the center of Agee's and Dostoevsky's experience and of their art, but the response of the two writers to this reality is utterly different. For Dostoevsky, the apprehension of death struck him most forcibly at age twenty-seven at the moment of his mock execution staged on the order of Czar Nicholas II. Immediately afterward, in the extraordinary letter that he wrote to his beloved brother Mikhail, Dostoevsky advises his older, but actually deferential and intellectually "younger," brother: "Look after yourself and your family, brother, lead a quiet and provident life." He then declares: "Life is a gift, life is happiness, every minute can be an eternity of happiness. *Si jeunesse savait!*" And he concludes the lengthy epistle with a spiritual prediction of a kind that turned out to be eerily prescient, for the trauma of Dostoevsky's encounter with death clarified an eschatological ethic to which he clung the rest of his life. "Now, at this turning point in my life," he wrote, "I am being reborn in another form. Brother! I swear to you that I will not lose hope and will keep my spirit and my heart pure. I shall be reborn to something better" (*Letters* 52–53). It is this eschatological vision, the understanding of the ultimate and precious value of one's time on earth, of the lives of others, and of the purposefulness of each moment of life, that lies at the center of Dostoevsky's moral vision.

Conversely, Agee never ceased to emphasize his sense of the purposeless nature of his life. From early on, his thoughts incline toward suicide; his own times appear to him "the darkest and saddest in centuries" (*Letters to Father Flye* 59). The "quiet and provident life" and the anxious care for oneself and one's family that Dostoevsky recommends to his brother are the very propositions that Agee despises above all. Speaking of Jonathan Swift's refusal to compromise with injustice, Agee informs Father Flye in August 1932 that he abhors those who are "kind and easy-living, and *resigned* to the expedient corruption of living quietly and happily in the world" (61). Lest one imagine that this is merely the histrionic despair of a young man who at nineteen felt "as if my mind were turning into a wart" (43), examples of a similar though deepening malaise can be cited throughout Agee's letters to Father Flye and throughout the entire body of his work. In a letter from February 17, 1936, Agee describes his mental condition as "not on the whole especially happy, or more than a fraction alive spiritually, and certainly seldom productive of any good, inside or outside me" (86). Then there is Agee's vivid description of his "drawing to a dead point" in a life in which he feels he has accomplished little: "Meanwhile I am thirty and have missed all the trains I should have caught" (125). In his letter of November 7, 1951, Agee speaks of his strong feeling "that this country is hitting somewhere along a new low" and of his thinking "it extremely unimportant who 'wins' the next war [presumably, the Cold War]" (196). Following a series of heart attacks in Los Angeles, Agee finds that he cannot moderate his habits as advised by his doctors because of his "caring much too little whether I live or die" (193). It is true that Agee spoke of an emerging religious inclination as he grew older—a "shapeless personal religious sense," as he characterized it (187)—yet this religious feeling was so much a reflection of his intensely anti-authoritarian suspicion of absolutes that it could never constitute a shared or stable religious system. It was, as Agee himself asserted, so "private" and inchoate as to be meaningless as a foundation of shared belief.

It is impossible to conceive of Agee's ever having proclaimed that "every minute can be an eternity of happiness." Agee's reaction to the force of death's reality was not eschatological; it did not point to faith in the purposiveness of the universe. Quite the opposite is true: it led to profound doubt, and thus to willful waste and self-destruction. The question that one must ask of Agee is the same one that Alyosha Karamazov puts to Lise Khokhlakova after she betrays her corrupt desire to have a man marry, betray, ruin, and desert her. "Have you fallen in love with disorder?" Alyosha asks (*Brothers Karamazov* 698). Yet, in reality, it is not merely disorder—it is destruction that appeals to Lise's dark imagination. In his innocence, Alyosha believes that she is simply too rich and too comfortable and that her nihilistic impulses are the product of a decadent ennui that could be alleviated by embracing the vows of poverty and service to others. In this, of course, he is not entirely wrong, but what he fails to recognize is the connection between Lise's self-destructive impulses and a larger cultural illness. Her desire to pursue evil for its own sake so that "there should be nothing left anywhere" is symptomatic of an imploding civilization shot through with self-contempt — the same civilizational demise that we have witnessed in the West throughout the past century.[2]

With so little to set against the destructive force of the period of cultural implosion in which he lived, Agee in his personal conduct demonstrated the same element of negation that appeared as a central theme in his writing, especially when writing about his autobiographical persona, Rufus Follet. In the well-known passage from Chapter Seven of *A Death in the Family* in which Rufus is portrayed as speaking with the figure of darkness, Agee's alter ego senses not only that "he would never know" his true identity, but, more damning, that he was not even the "little boy" that he appeared to be: "he was but the nothingness of nothingness, condemned by some betrayal, condemned to be aware of nothingness" (535). In this instance, a memory from earliest childhood, Rufus's terror is annealed by the appearance of his father, who comforts and sings to him, but the terror is real enough, and the implication is that once the father has been taken from him, the terror will never be silenced.

One consequence of Agee's rejection of inherited civilization was that, in rejecting a tradition that was the work of millennia, Agee took it on himself to construct from scratch a moral scheme and, indeed, a new mode of rationality — a task that philosophers from Aristotle to Hume had deemed impossible. The awareness that one is attempting a feat of this magnitude carries with it a grandiose sense of mission, and along with it that sense of what Dostoevsky, in the voice of the doomed atheist Kirillov in *The Possessed,* defined as the "new man." This new man, much like Nietzsche's post–Christian Superman, at the same time that he cares not "whether he lives or does not live ... will himself be

God" (*Demons* 115). As Kołakowski explained in "Revolution — A Beautiful Sickness," the millenialist dream that Dostoevsky represented in Kirillov, and in the entire circle of revolutionaries in *The Possessed*, involves "a belief that mankind can, as it were, free itself from all the burdens built up in its biological and social being over centuries, that it can wash away the sins of the past in the shock of a bloody revolutionary baptism, and begin everything anew from year one" (221). Inevitably, though, such sweeping revolutionary movements entail the clearing away of existing society and the purging of all those associated with it. "Starting from unlimited freedom," as Dostoevsky has it in *The Possessed*, one does indeed arrives at "unlimited despotism" (*Demons* 402).

It is possible to trace the consequences of this godlike, self-created persona in James Agee's life and art. Agee's notebook discussions of Christian sacraments and myth show him to be a sneering, malicious dissenter, one who speaks of the need to "keep God in His place" and who then asserts that "if a man makes a god in his own image; and then acts in no way to destroy his own self-respect, how can he go wrong?" (*James Agee Rediscovered* 196–97). Like the long tradition of Judas figures, beginning with Judas himself (whom Agee interprets as a "crushed Idealist," embittered by his loss of respect for Christ following Christ's triumphant victory over the Jerusalem "mob" [*James Agee Rediscovered* 195–96]), Agee never found a way out of his fatalistic negation. The best he could discover was support for a secularized ethics derived from Christian roots.

It was the implausibility of just this sort of demythologized Christianity, a humanized ethics derived from Christian principles as opposed to the irrational and inflexible demands of Christian mystery, that formed the central theme of Dostoevsky's major novels. As Frank stresses, "the crux of Dostoevsky's ideological preoccupations during the 1870s ... [was] the conflict between a worldly (Utopian Socialist and Populist) acceptance of Christian morality and one grounded in divine transcendence" (*Mantle* 49). Despite their tactical alliance with Christians, the dominant socialist thinking of Dostoevsky's time, as of our own, reflected an inflexible rejection of all forms of transcendence even as it attempted to preserve Christian "values" of charity, peace, and love. It was precisely this sort of attempt that Agee practiced throughout his adult life. There is

4. Agee and Dostoevsky

no doubt that Agee's fundamental ethics was derived from his Christian upbringing, but there is also little doubt that early in life he had come to question the redemptive force of Divine Incarnation, the essential mystery of Christian religion. Despite his assertion of secularized Christian values and his frequent employment of biblical imagery and language, Agee's ideology was based on a thorough-going philosophical materialism, one that entailed a deterministic conception of the human will. Again, in this respect we can locate Agee's thinking within the secularized liberal tradition that Dostoevsky despised above all else. Agee was merely a belated member of that numerous band whom Dostoevsky called those "trashy vulgar little liberals" (Dostoevsky's characterization of the radical writer G.Z. Eliseev, as qtd. in Frank, *Mantle* 229). As usual, Dostoevsky did not mince his words.

Agee's liberalism is on display everywhere in his work but perhaps most apparent in his treatment of the southern sharecropper class in *Let Us Now Praise Famous Men*, and, in fact, one of the most revealing contrasts between Agee and Dostoevsky lies in their differing views of the peasantry. For Dostoevsky, as Frank writes, the peasant "managed to preserve in his soul the highest and most sublime of the Christian virtues" (*Ordeal* 125)—that is, a humble acceptance of an inherited belief system. Similarly, despite the degradation of their physical surroundings and, to be candid, the self-wrought degradation of many among them, Agee's tenant families are presented in spiritual terms as embodiments of holiness. Yet this apparent similarity only attests to how different were Agee's and Dostoevsky's conceptions of the sacred, since, as a Slavophil who embraced an established religious tradition, Dostoevsky viewed the Russian peasantry as the living conduit of a traditional Russian Orthodox faith that had been abandoned or distorted by their social betters.[3]

One of the qualities that Dostoevsky associates most closely with the peasantry is the redemptive virtue of suffering, and since it represents the only pathway toward redemption of the self weighed down by egotism this virtue occupies a central place in Dostoevsky's attempt to reform the educated intelligentsia. The ultimate "purpose," so to speak, of suffering is to goad mankind toward redemption through Christ, an idea strongly suggested in the final sequence in *The Possessed* in which Stefan

Trofimovich is shown clutching the volume of the Gospels given him by Sofya Matveevna. As early as Part Two, Stefan intuited, if only in a superficial manner, the fact that "along with happiness, in the exact same way and in perfectly equal proportion, man also needs unhappiness!" (*Demons* 216). Yet it is only in confronting death that he comes face to face with the existential significance of his theory.

As Dostoevsky understood it, however, suffering can have little meaning in the absence of belief in a life after death. Again, it is Stefan Trofimovich who, quite unexpectedly, comes to understand more clearly than others the "necessity" of life after death. As he tells those gathered around his deathbed, "My immortality is necessary if only because God will not want to do an injustice and utterly extinguish the fire of love for him once kindled in my heart" (*Demons* 663). It is a "proof" frequently restated in various scenes throughout Dostoevsky's later fiction. As Frank notes, Dostoevsky argued that the afterlife "*must* exist as a necessary completion of human life on earth" if humans are to fulfill Christ's teaching of selfless and total love (*Stir* 297). Given human limitations, the completion of love as Christ prescribed it must come in the afterlife, not on earth; thus, the nonexistence of an afterlife rendered Christ's central commandment of love pointless. Faith in the afterlife was something about which Agee, on the other hand, was, as he repeatedly professed to Father Flye and others, quite doubtful.

Agee never pointed explicitly to Dostoevsky's conundrum that human life must be incomplete in the absence of certainty of eternal life, but he certainly registered it in fictional terms. In *A Death in the Family*, the rejection of the afterlife by several members of Mary Follet's family raises precisely this difficulty for young Rufus. Rufus's confusion following his father's funeral has everything to do with his uncertainty about life after death, an uncertainty communicated to him by all of the adults, including his insecure, self-righteous mother, but especially by his Uncle Andrew. Andrew's sudden shift from his famous set piece—a paean to the miracle of the butterfly on Jay's coffin ("almost enough" to cause him believe in God)—to a fierce, hate-filled denunciation of Christianity upsets Rufus by furthering doubts that were already established. It is not by any means merely a point of church policy regarding the burial mass

4. Agee and Dostoevsky

for Rufus's father that is at stake: the entire order of rationality is brought into doubt by the vast uncertainties that Andrew's outburst has underlined. How can Mary and Jay's love ever be "complete" in the absence of an afterlife in which their marital differences, so apparent in Agee's narrative, are reconciled? If this future reconciliation is foreclosed, how can Rufus's life be anything but a long meditation on the futility of human efforts to fulfill the central teaching of the Christian civilization in which he has been so carefully tutored, and continues to be tutored after his father's death? If Rufus's life is nothing more than a meditation on impossibility, how can he ever possess any conviction in the meaningfulness of any aspect of reality?

Agee's religious skepticism is also a key element in his treatment of the southern tenant class, whose fervent religious practices he completely ignores. The tone of the brief passage in which Agee describes the Gudgers' family Bible in *Let Us Now Praise Famous Men* seems constrained and petulant, turning into a sneer toward the end with the notation that the Bible "gave out a strong and cold stench of human excrement" (*Famous Men* 360). Does any reader of Agee's "documentary" work imagine that this depiction, brimming with hostility toward Bible-centered faith, represents an unbiased report of the religious experience of the sharecropper class? Nor would the tenants, one imagines, much care for Agee's meditation on the lovely simplicity of their lives. What they would prefer, in the same way that George Gudger prefers store-bought cigarettes to his hand-rolled ones (even if he believes that the hand-rolled cigarettes taste better), is a chance to enjoy the very same middle-class privileges that Agee appears to have rejected. Sadly, Agee's images of dirt, ignorance, improvidence, and sexual incorrigibility correspond more closely to the cultural stereotypes of an Eskine Caldwell, or a Dorothea Lange, than they do to reality. The documentary evidence provided by the vast collection of Work Projects Administration photographs from the 1930s and 1940s now available on the Library of Congress American Memory website suggests a people who, despite overwhelming poverty, maintain an impressive standard of cleanliness, self-respect, family cohesion, and personal ethics. The croppers were not Ishmael-like creatures exiled from the human community, as Agee imagined them to be (and thus aligned with his own project of bohemian exile): they were self-respecting, ambitious, moral human beings who aspired to the economic security and higher status of their "betters," and who in most cases regarded formal education (that warping institution, as Agee imagined) as their children's best chance in life. Descendants of the tenant class were soon to become beneficiaries of the postwar GI bill, and, in fact, in the postwar generation, few southerners, white or black, would remain in the tenant system. As Paul E. Mertz writes, "In the decades after the 1930s southern agriculture underwent massive changes that swept away tenancy" (qtd. in Wilson and Ferris 30).

Even that titular section from Ecclesiastics that Agee quotes near the end of *Famous Men* seems, by this point in the book, inappropriate and jejune. Those "famous men," those "fathers that begat us," men of "power," "leaders of the people," "rich men ... living peaceably in their habitations" (377), are not, of course, the object of Agee's interest in *Famous Men*. Agee's citation of this passage points toward a very different set of human beings, the very opposite of those celebrated in the biblical text. What Agee wished to discover among the tenants, and what he may have believed that he did discover, was a repudiation of the devout, highly regulated social order in which such righteous, powerful, rich men — those "virtuous " patriarchs of biblical tradition — hold sway.

To underline his opposition to the earnest moralizing of the biblical passage, Agee appends two sections that present his notion of the truly "divine" nature of the tenants and their surroundings: first, the description of two quite unceremonious and earthy young women, Annie Mae Gudger nursing Squinchy and Ellen Woods lying with her navel exposed to view; and, second, the description of what may be the mating calls of foxes in the distance — calls that suggest to the narrator a certain ecstatic "phase" of copulation (*Famous Men* 397). Both sections, of course, are intended to underline Agee's prioritizing of erotic joy, though of a fleeting and "lost" sort, over the seemingly static, heavy-handed authority of biblical hierarchies. Yet in this heavily loaded narrative arrangement, Agee was simply reasserting the Blakean notion that the authority of religious tradition constrains the freedom of the individual. Like Blake, Agee believed that the individual human being in his or her physical

4. Agee and Dostoevsky

dimension was divine, and that his or her sacred freedom was inviolable. For Agee, as for Blake, the authority of religious tradition, on the other hand, was "demonic" in its restraint of authentic being. Since he conceives of the tenants as existing outside of all society — outside the authority of religious, educational, cultural, and even legal institutions — they embodied the sacredness of "life" more fully than any other class.

As it turns out, this particular argument was quite familiar to Dostoevsky. The same tact of desacralizing the peasantry was a prominent feature of Russian liberal populist writing during the 1870s, and it was precisely this effort by intellectuals to divorce the peasantry, as they imagined it, from its most defining characteristic that Dostoevsky most strongly disliked. It is also the aspect of *Famous Men* that presents the greatest difficulties in Agee's treatment of the sharecropper class, for one of the crucial paradoxes of Agee's relationship to the sharecroppers is the extent to which his consciousness, however sympathetic it proclaims itself to be and however much he wishes to partake of and merge with the life of the tenants, remains distinct and apart from that of the croppers. This separateness is apparent in every nuance of the book: in Agee's "secretive" behavior, his voyeuristic posture relative to his subject, his habit of working through the night while the tenants sleep, his baroque style of description in contrast with the plainness of the subject, his educated urban intelligence in contrast with the untutored provinciality of the croppers, and so on. In contrast, Joseph Frank traces the tortuous road that led Dostoevsky, in the years of imprisonment and military service in Siberia, to identify himself with the values of Russian serfdom. In the nine years that he spent in Siberia, four as a convict and five as a soldier, Dostoevsky achieved a sense of identity with the ordinary people of Russia that he would never disavow.

Whether Agee actually "earned" a sense of solidarity with the southern tenant class is doubtful. In *Famous Men*, the tenants rarely articulate their beliefs, and when Agee puts words in their mouths, it is *his* words and *his* beliefs. This is the point of all those long interior monologues and expressionistic descriptive passages that take the place of articulation on the part of the sharecroppers themselves. In those passages in which Agee feels himself closest to the tenants, there is no speech at all: it is an assumed identity of feelings and thoughts, as in the scene in which Agee huddles with the tenants in the tiny cabin threatened by a dangerous thunderstorm. Yet even in this important scene (the "Introit" or beginning of the "worship" of the tenants paradoxically situated late in the narrative though chronologically near the beginning of the story), the "I" or Agee persona/narrator is the central character, not George or Annie Mae Gudger, nor even Louise Gudger, the most self-aware of the children and thus, necessarily in Agee's universe, the center of interest for the narrator. None of these characters, and certainly not the socially clumsy and hapless Ricketts, holds Agee's attention for long. It is the "I," Agee's own self, that man "from Mars" dropped into an alien environment, that is central. The narrator does not even remember what was said at this crucial meeting; he can only describe the physical scene "poorly" and "at a second remove" (*Famous Men* 343–44). What he does recall and can describe is the "I" himself, the "mysterious" visitor, the egoistic center of the children's and adults' attention, and even in her "quietly courteous" and "withdrawn" way, of Annie Mae (*Famous Men* 345).

It is not just that the Agee persona is apart: it is also *above* the subject. Unlike Dostoevsky, who embraced a theology of Christian kenoticism of the sort represented in the character of Prince Myshkin, Alyosha Karamazov, and preeminently in Father Zosima, the central virtue of humility seems lacking in the Agee persona in *Famous Men* and, for that matter, everywhere in Agee's writing. Even in his self-deprecation, the sense that he is "unfit" to live among the sharecroppers and that his art is a "failure," there exists the excessive pride of the martyr. Agee was more than willing to suffer indignity, poverty, ridicule, illness, and even death, but he was never willing to perform that one essential act of Christian contrition, the sincere and whole-hearted repudiation of egotism.

One of the remarkable facts about Agee's relationship to the tenants is just how brief was his residency among them in contrast with the lengthy period he spent fashioning his account. (Agee's work on *Let Us Now Praise Famous Men* occupied a period of five years following his brief visit in 1936.) Agee's extensive revision and refashioning of the sharecropper experience resulted in a highly idealized portrayal of the tenants, yet it is precisely in his idealization of the subject that Agee

4. Agee and Dostoevsky

seems less than truthful. According to his depiction, the sharecropper cabin was a "temple" because of its fragility and exposure; the marriage of George and Annie Mae Gudger was sacred, seemingly a replication of that of Joseph and Mary, not because it might engender a divine savior who would redeem mankind but because the marital life of the Gudgers was unguarded and unadorned. The Gudgers, since they could be nothing else and live nowhere else, seemed to Agee more "authentic" than middle-class families who could choose how and where to live, and their holiness had much to do with their presumed genuineness. They were sacred in the same sense that within romantic tradition a small child is, and, in fact, it was the tenant children, and especially ten-year-old Louise Gudger, who elicited Agee's greatest outpouring of sympathy.

In Book Two, "Colon: Curtain Speech," of *Famous Men*, Agee offers an intensely poetic evocation of the life of a sort of sharecropper everyman or everywoman. It is impossible to summarize the grand vision that Agee sets out except to say that the terms in which he portrays the life of the tenants suggest a strongly deterministic and materialist bias. Agee asserts that as the young sharecropper families face the inevitable hardships of their class, "the little slit graves of angelic possibility" will most certainly be "danced upon and defiled beyond memory of their existence" (*Famous Men* 105); likewise, he insists that the bitter facts of social inferiority and repression are unavoidable, as is the early acceptance of these facts by the victims. In offering this portrayal of an underclass "from all sides streamed inward upon, bombarded, pierced, destroyed" (*Famous Men* 106), Agee, however, was not offering fact: he was writing a deeply rhetorical, artfully constructed interpretation of social reality — an interpretation, in fact, that relied on certain rather familiar ideological assumptions of a sort that would have been entirely familiar to Dostoevsky.

Agee's first assumption in regard to the sharecropper class was the idea of economic determinism. However much he poeticizes the subject, Agee adopts the familiar framework of nineteenth-century social analysis with its assumption, as he states in "Colon: Curtain Speech," that money "at present is had at the expense of other spirits and of human good" (*Famous Men* 103). Apparently, all inequality of wealth must be traced to some act of victimization. The tenants are exploited because they do not possess the means of production, primarily land, equipment, and stock, and, in a vicious cycle of exploitation, they are forced further into debt with each new growing season. At best, they can only hope to survive. Nonetheless — and this is what distinguishes Agee from hard-line leftists and what has always exasperated them about his politics — Agee insists that the capitalist is also the victim of "diseases, so ghastly that one cannot in wisdom and honesty either envy or hate the image, say, of the landowner" (*Famous Men* 103). In reality, Agee's politics comprises a "soft" leftism that stresses the overall damage of capitalism to both proletariat and capitalist and proposes as a solution a new consciousness of the "true weight of responsibility which each human being must learn to undertake for all others" (*Famous Men* 104). On the surface, this remark suggests agreement with Dostoevsky's ethic of responsibility, for it uncannily mimics Father Zosima's dying advice that all human beings must accept personal responsibility for the sins of all others. There is, however, a crucial difference: the responsibility of which Agee speaks, as is made clear in what follows in *Famous Men*, is primarily social and economic. Though in his notebooks he frequently mocked Franklin D. Roosevelt's progressive politics, Agee's political perspective, as far as it goes, is hardly distinguishable from that of the social engineers of the New Deal, and this despite Agee's cool indifference to politics altogether.

Agee's notion of human responsibility, grounded on little more than a progressive sense of social ethics, reflects what Dostoevsky termed "universal dissociation" (Frank, *Mantle* 268), a condition in which a shared sense of tradition has been undermined and replaced by an ethics of personal empathy. It is perhaps for this reason that Agee seemed to possess no touchstone for responding to the horrendous political events taking place during the same period in which he worked to revise *Famous Men*. It was, after all, precisely during these years from 1936 to 1941 that the world witnessed the emergence of forms of savagery previously unknown to mankind, savagery about which Agee's writing, even as it belabors the injustice of the tenant system, is curiously silent: the election of Hitler to the German chancellorship in 1933; the passage of the Nürnberg laws and subsequent anti–Semitic repression leading up the drafting of the

4. Agee and Dostoevsky

final solution at the Wannsee Conference in July 1941; the great purges beginning in 1935 in the Soviet Union; and, of course, the beginning of World War II in Europe in September 1939.

In the context of this emergence of evil on a scale unknown in human history, Agee clung to a politics of isolationism, and he continued to do so even after America's entry into the war. He was not the only American intellectual to do so, but this does not lessen the shock of reading through Agee's published writing and notebooks from the late 1930s and 1940s and realizing, if we are to take him at his word, that he considered American capitalism equally as criminal as German fascism, nor does it excuse the fact that in all of Agee's considerable body of writing addressing current events, not one sentence was devoted to the Holocaust. In the notebooks published as *James Agee Rediscovered*, for example, there is no mention of any sort of oppression of the Jews; there is only a mischievous criticism, repeated over and over, of the Allied Cause. In Agee's draft of a poem entitled "Collective Letter to the Boss," Hitler, Mussolini, Roosevelt, King George V, William Randolph Hearst, Father Charles E. Coughlin, and John D. Rockefeller, among others, are cited as "the enemy" (*James Agee Rediscovered* 243), and, from what one can tell, all seem equally so in Agee's mind. Elsewhere, in a notebook draft of "America! Look at Your Shame!," Agee excoriates his native land for its apparent indifference toward the oppression of blacks, especially in light of the June 20, 1943, race riots in Detroit. Righting racial injustice "is one of the main things this war is about," Agee declares. "If it isn't about this we might as well not be fighting it at all (we might as well not indeed)" (*James Agee Rediscovered* 171). At this point, in the wake of some of the most savage events of the war (the Battle of Stalingrad in early 1943; the Warsaw ghetto uprising in April and May of the same year), Agee writes that he "began to be very sorry for all those people caught in the hopeless middle; even for Hitler and his damned idea" (*James Agee Rediscovered* 167). To feel sorry for the civilian victims of the war, even for those in Germany, is one thing; to feel sorry for Hitler is quite another.

It is for this reason that the second important assumption in *Famous Men*, the familiar concept of moral relativism, looms so large, for its existence made it impossible for Agee to form a judgment of the Nazi or Stalinist crimes. Repeatedly, Agee denies the possibility of moral distinctions, whether these pertain to prohibitions on crime, restrictions on personal behavior, or expectations of demeanor or appearance. Among the Alabama tenants, Agee asserts his belief that "degrees of dirt and the bearable or proper are in a sense so highly relative and social in conception" (*Famous Men* 175) that judgments cannot be applied. Agee's relativism, however, went far beyond matters of hygiene or personal appearance.

All of this was foretold in the horrific depths of Dostoevsky's imagination. In *The Possessed*, Shatov accuses Stavrogin of knowing "no difference in beauty between some brutal sensual stunt and any great deed, even the sacrifice of life for mankind?" (*Demons* 254). Although Stavrogin prevaricates in response, it is clear that this is a fair representation of Stavrogin's essential philosophy, and it is what makes possible a "stunt" that Dostoevsky considered the greatest crime of all: the corruption of a child. In the unpublished chapter relating Stavrogin's meeting with Father Tikhon, censored by the czarist authorities because of its graphic revelation of Stavrogin's seduction of his landlady's ten-year-old daughter, Father Tikhon asks Stavrogin: "If you are not ashamed to confess the crime, why are you ashamed of repentance?" (*Demons* 706). This question highlights a central failing of Stavrogin's character: a spiritual hubris that makes it possible for him to bask in the humiliation of his rejection by respectable society while at the same time repudiating the process of contrition and atonement that would assuage his guilt. At no point, I believe, is the figure of Stavrogin closer to that of Agee, whose ceaseless self-accusations and confessions of moral failing seem never to have led to repentance and expiation. In short, like Stavrogin, Agee was too stiff-necked and proud to humble himself before a religious ideal that demanded abnegation of the self, and like Stavrogin he ended his life a suicide in all but name.

Formulating his credo of skepticism, Agee asserts that "in terms ... of the manifestations of being, taken as such, which are always strict and perfect, nothing can be held untrue. A falsehood is entirely true to those derangements which produced it and which made it impossible that it should emerge in truth; and an examination of it may reveal more of the 'true' 'truth' than any more direct attempt upon the 'true' 'truth' itself"

4. Agee and Dostoevsky

(*Famous Men* 202). With this astounding assertion, much as Foucault would in succeeding decades, Agee has subjected all truths of existence to an acidic critique that leaves him with only an anarchic, irrational universe. Lacking the truths that Agee dismisses, society retains no common rationality, no shared moral assumptions, no inherited institutions or traditions, and no stable source of authority, and, lacking these pillars of order, it is plunged into a chaos in which the violent and strong oppress the peaceable and weak to a far greater extent than Agee ever imagined, even in what he thought he perceived in the southern tenant system. The result is far from the egalitarian innocence of which Agee dreamed.

A third and related assumption is Agee's dismissal of the rights of private property. Like the nineteenth-century Fourierists and anarchists, Agee thought in terms of a social primitivism that would eliminate material rights and obligations altogether. One worked when one wished; one shared what one had; one took what one needed. It was just this sort of utopian socialism that attracted Dostoevsky during the 1840s not only to the writing of Charles Fourier but to that of Comte Henri de Saint-Simon and Pierre-Joseph Proudhon, the very texts against which he reacted so forcefully following his return from Siberia. If we are to credit Zenkovsky's assessment, the question of human liberty, including the rights of property, is at the center of Dostoevsky's religious and ethical thought. In Dostoevsky's view, "freedom as such, isolated from the living impulses of love, contains the seed of death" yet freedom "may also lift man to the height of transfiguration" (Zenkovsky 135). Whether freedom leads to destruction or transfiguration is determined by human acceptance of an innate ethical nature that Dostoevsky viewed as a sacred mystery linking life on earth, as Dostoevsky voiced it in the words of Father Zosima, with "seeds from other worlds" (*Brothers Karamazov* 388).

As I have suggested, it may be that in some broad sense, Agee and Dostoevsky are comparable figures in that their idealism arose from similar fonts of compassion and from utopian hopes for mankind. Yet, though he may have began life in these idealistic terms, quite soon Agee found himself defeated and hopeless, an embittered and self-indulgent cynic unconcerned about his own future and that of his civilization. Dostoevsky, on the other hand, not only dreamed of paradise on earth;

he believed that he might contribute to bringing that paradise about, in moral and spiritual terms at least, through the embrace of inherited religious belief and established social order. Beginning life as a naïve idealist, Agee sank to the level where, in the final years of his life, he imagined a story written by God "reviewing the entire course of a hopelessly unhappy relationship" with "the human race" (*Letters to Father Flye* 203). Dostoevsky, on the other hand, having suffered infinitely more throughout a lifetime of parental neglect, imprisonment, poverty, censorship, and ill health, to say nothing of having to endure the mercenary demands of his parasitical relations following his brother's early death, pursued his life courageously and triumphed in the end with the completion of his masterpiece, *The Brothers Karamazov*, a magnificent gift to his adoring public. His was a faith in mankind's potential based not on some fleeting or sentimental empathy but on a realistic assessment of the strength of the instinct for life and the inherent nobility and goodness of human beings, all of which awaited only the transformative action of religious redemption. Dostoevsky and Agee were two writers initially possessed of the same utopian dream of paradise on earth. For Dostoevsky, this dream led to his acknowledgment of the dependence of human beings on a living God; for Agee, it pointed in the opposite direction toward an indictment of God and a half-hearted, uncertain claim of human sovereignty. While much can be learned from a comparison of Agee and Dostoevsky, in the end one must admit how little alike they were in essentials.

Notes

1. Unfortunately, some of Dostoevsky's critics have concluded that, in so forcefully asserting the arguments of the Grand Inquisitor, Dostoevsky must have been in "emotional agreement with Ivan" (Frank, *Mantle* 607). In various forms, in fact, this argument continues to surface even today, and it may have occurred to Agee himself as he read Avram Yarmolinsky's "good biography" of Dostoevsky (*Letters to Father Flye* 94). Yarmolinsky's biography advances an ambivalent, revisionist reading of Dostoevsky's novels. In Dostoevsky's scathing attack on nihilism in *The Possessed*, Yarmolinsky sees the operation of a "prejudiced mind" (305). According to Yarmolinsky, Dostoevsky "maliciously misrepresented both the goals and the strategies of the early radicals" (304). Another feature of Yarmolinsky's biography that might have appealed to Agee is its emphasis on Dostoevsky's supposed lifetime opposition to "the pathology of the

4. Agee and Dostoevsky

soul of man under capitalism" (420), as Yarmolinsky has it, and to the bourgeoisie everywhere. Several other aspects of the biography would have struck Agee: the general emphasis on Dostoevsky's sense of "disarray, disorder, chaos" and on "aberrant individuals" (422), and his grasp of the subconscious. All in all, despite his careful and generally restrained account of Dostoevsky's life, Yarmolinsky fails to take Dostoevsky's message seriously.

Another distortion of Dostoevsky, this time as a proto-existentialist writer, was popularized by William Hubben in his well-known book, *Dostoevsky, Kierkegaard, Nietzsche and Kafka*. Hubben's unsupported assertions, including the vague similarities that he points to between Dostoevsky and Nietzsche, actually obscure Dostoevsky's extraordinary distaste for Germanic abstraction. Hubben's comment that "Both writers are passionately occupied with tearing the masks from pretension and morality" (128), is simply a nebulous generalization. The underlying intentions of Nietzsche and Dostoevsky in removing the masks are, after all, quite different, and point towards different intentions. Nietzsche wishes to move mankind beyond the inherited beliefs of Western civilization, while Dostoevsky is constantly pointing to the shallowness of this very effort.

In the same way Hubben's assertion that both Dostoevsky and Nietzsche "regard the categories of moral good and evil as outworn and useless" (129), while it may be an accurate characterization of Nietzsche, is mistaken in the case of Dostoevsky. Hubben relies for evidence on passages in which the Grand Inquisitor is expressing his skepticism concerning the conventional morality of Christians, but Hubben does not pause to consider, as Dostoevsky explicitly informed his publisher and the public, that the Grand Inquisitor represents the epitome of evil or that the arguments of the inquisitor are thoroughly refuted in the chapters that follow in *The Brothers Karamazov*. In this way, Hubben is guilty of exactly the sort of misreading that Dostoevsky anticipated when he revealed to his publisher his fear that the Inquisitor's arguments had been presented too forcefully. Likewise Hubben's argument that "Nietzsche and Dostoevsky wrestle with faith and doubt without ever being able to separate the two" (130) can be refuted once again by Dostoevsky's own statements. As Dostoevsky revealed, his life was refocused in those supreme moments of faith in which doubt was *conquered*: in these moments, he realized the necessity of accepting the truth of Christ, even, as he said, if Christ's truth were "not true." This total submission to a religious authority is quite the opposite of Nietzsche's atheism.

Hubben's comparison of Kierkegaard and Dostoevsky is also based on a vague and speculative argument. For example, his assertion that Kierkegaard's either/or demand would lead to the conclusion that "Christianity's real enemies are not atheists, but we ourselves, the silent apostates, who are preparing the end of Christianity" (49) is hardly applicable to Dostoevsky, who, after all, opposed atheism in the strongest terms. The fundamental Kierkegaardian notion that the presence of doubt is a necessary ground of faith is quite alien to Dostoevsky's writing. Certainly, Dostoevsky recognized the element of doubt within European culture of his time, and even acknowledged the presence of doubt in his own psyche, but he also confirmed that he had rejected doubt. As Dostoevsky saw it, religion was a reaction against doubt, and this reaction pointed toward an unfettered embrace of naïve faith. This reaction is just the opposite of

Kierkegaard's, for in spite of a recognition of the widespread existence of doubt, it exhorts mankind to embrace religion not as a leap of faith but as a return to certainty. In Dostoevsky's terms, the return to faith was the consequence of a supreme realism based on an accurate assessment of the failure of atheism as he had seen it operate in the westernized Russian intellectuals of his time.

Kierkegaard's assertion, quoted by Hubben, that "one can be a Christian only in opposition" (41) is another point of difference with Dostoevsky. Kierkegaard's opposition to the institutional church of his time stands in opposition to Dostoevsky's embrace of the Orthodox Church, as well as to his support for the institution of the czardom, itself identified with Orthodox Russian tradition. The validity of the earthly institutions within which Christianity is embodied and transmitted, in other words, is a crucial element in Dostoevsky's thinking, and it is opposed to the iconoclastic radicalism of both Kierkegaard and Nietzsche.

2. In the manner in which he had "fallen in love with disorder," Agee resembles another of Dostoevsky's most compelling characters, Ippolit Terentyev in *The Idiot*. Like Agee, Ippolit is a dying rebel, and one who like Agee is quite conscious of his impending death. As Joseph Frank astutely points out, "Ippolit is revolting not against the iniquities of a social order but ... against a world in which death, and hence immitigable human suffering, is an inescapable reality" (*Miraculous Years* 331). What Ippolit lacks, as Frank makes clear, is a convincing religious faith that would place his and humanity's suffering in a mythological context beyond the level of the destruction of his personal ego. It is precisely this that is lacking in Agee's imagination as well. Ultimately, nothing can solace Agee or distract his imagination from the central and, as he perceives it, unjust fact of human mortality.

3. Interestingly, Dostoevsky's attitude toward the peasantry, so completely opposed to that of James Agee, was in some ways similar to that of the southern Agrarians, who viewed traditional society as a model of social order to which America might return. Like the southern Agrarians, the Slavophils and Populists in nineteenth-century Russia hoped to preserve the actual socioeconomic system of the peasantry "as uniquely valuable and precious in themselves and in their present form" (Frank, *Mantle* 77), not as proto–Socialist models of communal societies.

- 5 -

Flannery O'Connor's Conservatism: A Reading of The Violent Bear It Away

In a letter to William Sessions, a young instructor apparently much taken with Freudianism, Flannery O'Connor wrote that in her fiction she was aiming for a realm of truth beyond the sort of psychological "realism" that the Freudian interpreter might be seeking. O'Connor's scathing dismissal of the Freudian technique, a mechanical approach to reading that "can be applied to anything at all with equally ridiculous results" (*Habit* 407), was part and parcel of her rejection of other faddish critical approaches to literature. All of O'Connor's aesthetic principles were based on the fact that she saw literature as the product of human reflection grounded in enduring traditions of belief: in her case, in the established tradition of the Roman Catholic Church. In reaction to the rebellious intellectual culture of the late 1950s and early 1960s, a turbulent culture that sought self-knowledge through Freudianism, Marxism, and existentialism, among other ideologies, O'Connor responded with a mixture of bafflement and humor, as she did in her letter to Sessions. "My Lord, Billy," she wrote, "recover your simplicity" (*Habit* 407).

By simplicity, I believe, O'Connor implied an attitude of openness and directness that made possible the acceptance of the long-standing body of knowledge passed down within the civilization of which she was a part. The simplicity of which she spoke made it possible for her to see beyond the intellectual distractions of Freudianism and the like and to base her writing career on enduring truth. By stripping away what was ephemeral, and particularly what was alien and antagonistic to her traditional religious culture, O'Connor freed herself to gaze with an almost unbearable intensity upon the destructive and confused culture of her time. In her fiction and other writing, she attested the horrible damage of this culture on those who lacked the resources of a stable ethical and religious civilization. As O'Connor pointed out many times in her essays and letters, those who choose to approach life, or are led to do so as a result of their environment, with only the ad hoc resources of self-knowledge or a debased and ephemeral general culture have set forth unprotected and will be forced to learn through suffering. Had they access to the nurturing instruction of a stable body of inherited beliefs, much of their suffering might be avoided.

In the sense that she recognized the crucial importance of inherited traditions of belief, O'Connor was a natural conservative, but she was also a conservative in several more particular senses of the word. In truth, O'Connor had always been a social and fiscal conservative, and as she grew older, she displayed more interest in specific political issues including civil rights, federal aid to education, federal funding for the arts, and the concept of limited government. All in all, the evidence suggests that O'Connor possessed a sophisticated understanding of politics and that her political orientation was not dissimilar from that of intellectual conservatives like Russell Kirk or Senator Daniel Patrick Moynihan.

O'Connor's politics is a subject that major critics of her work have largely avoided or, if they have addressed it, about which they have distorted for reasons of their own. The names of the leading political figures of her time — Eisenhower, Nixon, Kennedy, and Goldwater — are absent from Richard Giannone's otherwise splendid book, *Flannery O'Connor, Hermit Novelist*, as they are (with the possible exception of Kennedy) from most interpretative books on O'Connor and even from *The Flannery O'Connor Companion* by James A. Grimshaw. The one book-length study to address O'Connor's politics, Robert Coles's *Flannery O'Connor's South*, focuses to a great extent on the author's conflictive feelings regarding the civil rights movement but muddies the waters when covering O'Connor's conservatism in a broader sense. Coles's brief discussion of the treatment of industrialism in "The Displaced Person," for example, suggests a rejection of "modern industrialism, a secular materialism gone viciously

5. Flannery O'Connor's Conservatism

berserk" (29). This sweeping generalization misrepresents O'Connor's position, which was not that materialism had gone "berserk" in America but that an exclusive focus on *any* ideology that departed from Judeo-Christian faith (including anti-materialist belief systems such as Buddhism or liberal bohemianism) was destructive to the audience she was addressing. Likewise, Coles's statement that O'Connor "placed herself politically in between CORE [Congress of Racial Equality] and the Young Republicans for Goldwater" (53) — a reference to a throwaway line in one of O'Connor's letters — fails to take her conservatism seriously. If O'Connor was in some sense "between CORE and the Young Republicans," it was closer to the Grand Old Party than to CORE — a group of activists that embraced black nationalism during the early 1960s and elements of which morphed into the Black Panther Party in the mid–1960s. Although Coles does point out O'Connor's "jabs" at "the entire liberal, secular world" (112), he fails to credit the central place of key conservative values in O'Connor's life and work: foremost among these values, respect for a stable, inherited belief system and caution with regard to social innovation and change. The cautious traditionalism underlying O'Connor's worldview was not simply a regional writer's unease with intellectuals and theorists: it was a Tory mentality that aligned her with a body of political thought that would serve as the intellectual ground of the Goldwater-Reagan wing of the Republican Party.

Politics, of course, was never O'Connor's overriding interest, nor could the sort of spiritual transformation that she sought be arrived at by way of political activity or institutions. But the fact that politics was always of secondary importance does not mean that O'Connor held no political opinions or that, as secular activity, politics was dismissed in favor of an all-engrossing devotion to religion. O'Connor was a writer whose life was primarily devoted to the pursuit of religious truth, but she was also an interested participant in the political life of her time. In both pursuits, she found herself returning again and again to an urgent need to discover the truth of things for herself and then to communicate this truth, through her stories, essays, and letters, to her readers.

Like many young people, in her student days O'Connor evinced traces of political idealism on such topics as civil rights, but as she grew older—she was never, of course, to grow "old," dying as she did at age thirty-nine—she expressed views that were closer to those of her conservative neighbors and, surprisingly perhaps, to those even of her mother. As Brad Gooch details, O'Connor frequently expressed distaste for the facile liberalism of intellectual friends, especially of those northern intellectuals who propounded easy solutions to the problem of segregation in the South while often overlooking the racial and other social problems of their own communities. Even as a student, O'Connor was deeply opposed to the kind of faddish leftism that was popular among American and European intellectuals, and she held views concerning American communists that were closer to those of Joseph McCarthy than to those of his detractors. During her stay at the Yaddo artists' colony in 1949, O'Connor was one of a small group led by Robert Lowell who objected to the left-leaning directorship of Elizabeth Ames and particularly to Ames's sponsorship of Agnes Smedley during her unusually lengthy stay at Yaddo from 1943 to 1948. As Gooch points out, Smedley, a strong supporter of Mao Tse-tung, spent her time at Yaddo "writing a biography of Marshal Zhu De, founder of the Chinese Red Army" (167). Smedley, who had been accused in the national media of being a Soviet spy in 1941 (an accusation that was quickly retracted), was clearly what McCarthy would have called a "communist sympathizer," and O'Connor, as her letters and other comments show, was deeply uncomfortable with Smedley's presence and with the political atmosphere at Yaddo in general. Days after leaving Yaddo, according to Helen Greene, O'Connor's history professor at Georgia State College for Women, O'Connor visited her office and spoke of her shock at finding so many atheists at Yaddo. According to Greene, O'Connor had found that many of those at Yaddo were communists (Gooch 176).

While O'Connor could be a vocal opponent of communism, during the 1950s she generally avoided voicing her opinions, other than to close friends, on the civil rights movement that was taking place all around her. Perhaps this was because, as Gooch puts it, O'Connor's perspective on the civil rights movement was "one of complex ambivalence" (333). Like many southerners of the time, O'Connor feared the effects of government attempts to force rapid desegregation. She supported John F.

5. Flannery O'Connor's Conservatism

Kennedy in the 1960 presidential campaign not on the basis of his overtures toward black voters but because of her loyalty to Kennedy as a Roman Catholic. Kennedy, of course, had a reputation as a committed anti-communist and, despite his popularity with blacks, his campaign put forward little in the way of specific proposals for civil rights legislation — landmark legislation that would be crafted and passed by Lyndon Johnson only after Kennedy's death. O'Connor was overwhelmed by grief following Kennedy's assassination, but she showed little enthusiasm for the liberal initiatives that were later associated with his presidency.

The upshot of this gradual political evolution was that by July 10, 1964, weeks before her death, O'Connor was urging her long-time friend, Maryat Lee, to vote for Barry Goldwater, the conservative Republican candidate for the presidency. (The inverted "Vote for Goldwater" line, which appears in a letter of July 10 published in the *Collected Works* [page 1215], was inexplicably removed from the version of the same letter published in *The Habit of Being* on pages 591–92, a significant editorial decision since there are only a few references to Goldwater in O'Connor's letters.) The 1964 election presented voters with a clear choice between Goldwater, a social and fiscal conservative and a defense hawk, and Johnson, a southerner but one whose entire public life was shaped by the liberal politics of the New Deal and by his connection with the left wing of the Democratic Party. The fact that O'Connor had come to the point of openly favoring the deeply conservative Goldwater over Johnson, who after all had inherited Kennedy's liberal agenda and rammed it through Congress in the first months of his own administration, said a great deal about where her true sympathies lay. To support Goldwater over Johnson at a time when the nation was still mourning the death of Johnson's beloved predecessor and when Johnson was viewed as a loyal supporter of Kennedy's New Frontier policies, if not exactly as a Kennedyite himself, was to declare oneself conservative indeed. It was an indication that one had rejected the thirty-year-long ascendancy of liberal politics beginning with FDR in 1933 and that one was looking to change the ideological discussion from the assumptions of statism to that of limited, constitutional government. Although Goldwater stumbled badly in the 1964 campaign, many of those working on his campaign and many inspired by his unapologetic conservatism (including Ronald Reagan and Karl Rove, the future political adviser to George W. Bush) went on to shape the direction of American politics in the next half-century. In supporting Goldwater, O'Connor was casting her lot with this conservative groundswell. In contrast to Johnson's liberal program of government expansion and control of education, culture, employment, housing, and other facets of everyday life, Goldwater campaigned on a platform of limited government. O'Connor's choice of Goldwater over Johnson must therefore have been based, in part at least, on her own identification with a constitutional view of enumerated powers.

It is not only in her fiction, of course, that O'Connor registered her identification with conservative politics. As her biography reveals, O'Connor's everyday milieu, that of middle Georgia in the midst of the civil rights movement and at the onset of Johnson's Great Society push toward Big Government, was an intensely conservative one. In her relations with family and friends, O'Connor reveals a cautious conservatism both in terms of her social views and her management of fiscal affairs. Her letters to friends and associates are filled with warnings of the dangers of social innovation and of too great a measure of personal freedom. As she affirms in these letters and in her essays, most of which were presented as talks before university and civic groups, O'Connor accepted the ethical teachings of the Catholic Church, even those teachings and practices that she found somewhat difficult to accept, as for instance the Church's censure of certain books that O'Connor valued. Despite some misgivings, O'Connor understood that the Church's ethical guidance was liberating in that it opened her mind to the consideration and acceptance of spiritual realities that she might otherwise have overlooked or underappreciated. The Church's teachings on the sanctity of life and the centrality of the family, as well as its assertion of the dignity of every individual, were the basis of much if not all of O'Connor's conservative principles. Russell Kirk, one of the leading conservative writers of our time, has traced the political institutions of liberal democracy to these same tenets of Judeo-Christian belief. As Kirk writes, "European and American civilization has been erected upon the foundation of the dignity of man — upon the assumption that man is made for eternity, and that he possesses

5. Flannery O'Connor's Conservatism

dignity because he has some share in an order that is more than temporal and more than human" (233). O'Connor, who was an acquaintance of Kirk and an admirer of his thought, would certainly have agreed with Kirk's analysis, though she would probably not have expressed her conclusions in such an abstract manner.

It was not just the Church, though, that O'Connor conceived of as liberating. Critics have perhaps underestimated the extent to which her regional affiliation — her love of the South as a place that was heavily populated by conservative, non–Catholic evangelical Christians — influenced her thinking and her work. O'Connor expressed this regional affiliation in innumerable ways, including her love of the southern dialect as replicated in her fiction, her loving depiction of the southern landscape, and her proclivity for selecting evangelical Christians as protagonists. O'Connor was entirely serious when she insisted on more than one occasion that living in the South had lent sophistication to her writing: in fact, that it had made her writing possible in a way that would not have been possible in New York or San Francisco. In a letter to Elizabeth and Robert Lowell, O'Connor urged her friends to bring their daughter Harriet "to see this region and me, so as my kinfolks say, 'she would be broad'" (*Habit* 251).

Like the Church, O'Connor was particularly opposed to the intrusion of government into the personal realm of life. This was especially the case when the state was seen as intruding in matters of family life and education. Of course, one has to ask *which* Church O'Connor aligned herself with, especially in the period in which the Catholic Church was engaged in a process of sweeping self-examination connected with the Vatican council convened by Pope John XXIII and concluded by Paul VI. The changes in liturgy and ecumenicalism that resulted from the second Vatican Council were not implemented until after O'Connor's death, but a changing sense of the Church's mission and of the religious life in a more general sense was clearly in the air throughout the 1950s and 1960s. Several of O'Connor's acquaintances, including her friend Maryat Lee and her visitor Robert Coles, felt that their faith demanded participation in or at least sympathy for activist causes. Yet there is little evidence that O'Connor shared their view of Christian service. Her sense of her obligation as a Catholic was expressed in a letter to Betty Hester, the correspondent who for many years was identified as "A." in collections of O'Connor's letters. O'Connor wrote that "You do not write the best you can for the sake of art but for the sake of returning your talent increased to the invisible God to use or not use as he sees fit" (*Habit* 419). This was a definition of the writer's vocation that differed radically from many of O'Connor's contemporaries, even from that of Catholics such as Mary McCarthy. The general direction of writing at the time was toward political engagement, with a decided tilt toward liberal if not radical affiliations. O'Connor was not merely skeptical of this course: she was certain that the self-liberation sought by her contemporaries was a false path that would lead to destruction.

Some have argued, of course, that O'Connor's thinking was so closely bound to that of the Church that she did not think independently on secular matters: in other words, that she simply consulted the teachings of the Church and conformed her opinions to them. While it is true that O'Connor accepted the guidance of the Church in essentials, it is also fair to say that, like all believers, she was forced to interpret her everyday experience in terms of these teachings. Instead of limiting her imagination, O'Connor insisted, her orthodoxy opened her mind to experience in ways that were unavailable to agnostics and atheists. Perhaps the most important instance of this need to comprehend the Church's teachings in relation to the unchartered waters of postmodern experience was O'Connor's reaction to the spreading apostasy of secular humanism, a worldview taking many specific forms but one grounded in the basic faith in progress and on faith in the liberation of mankind through education and political emancipation.

In writing *The Violent Bear It Away*, as O'Connor told John Hawkes in a letter of 13 September 1959, her intention (as always in her fiction) was to dramatize "the conflict between an attraction for the Holy and the disbelief in it that we breathe in with the air of the times. It's hard to believe always but more so in the world we live in now" (*Habit* 349). This statement was highly significant because it clarified the relation between O'Connor's overriding religious convictions and her determination to explore the contemporary condition of the fallen world. As she made clear to Hawkes, her "attraction for the Holy" did not in any sense separate her art from the world of experience: it compelled her to probe more deeply and to "stare" more intently at the often disconcerting facts of a world that was permeated with disbelief. Her mission was a prophetic one: to expose and help to reverse the confusion and violence that accompany the loss of belief.

These intentions are apparent in *The Violent Bear It Away*, in which there exists a fundamental opposition between two main adult characters: the arch-conservative, Mason Tarwater, and the oblivious liberal, Rayber. Caught in between the opposed and mutually exclusive worldviews of these two figures is Mason Tarwater's great-nephew, Francis Marion Tarwater. The novel's dramatic action turns on a fundamental debate between the religious conservative perspective of the elder Tarwater and the secular humanism of Rayber, the "schoolteacher"—a role that O'Connor, like many conservatives before and after, associated with the propagation of a misguided program of progressive thinking in the young. In the end, O'Connor resolves this conflict by forcing young Tarwater to confront the consequences of liberalism and, thus, to fall back on the conservative worldview of his great-uncle.

The world that Tarwater enters after the death of his great-uncle is immediately revealed to be the fraudulent realm that O'Connor associated with secular humanism. Tarwater's meeting with Meeks, the salesman who uses love as "the only policy that worked 95% of the time" (*Collected Works* 362), is only the first in a series of encounters culminating in Tarwater's rape by the flamboyant pederast who merges with the figure of "the stranger," the faithless double of himself who has stalked him all along. Meeks, whose name suggests a time-server who lives comfortably within his own small sphere, is a carefully drawn representative of the secular materialist. He is a person who worships success and who takes an interest in machines of all sorts, for it is machines, along with the slick mendacity of his approach to sales based on "love," that are his means to success. Had O'Connor written the character in today's terms, she might well have shown Meeks engaged in social networking, outfitted with an iPad and the latest generation of cell phone.

While O'Connor had no interest in the sort of realism that engages in representation of quotidian experience for its own sake, she was determined to make Rayber's fallen nature palpable. This, as she frequently noted, was the most difficult part of the novel for her to write. After completing a draft of the novel in 1958, O'Connor spent the next eighteen months focusing on revision of the sections dealing with Rayber, the "liberal, atheist, do-gooder" (310), as Gooch characterizes him, whose character is diametrically opposed to that of O'Connor herself. Rayber's worldview is mired in the sort of evil that converts every moment of life to a form of enslavement to the materialistic norms of efficiency, self-gratification, and service to the state. Cloaked in the language of the modern social sciences and of educational testing in particular, Rayber's vision forces one to participate in a deadening collectivist mentality. Sensing this loss of individualism early on, Tarwater mocks Rayber's dependence on a hearing aid and thick glasses, for he senses that in some deeper sense Rayber is deaf and blind to reality itself. Rayber's deafness becomes the special focus of Tarwater's attention, in part because of the contrast with his great-uncle, a prophet who "heard voices" without the need of a mechanical prop.

Evidence of Rayber's corruption, and of his corrupting influence on the young, is scattered throughout the novel. Rayber's house, for instance, is a structure of "pale yellow brick" (*Collected Works* 349), a color that suggests both the weakness of Rayber's commitment and the evil of his cause. Unlike Mason Tarwater, who insists on calling his great-nephew by his full name, Rayber employs the familiar form of naming: Francis, a dignified-sounding name carrying a noble quality (as well as a reference to the Revolutionary War hero, Francis Marion), becomes "Frankie," a moniker suggestive of a decadent popular culture. Another indication that Rayber is living an inauthentic existence is apparent in his marriage to Bernice Bishop, a person twice his age whom Tarwater calls "the welfare woman" and who bears him a "dim-witted" son (*Collected Works* 334) before abandoning him. It is hard to imagine that this relationship is a genuine marriage based on a lifelong commitment since Bernice abandons both Rayber and Bishop at the first sign of difficulty. Nor is it possible to imagine that Rayber, for his part, based his relationship to Bernice on anything other than expediency of one form or another.

5. Flannery O'Connor's Conservatism

Even by his own standards, Rayber is guilty of bad faith. When Old Tarwater abducts Tarwater and "adopts" him, Rayber makes little effort to reassert his claims of guardianship, partly out of fear of the old man's resistance. In fact, even as he lives by the norms of unbelief, Rayber is not fully committed even to these standards. He is not so much the champion of secular ideals as the weak adherent of a compromised modernism that he does not fully understand. He certainly does not understand the implications of his statement to Tarwater that he does not "believe in senseless sacrifice." As he says, had he attempted to take the boy from Old Tarwater and been killed, "A dead man is not going to do you any good" (*Collected Works* 395). That, of course, with its unwitting reference to Christ as the "dead man," is a telling expression of his atheism, but it is not at all what Tarwater needs to hear. Nor does Rayber's mission to "reform" Tarwater, after the boy arrives unexpectedly at his door, persist for more than a few days.

Young Tarwater, who carries the "seed" of his great-uncle in every sense of the word and who pits himself against Rayber from the start, has the effect of upsetting the schoolteacher's fraudulent equilibrium, a sense of "serenity" based on feeling "nothing" (*Collected Works* 454). Within five days Rayber has decided that Tarwater must accept *his* terms, which include conformity to the liberal ideals of secularism, educational improvement, and social adaptation, or leave his home. The fact that Rayber gives so little of himself in his relationship with Young Tarwater is evidence of his unfeeling nature. Far more important, however, is Rayber's hollow response to the suffering and, ultimately, the death of his own son, Bishop. Even though Bishop is able to perform most everyday functions on his own, Rayber finds his presence almost unbearable. The reason for this, strangely enough, is that Bishop's presence awakens an agonizing love — love of a sort that is closely associated with religious faith and that upsets Rayber's entire secular scheme of thinking.

One of the remarkable aspects of Rayber's character as O'Connor develops it in the novel is that it reveals a heartless atheist who is at the same time the victim of his own unbelief and who, despite his destructive rejection of love, makes a certain claim on our sympathies. Despite all that he stands for, Rayber is not so much a demon as he is the victim of a demonic culture in which he participates and which he promotes. In the end, while he may well be beyond rescue, he is at the same time the agent of evil and the weak and confused product of the evil of secular humanism. As O'Connor writes, at those times when Rayber is moved by love for Bishop, "he would be left shocked and depressed for days, and trembling for his sanity" (*Collected Works* 401). Rayber, in fact, experiences a surrender to love not unlike that of his uncle, Old Tarwater, and for this reason Rayber fears and suppresses his love for Bishop and is ultimately complicit in Bishop's death. To admit the depth of his love for his son would amount to an admission that Old Tarwater is right and that everything that Rayber values in everyday experience, his study of behavioral science and his commitment to social development, is pointless in light of God's transformative love for His creation. Thus, in the climactic scene in which Tarwater drowns Bishop while baptizing him, Rayber, who fully realizes what has happened, manages to block out all feeling at the loss of his son.

Rayber is, in reality, a character-type about which O'Connor wrote a great deal throughout her lifetime: the obtuse liberal do-gooder who cares more about humanity in the abstract than about those actual human beings who are closest to him. Despite the fact that Bishop cries out for his father's love, Rayber spends far more time and energy attempting to impose his narrow-minded form of social engineering on humanity in general. Like Bishop, Old Tarwater, the uncle who briefly comes to live with Rayber, attempts to engage the schoolteacher's emotions but finds himself cast aside, the object of Rayber's "scientific" study designed to prove that the old man suffers from a mental disorder. Interestingly, Rayber's response, or lack of response, to his uncle is in this way parallel to his treatment of Bishop, whom he is incapable of viewing other than in the vocabulary of disability.

Rayber was obviously a character type that was deeply troubling to O'Connor, since variations of the character appear in "A Good Man Is Hard to Find," "Everything That Rises Must Converge," "The Enduring Chill," "The Lame Shall Enter First," and other stories. Ironically, while Rayber spouts a utopian vision of social justice and universal betterment, it is Old Tarwater who expresses a compelling "vision of a world tran-

5. Flannery O'Connor's Conservatism

sfigured" (*Collected Works* 401). O'Connor understood that it was the work of social scientists that formed the basis for the expansion of federal welfare and education programs during the 1950s and 1960s. O'Connor recognized that these state programs threatened human liberty, which availed itself only to those who lived beyond state control. For this reason, she directed her fiercest satiric assaults at the figure of the social scientist. In such stories as "The Enduring Chill" (1958), "Everything That Rises Must Converge" (1961), and "The Lame Shall Enter First" (1962), O'Connor satirized protagonists whose liberal humanism blinded them to the broader mysteries of existence and led to their acceptance of a deadening materialism. At the same time that she satirized the destructiveness of liberalism in her fiction, O'Connor provided a more analytical critique in several important essays including "The Regional Writer" (1963) and "The Catholic Novelist in the Protestant South" (1963). It is interesting that no less a conservative than Caroline Gordon, O'Connor's lifelong literary confidante and adviser, recognized the increasingly programmatic quality of O'Connor's later fiction and urged her protégée to return to an aesthetically "pure" form of writing. While Gordon was equally conservative in her social and religious views, she maintained the New Critical doctrine that narrative art must be the product of a sensibility distanced from the immediacy of experience, especially that of politics. I would maintain that O'Connor came to reject this aesthetic doctrine.

It is in *The Violent Bear It Away* that O'Connor arrived at the fullest and most compelling expression of her conservative view of the world. In this novel Old Tarwater's opposition to Rayber's progressive program of education is based on his knowledge that such an education, focused on a secular and liberal view of life, is a destructive exercise in indoctrination that ends in the destruction of liberty. In place of the statist education that Rayber promotes, Tarwater offers his nephew a "well rounded education covering Figures, Reading, Writing, and History, beginning with Adam expelled from the Garden and going on down through the presidents to Herbert Hoover and on in speculation toward the Second Coming and the Day of Judgment" (*Collected Works* 331). Tarwater's educational curriculum reflects his deep and protective love for his nephew in the face of what he, Old Tarwater, knows to be the deadening materialism of an atheistic society. Unlike that of Rayber, which would perhaps prepare Tarwater for a hollow existence as the servant of a state bureaucracy or some other collectivist organization, this teaching is intended to train young Tarwater in the vocation of prophecy, and, more specifically, to prepare him to complete the unfinished work of baptizing Rayber's son, Bishop. The lessons that he has to teach, unlike those of Rayber's secular schooling with its focus on healthy adjustment and positive self-image, are painful and difficult. It is understandable that Tarwater should rebel against his great-uncle's teaching since that teaching unmasks the unpleasant facts of everyday life and thus results in what many would regard as a condition of alienation. After having been "burned clean" (*Collected Works* 332) in preparation for his Christian service, the future that Old Tarwater envisions for his young charge, Tarwater will never again "fit in" within the faithless confines of liberal society. He will, however, have gained the life-sustaining knowledge of his true purpose within a divinely created universe.

Mason Tarwater's effort to convey this truth to young Tarwater is evidence of his deep compassion and humanity. His teaching, in fact, reflects a much broader understanding of the philosophical limitations of the modern world than would appear to be the case. In effect, Tarwater has distilled a lifetime of shrewd reflection on the failings of secularism, humanism, and statism and has formulated his own response to modernity based on his extensive knowledge of biblical texts and human experience. In contrast to the enslaving philosophy that governs the secular world, Tarwater's religious teaching is joyful and liberating. As he tells Tarwater: "'I saved you to be free, your own self!'" (*Collected Works* 339). What state education has to offer, on the other hand, renders children "one among many, indistinguishable from the herd" (*Collected Works* 341). As Tarwater comes to understand at the end of his painful journey of self-discovery, his great-uncle was the most sophisticated and knowledgeable individual he has ever met or is likely to meet, and despite the burden of his prophetic mission, the most joyful and fulfilled.

Not only does *The Violent Bear It Away* embody O'Connor's conservative defense of the family and of localism — the powerful depiction of nurture and self-sufficiency associated with Powderhead — it reflects the central role of religious orthodoxy in O'Connor's moral imagination. In the forefront of the novel is the conflict between the expansive role of government as represented by Rayber, spokesman for the state, and the traditional role of individual responsibility and religious faith represented by Old Tarwater. Had she lived to witness the passage of *Roe v. Wade* in 1973, O'Connor would certainly have sided with the Right to Life movement that worked to overturn the court's decision on abortion rights. Long before *Roe v. Wade* introduced the particular arguments for and against abortion into the general political debate, O'Connor had reflected on the ethical implications of abortion in considerable detail, and based on her understanding of the issue, she had become an unequivocal supporter of the Right to Life well before that phrase was invented. O'Connor's view of abortion was identical to that of the Church, as was her view of birth control: the destruction of life was abhorrent and inexcusable, and it was the responsibility of the living to protect the rights of the unborn. As O'Connor wrote to Betty Hester on 27 June 1959, "The Church's stand on birth control is the most absolutely spiritual of all her stands" (*Habit* 338).

Though critics such as Richard Giannone have understandably focused on her religious convictions in a strictly theological sense, O'Connor was a conservative in nearly every sense of the word. In the terminology that emerged after her death, she was most assuredly a "religious conservative": one who viewed abortion in precisely the same terms as did the Catholic Church but also in the terms of the Religious Right of the last few decades. She was also a conservative on national defense — a patriot who was appalled by the left-leaning stance of so many writers and intellectuals of her generation and one who characterized communism in her letters and essays as an ungodly "evil empire" intent on the destruction of liberty.

O'Connor was also a social conservative. While O'Connor was in no sense a racist, she echoed the "go slow" policy of southern conservatives who believed that federal enforcement of integration would lead to violence in the South. She was also a social conservative in terms of the various movements toward personal liberation that flourished in the postwar decades. O'Connor was well aware of the publications of the Beat writers centered in San Francisco, and she had worked out in her own mind the destructive implications of their mantra of unlimited personal freedom. In a letter to Maryat Lee of 6 September 1959, she spoke of the Beats as "revoltingly sentimental about their own bohemianism" (*Habit* 349), but it was not just the aesthetic fraudulence of the Beats' bohemian posture that troubled O'Connor. There was danger to society and to the soul in the moral confusion resulting from the belief that one's identity was self-created and that it could shift at will from one perspective to another. In a letter of 6 September 1959, O'Connor mocked Allen Ginsberg's notion "that the way to reach God is through marijuana" (*Habit* 349). More seriously, O'Connor recognized the harm of writers such as Iris Murdoch, a British humanist who served in some respects as O'Connor's nemesis throughout the last years of her life (even seducing O'Connor's closest friend, Betty Hester, away from the Church and toward belief in godless self-discovery). Although she at first held a very favorable opinion of Murdoch's writing, O'Connor came to view Murdoch's writing as essentially pointless. Having read *The Severed Head*, O'Connor commented that "when I got through I did not see that it added up to anything. In fact, I found it completely hollow" (*Habit* 439).

It was not just Ginsberg or Murdoch that O'Connor had in mind, either. The entire post–Nietzschean movement toward rebellion against inherited beliefs was the object of O'Connor's searing analysis. One level of the narrative in *The Violent Bear It Away* develops quite clearly from this aspect of O'Connor's sensibility as O'Connor channels her own scathing criticism of modernist experimentalism through the character of Old Tarwater and through that of Tarwater himself, as he is at the end. For example, at Cherokee Lodge, where Rayber takes Tarwater and Bishop for a "holiday," Tarwater observes the latest fad of dancing to jukebox music. As he watches four couples of his own age gyrating to the atrocious noise, it seemed that "they might have belonged to a different species entirely" (*Collected Works* 447). Staring past the boys and girls, nearly indistinguishable by gender, Tarwater watches the couples dancing with a "furious stern concentration" (*Collected Works* 447). As O'Connor writes, "They might have been insects buzzing across the surface of his vision" (*Collected Works* 447).

5. Flannery O'Connor's Conservatism

In this heavily loaded narrative language O'Connor stresses the unnaturalness of what Tarwater witnesses. As O'Connor depicts it in this scene, the popular culture of American youth is evolving toward something cold, inhuman, and merciless. The tribal quality of the music is bad enough, but along with that is the closed-minded "concentration," which, of course, is really a sort of willed lack of concentration, and the determination to repress natural differences of gender. Clearly, O'Connor was well ahead of her time in these observations, as in everything she undertook. The upshot of this drift toward an inhuman popular culture was the loss of personal expression and liberty, and a decline in adherence to convention and to traditional belief.

It is not merely the loosening of conventional standards that O'Connor satirizes in this scene, however: something more important is at stake. What the dancers represent is not just rebellion against convention or relaxation of moral codes: it is something akin to what Jonah Goldberg would later call "liberal fascism." After the music stops, Bishop begins to wail in disappointment. Noticing Bishop for the first time, the response of the dancers to this seriously disabled child is "shocked and affronted as if they had been betrayed by a fault in creation" (*Collected Works* 448). Here O'Connor is pointing to the inability of the liberal culture, intent as it is on maximizing "happiness" and self-fulfillment, to accept human imperfection — an inability that results in all sorts of collectivist schemes to "correct" whatever falls short of perfection and, failing that, to shut off from view or even to do away with that which is imperfect. The attitude of the dancers is not pity or compassion but anger stemming from the fact that their self-serving idealism has been upended. The liberal mind, in other words, is incapable of accepting the world of suffering and loss that Hannah Arendt characterized as "the human condition" or that V.S. Naipaul had in mind when he wrote that "the world is as it is."

O'Connor's conservatism extended as well to fiscal matters. Unlike many artists, perhaps in her case because of the perilous state of her widowed mother's finances and the ever-present need to economize, O'Connor was keenly interested in the depth of human necessity and, thus, in the role of money in human society. Unlike many liberal writers, O'Connor was far from indifferent to the needs of ordinary human beings, perhaps because she herself had experienced poverty much of her life, albeit lightened by the charity of more affluent relatives. O'Connor possessed a clear understanding of the necessary role of monetary exchange within human affairs. One can say that O'Connor took a significant interest in and was an ardent supporter of (as landlord, investor, and literary entrepreneur, participant in) the capitalist system. Unlike many of her radicalized contemporaries, from Jean-Paul Sartre and Samuel Beckett to Heinrich Böll, there is no sense in O'Connor's writing of a critique of capitalism, whether from a Marxist or existentialist point of view.

In many respects, O'Connor was not anti-materialistic at all, but prudently realistic about the need to increase revenues from her publications and appearances and to reduce farm and domestic expenditures. She was, after all, in a sense "co-owner" of Andalusia. Although she did survive her mother and so never took title to the farm, O'Connor's perspective might be characterized as typical of the rentier class, however limiting she sometimes depicted that perspective in her fiction. Like her mother, O'Connor understood that employees could be a burden as well as an asset and that taxes were the bane of a property owner's existence.

In some fundamental sense, in fact, human liberty as O'Connor understood it was tied to the ownership of property, and so property rights were to be considered sacrosanct. Tarwater's rural acreage, Powderhead, constitutes a self-sufficient world in which he and young Tarwater are free to spend much of their time in reflection and prayer. This independent lifestyle is greatly superior to the wage slavery that O'Connor associates with the city, and especially with those such as the schoolteacher Rayber who owe their livelihood to the state. Old Tarwater is fully aware of the virtue of land ownership, for every time that he and Tarwater return to Powderhead after one of their brief trips, Old Tarwater gazes lovingly at his property. As O'Connor described it, "He might have been Moses glimpsing the promised land" (*Collected Works* 474).

For Tarwater's kind of independence to continue, however, property rights must be protected not just from illegal seizure but from confiscation via taxation. O'Connor understood quite well the process by which excessive taxation threatened the dignity of mankind. Human liberty could not continue to exist in a society in which much of the earnings of the

5. Flannery O'Connor's Conservatism

citizenry were confiscated by the state, which then used those revenues to impose further controls over the lives of its citizens. Unfortunately, as O'Connor understood, the power of the state was rapidly expanding during her lifetime and with this power came the decline of individual liberty. Just as the freedom to express oneself openly was curtailed in an educational establishment which was controlled by state funding, the freedom of the artist was restricted within a culture in which government funding of the press and the media influenced the reception that the artist might receive and even limited the artist's ability to publish at all. One of O'Connor's most remarkable qualities in this regard, and one not full appreciated by her critics, was her courage to risk popularity — indeed, to risk her career — in the service of truth. As an unapologetic critic of the prevailing liberal culture, O'Connor was taking a chance on never finding a publisher and on having her work roundly denounced by critics, as in fact it was by many.

It was especially in the liberal North that O'Connor detected support for the expansion of the state and with it the curtailment of liberty. The dangerous collectivism that ruled much of the world — that formed the basis of European fascism and communism — now influenced much of the intelligentsia in America. While it may be something of a stretch to see Rayber as the representative of totalitarianism, his thought processes are every bit as destructive, and are destructive in the same ways, as those of the loyal communist apparatchik. In Rayber's thinking, there is no place for the dignity of life. He is therefore capable of destroying life at will if doing so serves his ideological purposes. As Mason Tarwater tells his great-nephew, "every living thing that passed through [Rayber's] eyes into his head was turned by his brain into a book or a paper or a chart" (*Collected Works* 341). This inhumanity includes Rayber's inability to respond to nature. When Rayber later returns to Powderhead with Tarwater and Bishop during their stay at Cherokee Lake, he represses his awed response to the virgin forest: after a moment's reflection, "he reduced the whole wood in probable board feet into a college education for [Tarwater]" (*Collected Works* 444–45).

It is not just Rayber's own thought process that is destructive, however. As with all forms of collectivism, the end game for Rayber is enforcement of strict conformity of thought and action on others. It is, in other words, essentially totalitarian in nature since its underlying motive is total control. In fact, at those times when he is unable to control others, Rayber becomes possessed by a sort of rage that finds an outlet in violence. This is certainly the case when, unable to deal with the emotional demands that his son's need for love make upon him, Rayber attempts to drown Bishop at a beach far from the city. This travesty of baptism is, of course, contrasted with Old Tarwater's attempt to baptize Bishop and with Tarwater's unconscious compulsion to fulfill his great-uncle's wishes by doing so himself.

In taking Tarwater and Bishop to Cherokee Lake, a rustic resort just thirty miles from Powderhead, Rayber carries out an "experiment" of returning Tarwater to the site of his upbringing. By forcing Tarwater to confront his past, as he thinks, Rayber will expose the false teachings of Old Tarwater and so restore Tarwater to the "health" of atheism and unbelief. One could argue, of course, that unconsciously Rayber may be operating on the basis of any number of confused motives: to provide the opportunity for Tarwater to baptize Bishop, to cause the drowning of Bishop, or even to reconnect with Old Tarwater himself. Rayber's peculiarly haunted appearance, "like something human trapped in a switch box" (*Collected Works* 426), certainly suggests a duplicitous motivation.

Cherokee Lake may provide Tarwater an opportunity to "confront" his past — eventually, of course, it does — but one need that it cannot satisfy is the mounting hunger within Tarwater for something beyond what Rayber can supply. The hunger that has tormented Tarwater all along comes to a head in the final sections of the novel. As it is, Tarwater has hardly eaten since leaving Powderhead because the food he receives at Rayber's table is tasteless and less than nourishing in comparison with what he received from his great-uncle. "If the old man had done nothing else for him," O'Connor writes, "he had heaped his plate" (*Collected Works* 430). In contrast with the meat and biscuit provided by his great-uncle, Rayber offers Tarwater dry cereal, lightbread sandwiches, and foreign restaurant food. The obvious symbolism of Tarwater's hunger, a spiritual need as well as a physical one, is carried through until the end of the novel.

5. Flannery O'Connor's Conservatism

Tarwater's spirituality finds one avenue of expression in his seemingly unconscious compulsion to baptize Bishop. Paradoxically, this compulsion, planted in his character by Old Tarwater, results in Bishop's drowning but is closely connected with the reverence for life that Tarwater's great-uncle preaches throughout the novel. The baptism scene, recalled after the fact by Tarwater, is filled with the Christian symbolism of the blood-like "red globe" of the setting sun, the dark water of life of Cherokee Lake, and the star-filled night sky suggesting the transfiguration that O'Connor associated with the peacock. As he reenacts the scene in a series of broken thoughts and images, Tarwater moves in a phantasmagoric manner from the condition of rebellion toward the state of grace. Prodded by the voice of the stranger urging him to rid himself of Bishop, Tarwater, whose very name specifies the rich dark blood of life, carries out the shocking baptism via murder. The scene is recalled in a hazy, disjunctive, magical style of narration, but then O'Connor was not writing "realism" of a representational sort: she was aiming for a higher form of realism that she connected with Hawthorne and the romance tradition. In this form of moral romance, a reverence for life might well coincide with an act that might be termed "murder." In truth, the killing is, and is not, murder: the very fact that Tarwater's action transcends a legalistic reading points to the all-important nature of baptism as the path to life, besides which murder seems, in the terms of moral romance at least, trivial.

In the novel's final sequence, Tarwater returns to Powderhead following the murder/baptism of Bishop. On the way, against the remembered warnings of his great-uncle about riding with strangers, he accepts a ride with a driver in a "lavender and cream-colored car," "a pale, lean, old-looking young man with deep hollows under his cheekbones" (*Collected Works* 469): in other words, a double of himself but one now becoming distinct from his true nature. After he joins the malevolent-looking stranger, Tarwater accepts a marijuana cigarette and a drink from a bottle of drugged alcohol that he opens with the corkscrew-bottleopener, a gift from Rayber that Tarwater boasts will "open anything" (*Collected Works* 470). This, of course, is exactly the point: the corkscrew-bottleopener, opening what a liberal writer like Aldous Huxley might term the "doors of perception," enables Tarwater to drink from a drugged mixture that renders him "irresponsible" and leads to his rape at the hands of the stranger. The degradation of this rape is the decisive event leading to the transformation of Tarwater from a confused and rebellious young man questing for self-knowledge to a prophet certain of his relationship to a stable body of inherited belief. At this point, following the rape, Tarwater begins to separate definitively from the tempter who has shadowed his existence ever since the death of his great-uncle, though the separation will not be complete until Tarwater returns to Powderhead and burns the woods containing the spirit of the stranger. Yet even now, as if cleansed by the same fire that had burned clean Old Tarwater, Tarwater's eyes take on the haunted expression of one who sees beyond the trivialities of the present. He has entered upon a vocation that will return him first to Powderhead and then back to the secular city where he may save a few others but will undoubtedly suffer at the hands of unbelievers.

The scene of revelation at the end of the novel clarifies the path that Francis Marion Tarwater will follow in the future. In a vision of Christ on the Mount feeding the multitudes with loaves and fishes, Tarwater becomes aware for the first time that his is a deep spiritual hunger that can only be nourished by sacrifice and service. At this point Tarwater becomes, like his great-uncle, one in a long line of prophets including Daniel, Elijah, and Moses. It is a joyful and glorious ending to a torturous narrative, the most difficult undertaking of O'Connor's career.

It is worth considering, however, just what form Young Tarwater's preaching will take once he returns to the secular city. The symbolism of blood, fire, bread, and rebirth in the novel's final pages points clearly to Tarwater's future as a prophet of redemption, one whose vocation is to warn mankind of "THE TERRIBLE SPEED OF MERCY" (*Collected Works* 478). But if Tarwater's vocation is to preach the fundamentalist truth that one must be born again, it assumes, as O'Connor pointedly tells us in the novel's final phrase, that in their secular lives "the children of God lay sleeping" (*Collected Works* 479): that is, that they are asleep to the mercy that awaits them once they have embraced a stable and coherent belief system. As O'Connor suggests repeatedly in *The Violent*

5. Flannery O'Connor's Conservatism

Bear It Away (and as she had dramatized in horrific detail in her first novel, *Wise Blood*), the Christian prophet in the secular city will suffer at the hands of a majority who prefer the comfortable sleep of atheism, relativism, and liberalism to the religious orthodoxy that O'Connor had in mind. But the remainder of Young Tarwater's life will be devoted to spreading the same conservative message as that of his great-uncle: the message of liberty, responsibility, and love that Old Tarwater has taught his great-nephew. This message is much broader — it is different, in fact — than the religious teachings of any particular Protestant denomination since, as O'Connor stressed, Old Tarwater was "not a Southern Baptist, but an independent, a prophet in the true sense" (*Habit* 407). Significantly, she insisted that the mainstream Protestant churches in the South "are evaporating into secularism and respectability." What is taking their place, she wrote, is the emergence of "all sorts of strange sects" (*Habit* 407) in reaction to the spiritual disturbance of a radically tolerant and faithless culture.

As difficult as it is for some critics to admit, O'Connor was deadly serious in her presentation of Mason Tarwater and Rayber as representatives of opposed and competing civilizations. As prophets of a coherent system of inherited beliefs, Old Tarwater and his great-nephew after him are men who are intensely aware of the damage of secular humanism. Their vocation in life is essentially the same as that of O'Connor: to warn the unbelievers of their time of the destructiveness of atheism, relativism, and liberalism, and to plead for a return to the sensible, if demanding, teachings that Mason Tarwater enunciates in the early chapters of the novel. O'Connor found that Old Tarwater's character came easily to her, but it was more difficult to write that of Rayber because, although she knew a great deal about secular humanism from the outside, she found it impossible actually to fathom an existence so completely alienated from God. In writing the character of Old Tarwater, on the other hand, she was simply recording a version of herself. As she wrote to John Hawkes on 13 September 1959, "The modern reader will identify himself with the schoolteacher, but it is the old man who speaks for me" (*Habit* 350).

- 6 -

Naipaul's Turn in the American South

J.M. Coetzee once suggested that V.S. Naipaul's major contribution to English literature might well be "a mode of writing that Naipaul has perfected over the years, in which historical reportage and social analysis float into and out of an autobiographically colored fiction and travel memoir" (*Razor's Edge* 9). As travel writing of a kind that weaves together the author's direct observations, anecdotes, interviews, reflections, and long-standing moral concerns, *A Turn in the South* clearly falls within this mode. Yet writing of this order possesses a thematic and narrative coherence that renders it an imaginative creation on the same order as Naipaul's fiction, so much so that Coetzee's term, "travel memoir," with its mildly patronizing suggestion of some sort of diary account, is hardly adequate as a description of the appraisal of human civilization that Naipaul was writing, nor does the inexact phrase "autobiographically colored" do justice to what Naipaul has achieved in this genre. For one thing, Naipaul's "travel memoirs" employ a sophisticated narrative persona that plays off against the documentary subject. The Naipaul persona, who appears in both the travel writing and in such novels as *The Enigma of Arrival* and *A Way in the World*, is a complex imaginative figure deployed as a means of mediating between the seemingly incomprehensible chaos of the world that is Naipaul's subject and the stable core of principles at the center of Naipaul's vision.

Naipaul had never visited the South prior to 1984, when he arrived in Dallas, Texas, for a journalistic assignment at the Republican National Convention. Dallas itself, though hardly a representative southern city,

6. Naipaul's Turn in the American South

was pleasing to Naipaul: "I liked the new buildings, the shapes, the glossiness, the architectural playfulness, and the wealth that it implied" (*Turn* 24). But this brief visit to Dallas afforded only a superficial and oblique impression of a region that he had previously known only second-hand by listening as a child in Trinidad to the southern evangelical radio station of which his grandmother was a devoted follower. Whatever else he knew about the region centered on its unenviable reputation for racial conflict, and while this history was surely significant, it did not constitute a complete portrait of life in the South. In fact, when he does arrive in the South for the extended visit that would last through the spring and summer of 1987, Naipaul discovers that he must overcome his preconception that the race issue dominates every aspect of southern life: for Naipaul, as for so many others (particularly international commentators), "southern racism" is a reified concept that can only be overcome, if at all, by actual experience. Once he begins to explore the South with the help of a series of personal contacts, Naipaul finds that racial conflict is no longer an overriding problem in the South. The ordinary lives of most southerners are more focused elsewhere — on family, faith, work, and a love of the outdoors.

Naipaul's overall paradigm, and one that determines the book's central themes, is announced in the title, *A Turn in the South*. Like many observers before him, Naipaul focuses on the "turn" or changing nature of southern society from an agrarian civilization to a modern industrial culture. (The title, of course, also evokes an old-fashioned, leisurely walk or "turn" of the sort that one might encounter in a novel by Jane Austen.) The major themes that Naipaul explores are not unlike those developed in the classic histories of the New South by C. Vann Woodward or George Brown Tindall, or, for that matter, in the contributions of Allen Tate, Andrew Lytle, and Robert Penn Warren, among others, to the classic anthology, *I'll Take My Stand*. In his own way, each of these commentators address a similar set of conservative concerns: the mythic beauty of the southern landscape threatened by industrial development; the personal quality of social relationships within an "organic" society replaced by regimentation and estrangement; the prominence of the family weakened by modern ideas of self-liberation; the centrality of religion undermined by secularism. As in Tate and Lytle, there is the predictable warning of the decline of a unique way of life as agrarian ways and traditional patterns of belief are displaced by industrial culture, but to this familiar paradigm of agrarian-industrial conflict, Naipaul affixes a distinctive vision, one based on a broad and complex understanding of history resulting from his Indian ancestry, his Trinidadian childhood, and his long residence in Britain.

Naipaul brings each of these cultural perspectives into play, and at times it is difficult for him to avoid viewing the South as a former "internal colony" of the United States, a region that has suffered the same forms of deprivation that Naipaul has dissected in his many books on the Caribbean, Africa, and India. Indeed, one of the intriguing, and at times perplexing, aspects of *A Turn in the South* is the extent to which Naipaul falls back on a tropical paradigm in his perception of the American South ("how close, in the slave days, the slave territories of the Caribbean and the South were" [*Turn* 87]), and how close they might continue to be in Naipaul's reading were it not for the fact that the experiential level of the narrative so often contradicts and in the end is permitted to override even Naipaul's outdated generalizations. At one point, for example, Naipaul's reaction to the late summer heat causes him to compare the South to India. Driving to visit friends in north Georgia, he writes: "In a pond beside the road on the way to Fort Oglethorpe cattle stood in muddy water up to their bellies — one might have been in India" (*Turn* 265). And yet, as Naipaul quickly notes, he is *not* in India, nor in a colonized or formerly colonized region. He is in the most entrepreneurial, business-friendly region of the United States, a landscape imbued with automobile plants, expressways, and a solidly middle-class population. Beginning with only broad stereotypes, Naipaul broadens and refines his understanding based on observation and experience: he is too fine a realist to avoid seeing and recording what stands before his eyes. Like everything else Naipaul has written, *A Turn in the South* is a book about the confusions and contradictions of perception and understanding, and it reveals the way in which stereotypes and ideological assumptions, especially, in this instance, those of the Naipaul persona himself, constitute obstacles and temptations that stand in the way of

6. Naipaul's Turn in the American South

one's grasp of reality. Gradually, Naipaul's experience leads him to qualify and all but reject the postcolonial interpretation. Not long into his journey Naipaul sets aside most of his outdated assumptions and is carried along by his irrepressible realism into a less tidy but far more truthful depiction. Gradually, Naipaul suppresses his tendency to read the South through the lens of the other colonial or postcolonial societies he has studied, discarding this view along with much of the racial paradigm that he originally brought to the subject. By the end of the book, he arrives at a sense of the South as a socially conflicted, historically complex, and rapidly changing region.

Lacking previous experience of the South, Naipaul adopts the role of student of southern culture — seeking out contacts; reading and rereading books such as *Up from Slavery*; filling notebooks one after another with the records of interviews, observations, and experiences. One of the points about which Naipaul must inform himself, for example, is the complex class structure that exists in the South. Although he had only an indistinct idea of the meaning of the word "redneck" before arriving in the South, Naipaul quickly grasps the significance not only of the term but of an entire culture of "the pickup trucks dashingly driven, the baseball caps marked with the name of some company" (*Turn* 212) and a stubborn, at times aggressive, assertion of independence in the very posture of poor white males. With his open-minded wonder and appreciation for the South, Naipaul (in this instance, with the aid of his guide, a local man named Campbell) comes to distinguish "pride and style and a fashion code [and even "poetry"] where I had seen nothing" (*Turn* 212). It is one of numerous instances where the Naipaul persona engages in self-correction; it reveals a remarkable propensity for truth-seeking that leads him further and further into the sometimes damaged and irreconcilable nature of southern society and, for that matter, of all human societies.

Naipaul's encounter with southern aristocracy is a revelation as well. In its own way, the southern elite constitutes a distinctive culture, and one entirely as outlandish as that of the poor whites. As he spends long hours talking with "Mary," a middle-aged descendent of Delta plantation owners, Naipaul begins to understand the importance of a particular set of manners as a mark of aristocracy ("in the poverty of the South, class was something in the mind and consciousness of the family, related to an idea of good behavior and seemliness" [*Turn* 170]), and in her liberal attitude toward racial integration, he perceives a continuing sense of noblesse oblige. Mary is proud of her southern background but hardly oblivious to the challenges of poverty and race that have existed in the region. Born in 1944, she can recall the Emmett Till murder, which took place in 1955 not far from her hometown of Greenwood, Mississippi. Nonetheless, in the face of this history Mary maintains a firm sense of superiority, not only toward the poor whites who are her neighbors but also toward people in the North. In the intricate mental ledger of social relationships to which she clings, Mary balances her pride in southern identity, her stature as a social reformer, and her undying disdain for poor whites. For her, the South, with its extraordinary culture, great literary tradition, and graceful society of manners, is superior to anything in the industrial regions of the North, but her aristocratic milieu positions her family at the top of southern society as well. From her perspective, it is the poor whites who have perpetuated a climate of racial conflict and who are to blame for any number of southern failings. Those families who are transient, who say "ain't" and "nigger," and who lack basic table manners, are the ones to blame for the South's fall from grace.

Despite his appreciation of Mary's personal qualities, Naipaul appears to interpret her conception of aristocracy as a static and defensive code of behavior intimately connected to the threat to her own position within a dynamic social order. A heightened sense of social distinctions is to be expected within a socially fluid society, such as that which surely existed on the nineteenth-century southern frontier of Alabama and Mississippi. In this frontier society, wealth would otherwise constitute the surest indicator of class position. However civilly he behaves toward this aging remnant of fine manners and deft snobbery, Naipaul cannot help but sense that Mary's view of the world is wrong, not because it is artificial — what form of human cultivation is not? — but because it is so obviously biased in favor of her personal advantage. Like the hermetic world of the Tulsis in Naipaul's great novel, *A House for Mr. Biswas* — a world also dominated by an aging matriarch — Mary's world is static and defen-

6. Naipaul's Turn in the American South

sive. In the context of the ever-present social disorder in which southerners have lived since the Civil War, and, indeed, within the volatile frontier society that preceded the war, a code of manners served to distinguish the gentry from the rest of society. In the contemporary context of rapidly increasing affluence and opportunity, Mary's pretensions seem completely pointless.

Mary would undoubtedly protest that one indication of her own more refined background and that of southerners in general is a greater refinement of religious practice. Naipaul himself becomes keenly aware of the variations of southern religious experience, and, given his general skepticism concerning all religious institutions, southern religion is sure to attract his critical gaze. Once again, experiential reality tends to undercut his preconceptions, though in this case one feels that it is more difficult for Naipaul to control his prejudices. Naipaul is deeply disturbed by the fanaticism and emotionalism that he sees in evangelical services, but he is surprised at the "formality" that he finds in mainstream churches, and especially in the African Methodist Episcopal (AME) church service that he attends in North Carolina. Everywhere he travels in the South, Naipaul discovers an extraordinary religious inclination among the people whom he meets. As he writes: "In no other part of the world had I found people so driven by the idea of good behavior and the good religious life" (*Turn* 164).

In the case of the many fundamentalist Christians whom he encounters, however, Naipaul reacts to their fervid religious practices in a predictably unsympathetic manner. One of Naipaul's lifelong bogeymen, after all, has been religious fanaticism of the sort that he detects in certain sects of Islam, in various forms of mysticism, and in Protestant fundamentalism. Because of his fear of religious fanaticism, Naipaul fails really to comprehend the importance of fundamentalist belief for many southerners. What Naipaul fails to admit is that in the absence of belief systems capable of holding conviction, a preponderance of the American public, not only in the South but everywhere (and truth be known, in all human societies), would find themselves at a loss, lacking a spiritual ground of purpose and belonging. This is the case of his encounter with Paula, a young waitress on her last day at work in a Research Triangle restaurant.

For her part, Paula believes that faith provides solutions to problems that arise in a culture in which marital roles are not clearly defined. Her religious faith has taught strength and forbearance, and these virtues make possible a drastic improvement in her life as she rejoins the husband from whom she has been separated. Unfortunately, Naipaul interprets her reliance on faith as weakness, "a medieval idea of chaos, and the solitude and helplessness of men, and the necessity for salvation" (*Turn* 282–83). In this instance, it would seem that Naipaul has given in to his own prejudices and forsaken his talent for close observation. His comparison of Christian fundamentalism with Islam, both reflecting an identical "need for security" (*Turn* 285), is a simplistic reading of both faiths.

In his travels Naipaul detects an eagerness among southerners to make sense of their experience not only through vigorous religious expression but through storytelling and talk, a feature of southern life that Fred Hobson analyzes in his superb book, *Tell About the South*. Among ordinary people as among the many artists, politicians, and celebrities whom Naipaul interviews — elder statesmen like Will Campbell and writers such as Anne Rivers Siddons and James Applewhite — there is a similar compulsion to evoke "a kind of complete world" (*Turn* 301). The southern talent for storytelling was, in Naipaul's opinion, quite opposed to the heartless world encountered in the work of Salinger, Cheever, and Updike — all of them authors specializing in the representation of middle-class society of the urban North. As Naipaul wrote in a review of *Stories from the New Yorker: 1950–1960* which appeared in *New Statesman* on December 22, 1961: "It isn't only that so many of its American stories are indistinguishable in style, sensibility and mood; it is that these stories, when read in bulk, seem to have issued from a civilization so joyless that it must be judged to have failed" (qtd. in French 190). In heartland America, Naipaul encountered something quite apart from the grinding anomie of the northern suburbs. Among the southern storytellers whom he encountered in the South, there existed the same acute penchant for meaning and order that was undoubtedly the basis for the literary success of so many fiction writers in the South. What writers such as Faulkner, O'Connor, and Welty have accomplished in imaginative works of fiction draws on an essential feature of southern society, the everyday need of

6. Naipaul's Turn in the American South

southern people to explore the meaning of their lives through narrative, and Naipaul may well be correct that the intensity of this need results in large part from the history of anarchy, disorder, and loss that shadow the South.

Perhaps also in response to this turbulent history, the South, as Naipaul understands it, is the last bastion of quintessential American values of optimism and personal responsibility. In a section of the book that deals with catfish farming — a classic example of the author's ability to merge concrete observation with an allegorical level of meaning — Naipaul communicates a profound understanding of the role of private initiative and accountability in southern identity. There are no windfall profits and no assurance of success in catfish farming, a vocation that requires the most careful, hands-on management and that is subject to every sort of mishap. Again, like human civilization as a whole (within which, in the South at least, it plays its own modest part), the success of a catfish operation rests on the intelligence, assiduousness, and effort of those engaged in it. Like civilization in general, the success of catfish farming also depends on an inherited body of knowledge, methods, and customs that have evolved over time ("how much experimentation and accident and loss — had gone into the rearing of those fish being loaded that early morning into the trucks of the processing plant!" [*Turn* 174]). Naipaul's evocation of the catfish culture is, in sum, a brilliant *tour de force* that embodies his deepest convictions concerning the role of inherited knowledge, rationality, initiative, and self-control within human civilization. As it traces the harvesting and processing of catfish from egg to marketable product, the passage also reveals Naipaul as a writer whose own labor exhibits the identical virtues of patience and intelligence.

"De-heading," as Naipaul points out, is a word perfectly suited to its meaning — the sort of word that Naipaul savors: "A man can be beheaded; a man is not de-headed any more than a fish is beheaded; and 'de-headed' suggested the industrial process involved" (*Turn* 175). A wry humor, in fact, underlies the entire unreal passage, as if the writer can hardly believe the situation he finds himself in, reporting on the growth of an important new industry whose success depends on its efforts to enhance the palatability and image of a lowly species of bottom feeder.

Yet civilization itself is not much different: art, education, and industry all depend on a continual effort carried out over centuries to improve the elemental condition into which human beings have been born. And like catfish farming, the slightest inattentiveness—a problem with aeration of the ponds, feeding too much or too little, a mistake in the timing of a harvest or a delay in processing—can spell ruin. The "paradox of civilization" (*Turn* 275), as Naipaul points out in a later passage devoted to the cultivation of tobacco, is that human beings are able to take something as distasteful as catfish (or tobacco, or human nature in its rudimentary form) and translate it into something of worth. It does not escape Naipaul's notice that the word "cultivation" can be applied to two quite different but, in essential respects, identical spheres: the act of "cultivating or tilling," and "culture or refinement." We are at risk once we lose sight of the connection.

The virtues that Naipaul identifies in the farming of catfish or tobacco are part of the same moral vision that grounds all of his writing. This vision of "the universal civilization" involves, above all, an appreciation of reason and order in the face of the destructive potential for impassioned self-interest and anarchy. In Naipaul's judgment, only the sort of liberal democratic civilization that has existed in the West during the last several hundred years can ensure human liberty and at the same time support a vigorous market for human effort and creativity, and only within such a civilization are the values of human dignity, privacy, and security likely to be protected. Herein, however, lies another paradox, for the sheer scale of modern industrial and postindustrial culture—a product in itself of the success of western market capitalism—appears to generate forms of alienation and atomization that undercut the values of reason and order that Naipaul prizes. The great wealth and extent of cities like Dallas and Atlanta are impressive, but urban-industrial society, with its abstraction of human beings from nature and from intimate social contact and negotiation, engenders a pernicious form of anomie. Naipaul values the neighborly scale of smaller cities and towns not for nostalgic reasons but because the human scale of those communities reins in the abstract intellect and humbles human ambitions. Naipaul seeks to perpetuate the tolerance, restraint, and civility of liberal democracy,

6. Naipaul's Turn in the American South

qualities that too often seem at risk within the inhuman scale of urban-industrial development.

A comparison of *A Turn in the South* with his fictional works shows that Naipaul is well aware of this difficulty, for one of the major concerns of his fictional works is the importance of this same human scale that has been lost in the urban-industrial organization of society. By its very nature, urban crowding discourages the slow, civil interchange and obstructs the natural meeting places — the country lanes, walkways, watering holes, and marketplaces — that gave encouragement to social exchange in the past. The regimentation of daily life has detrimental psychological effects, including a rise in the sense of disaffection and anomie. There are economic and environmental consequences as well. In the preindustrial agrarian economy, Naipaul finds a greater balance was maintained in market prices for crops, and he speculates that the smaller scale of agriculture, before the advent of large-scale cultivation and the widespread use of pesticides, may also have prevented large-scale disasters by ensuring the presence of "disease that redressed the balance" (*Turn* 84) among crop plantings. The increasing abstraction of modern existence, as Naipaul views it, explains the melancholy awareness of impermanence and ruin that pervade his writing ("Naipaul's serious devotion to his own gloom" [29], as Michael Wood put it in a review of *Half a Life* and *Magic Seeds*). For example, in *The Enigma of Arrival*, Naipaul's narrator traces the ruin of his temporary home on the Wiltshire estate where he resides as the retiring tenant of a remote, eccentric owner. When he finds the droveway along which he has enjoyed walking partially fenced in, Naipaul's narrator understands that this "fencing in" is the beginning of a process of constriction and loss that will eventually ruin the happiness of his Wiltshire home: "It caused me pain. But already I had grown to live with the idea that things changed; already I lived with the idea of decay" (*Enigma* 23). In the experience of many southerners, Naipaul perceives a close parallel to his own sensibility: they too have found "things changed" and have often interpreted that change as a process of decay.

This sense of loss points to another of Naipaul's central concerns, again one that is not by any means limited to his experience in the South:

his understanding of the vulnerability of human civilization and the consequent need to resist the voracious forces of change that seem to threaten its survival. This careful, prudent, conservative attitude, one that Jeffrey Meyers misconstrues as "instinctive mistrust" (47), testifies to an extraordinary concern for human welfare in the face of uncertainty and insecurity. In part, this concern is something that Naipaul inherited from his father: the father's "fear of extinction" as a human being and as a writer that could be opposed "only by the exercise of the vocation" of writing that he shared with his son (*Literary Occasions* 111). In this sense, Naipaul's exploration of the South — like his exploration of Africa and India in other books — would seem to result from a kind of filial obligation to address the legacy of fear that he shares with his father.

A legacy of fear is something that most southern writers and critics can appreciate. In the fiction of William Faulkner, it is the underlying cause of Quentin Compson's pathology and his suicide, and it is the impulse behind Joe Christmas's "contemptuous attitude" (Faulkner 35) toward Byron Bunch's offer of food or Thomas Sutpen's desperate attempts to found a dynasty in response to the social rebuke that he suffered as a youth. A similar sense of the "scarcity" of existence, of how constricted and unrewarding life at times can seem, underlies what Flannery O'Connor meant when she spoke of "how deep in you have to go to find love" (*Habit* 308). Within southern criticism, the stress on the concrete word or image reflects this appreciation of the finiteness of life. Within Allen Tate's aesthetics, as reiterated by R.P. Blackmur and others in the New Criticism, the poetic imagination "restores the speculative or abstract imagination to the condition of the concrete and the actual" (Stallman 44). Like Naipaul, with his acute fear of the fragility of human civilization, southern writers and critics have had to live with the threat of extinction.

Given Naipaul's background of growing up within an impoverished and sometimes violent multiethnic society, one that was "at once exceedingly simple and exceedingly confused" (*Literary Occasions* 183), it was inevitable that he should take an interest in the harsh and unsettling aspects of southern culture: the hardship of the frontier, the racial history of the South, the Civil War and its aftereffects, the Great Depression, the recent influence of religion in politics, as well as on the often harsh

6. Naipaul's Turn in the American South

physical environment of the South. In the brutal confluence of southern climate and history, Naipaul finds confirmation of his overriding conception of the human condition. The early European settlers had come to the South "with very little, had started in the wilderness perhaps with only an idea of civilization" (*Turn* 198). Southern history, in this reading, with its conception of a brutal history of settlement that continues to influence contemporary life in damaging ways, approximates Naipaul's view of human civilization as a whole. In the South's tortured history of frontier settlement and slavery, Naipaul finds confirmation of his prior conviction that existence has never been anything but perilous. An endless tally of victims is inscribed on the southern consciousness, a history of sacrifice attested by small-town monuments to the dead and broad swaths of inner city and rural poverty. Even in the South's more prosperous and gentrified districts, Naipaul discovers abundant evidence of a continuing damage. In the constriction and regimentation of a gargantuan automobile factory in Tennessee, he suggests there exists a decline in the quality of life. In the enormous scale of industrial and modern agribusiness, Naipaul finds evidence not only of cultural decline but of a violation of a fundamental order of being.

In the end, the key to Naipaul's interpretation of the South is this overriding sense of loss, and Naipaul is at his best in his sensitivity to what he calls "the past as a wound" (*Turn* 99). It is a sensibility with which Naipaul was intimately familiar long before he visited the South, as in his nonfiction and historical/autobiographical fiction Naipaul has documented other cultures similarly wounded. The island of Trinidad, passing from the control of its native inhabitants to the Spanish conquerors, from the Spanish to the French, then to the British, and most recently to the political control of an Afro-Caribbean majority; Venezuela, having suffered and continuing to suffer, as Naipaul sees it, two hundred years of anarchy and ruin, the aftermath of an precipitate independence from Spain; India, having endured five hundred years of conquest — the Mogul invasion in 1526 followed by the British in 1857 — and then emancipated, as Naipaul believes, into a condition of ruin, squalor, and ethnic and class division. It is hardly coincidental that all of these cultures share a legacy of slavery of one form or another.

One of the deleterious effects of this sense of "the past as a wound" is the tendency to monumentalize the past. Like many cultures that have suffered loss in a major war, the South retreated into a psychosis of denial. What if Douglas had defeated Lincoln in 1860? What if Britain had come to the defense of the South, breaking the northern blockades and resupplying the southern armies? What if Jackson had not been killed at Chancellorsville, the victim of friendly fire from one of his own men? What if Lee had not ordered Pickett's charge at Gettysburg? The problem with such fantasies is that they lead to an endless regression of historical revisionism, requiring not only the supposition of improbable military victories but a shift toward more and more unrealistic justifications of the war. In this evasion of reality, the war is refigured as the gallant "Lost Cause," but, as Naipaul wryly notes, among those who enshrine the Lost Cause, "the cause itself [is] never defined" (*Turn* 104).

Everywhere he looks Naipaul finds, quite literally, that the southern landscape is dotted with monuments to its own defeat. Among these, Naipaul visits the monument to the Confederate dead on the statehouse grounds in Columbia, South Carolina; Missionary Ridge in Chattanooga; Chickamauga battlefield; and even an unadorned monument to the contributions of slaves to the Lost Cause in the small town of Canton, Mississippi. Naipaul also records a contemporary landscape filled with its own monuments to human defeat: the inner-city slum that Naipaul tours in Chattanooga attests a continuing history of human damage, as does the ghostly abandonment of so many southern small towns. To a vegetarian of South Asian descent, the high rate of obesity among so many southerners is another symptom of continuing damage. The music of the South — whether the black blues or white ballad tradition — also testifies to this sense of loss. Influenced by the Scotch and Irish ballad tradition, the country music that Naipaul hears playing throughout the South conveys "the melancholy of a transported people" (*Turn* 233) who in their ancestral memory preserve the consciousness of a tragic past.

Still, in spite of his inclination to focus on the wound in southern history, Naipaul finds the South in other respects to be a miraculously rich and appealing culture. One of the paradoxes that Naipaul considers is the fact that the South, another of the "half-made societies" (*Literary*

6. Naipaul's Turn in the American South

Occasions 170) of the sort that he has so often analyzed, should at the same time comprise an integral part of the United States, the world's only superpower. Despite the veritable bellyache of history evident in every courthouse square with its inevitable monument to southern gallantry and defeat, the South has been reborn into a culturally and economically vital region. Naipaul's journey throughout this fertile, productive sector of America — from his arrival in Atlanta, his visit to Charleston, to his travels in Florida, Alabama, Mississippi, Tennessee, North Carolina, and Virginia — affords "great pleasure" (*Turn* 221), and the South even holds "romance" (*Turn* 221), not just in the touristy sites of old Charleston and the Delta pilgrimage homes but in the small pleasures of contemporary life. The wooden deck and wooded backyard of one of his hosts in northwestern Georgia seems glamorous, a rare luxury of affordable space in an increasingly crowded world.

For a writer who hails from the small island of Trinidad, even for one who has resided in Britain for over three decades, the sheer dimension of southern agricultural production is also impressive. Naipaul's awareness of this dimension affords him a clearer understanding of what must have been the enormous if brutalizing productivity of the southern plantation system and also the scale of its demand for slave labor. On this point, however, as he suggests that the southern slave system depended on far greater numbers of slaves than did that of the Caribbean, Naipaul is simply wrong. His view that "the slavery of the British Caribbean islands began to seem small-scale, even domestic" (*Turn* 118) in comparison with that of the South overlooks the reality that Caribbean slavery was anything but small-scale. In contrast to the approximately one half million slaves who were brought to the United States before importation ended in 1808, the European colonies in the Caribbean imported a total of over two-and-a-half million slaves. Among the former British colonies of the Caribbean, the evidence of a large-scale slave economy is unavoidable: it is manifest today, in Trinidad as in Barbados, Jamaica, and elsewhere, in the presence of a large Afro-Caribbean majority population. Nor can one accept Naipaul's view that racial violence of the sort that existed in the South after Reconstruction never existed in the Caribbean. In the post-slavery period, following 1833 in the British colonies and 1865 in the South, southern racial violence was paralleled by civil unrest, poverty, and oppression in the British Caribbean (in Jamaica, for example, one hundred years of periodic unrest culminated in the large-scale riots of 1938). Naipaul's suggestion that racism of the sort practiced in the South did not exist in the British Caribbean colonies is, in fact, belied by his own accounts in such novels as *Guerrillas*. In the fictionalized Caribbean island in which the events of the novel take place, the political coup of an independence faction is associated with an ominous foreboding of violence, not only for whites who flee the island but for those blacks such as Jimmy Ahmed who almost certainly face execution. For colonial peoples like Jimmy, there is a constant sense of unreality: he is one who lives with "the sands shifting under [him] and there's nothing to cling to" (*Guerrillas* 254).

In essentials, however, Naipaul's understanding of the South is remarkably insightful. What Naipaul finds especially disturbing is the sense of a loss of moral clarity within present-day southern and Caribbean black society. In what amounts to "the final cruelty of slavery," Naipaul discovers the contemporary condition of African Americans and Afro-Caribbeans to be "without the supports of faith and community evolved during the last hundred years or so" (*Turn* 135). In the South of the late 1980s, Naipaul uncovers an African American population still mired in poverty, living amid a high incidence of crime and "horribly lost" (*Turn* 135), as a black convict informs him. This view of African American society (which Naipaul reiterated in a 1992 interview in which he spoke of the lack of responsibility evident in "the rioting, looting, violence and murder in Los Angeles" [Meyers 39]) appears to be confirmed by a visit to Tuskegee Institute (now Tuskegee University), an apparent "oasis" of order and decency in the midst of a troubled landscape of poverty and violence. Yet even the Tuskegee campus, Naipaul discovers, has entered a period of decline as the community appears to be living off the borrowed capital of a legendary past. In the accommodation he is assigned, elevators have ceased operating years before, window screens are missing, and air conditioning is nonexistent. Despite his enormous respect for Booker T. Washington and his admiration of *Up from Slavery* as a sophisticated, multi-leveled work of art, Naipaul believes that Washington's legacy has been lost sight of.

6. Naipaul's Turn in the American South

In a thoughtful critique of *A Turn in the South*, Arnold Rampersad questions the soundness of this account of black southern society. According to Rampersad, Naipaul presents a "hostile picture of the black Southern world" (32): the depiction of Albert Murray at the beginning of the novel trivializes and demeans this important black writer; the account of Howard's home in North Carolina focuses on the black community's poverty and dependence; and the book ignores black writers, artists, musicians, and community leaders while concentrating on whites. Rampersad connects Naipaul's attitudes toward the South with those of the Nashville Fugitives; he objects that Naipaul admits an interest in "redneck" culture while ignoring its "cultural counterpart among blacks" (35); and he takes issue with Naipaul's description of Memphis as two cities: the black city one of "desolation," the eastern suburbs "under siege." Rampersad's analysis is considerably more far-reaching than these examples would suggest and, though it focuses primarily on the issue of racial depiction, presents an intriguing thesis concerning the autobiographical elements in *A Turn in the South*—a relation to the South as a means of coming to terms with the Caribbean past that Rampersad terms Naipaul's "truce with irrationality" (39).

While it may be excessive to conclude that Naipaul actually "attacks the black South" (Rampersad 32), it is fair to say that Naipaul's book contains little that is positive and leaves much ground unexplored. Still, it is important to distinguish between Naipaul's judgments of the historical evolution of cultures, which can seem harsh and offsetting, and his response to human beings as individuals, which seems fair and open-minded. For example, while his friend Howard's black community is depicted as impoverished and shabby, as apparently it is, its black church is represented as gracious and culturally imposing: "I began to feel the pleasures of the religious meeting: the pleasures of brotherhood, union, formality, ritual, clothes, music, all combining to create a possibility of ecstasy" (*Turn* 15). For Naipaul, a lifelong religious skeptic, the sense of order and purpose in the southern black church service comes as a pleasant surprise, particularly considering his preconceptions of black religion based on his childhood experience in Trinidad. As he admits, he had always thought of black religious expression in terms of "ecstasy and trance" (*Turn* 65). Again, while jazz and blues are largely ignored, at no point does Naipaul suggest that country music is "superior" to African American musical genres. While one would hope that Naipaul experienced more of the black South than the impoverished inner city of Memphis or Chattanooga, in point of fact a serious socio-economic and racial division did exist in these cities at the time of Naipaul's visit. In the final analysis, Naipaul's jaundiced view of African American society can be explained in large part by his own predisposition to dread whatever appears disordered, exposed, or not fully formed. This innately skeptical temperament has led Naipaul to write highly critical reports on various societies in the Caribbean, Africa, India, Latin America, and the Middle East, but it has also contributed to an incisive critique of contemporary British society in *The Enigma of Arrival*. Naipaul's treatment of African American society is, if anything, less critical than these reports, nor does Naipaul spare himself. The "Naipaul" persona which appears in a number of works is held to the same standard of dedication, diligence, and self-restraint, and often found lacking.

Naipaul's journey ends in Stantonsburg, North Carolina, in the company of James Applewhite, a southern poet whose work Naipaul especially admires. What Naipaul finds in Applewhite's poetry, and what he most admires in the South, is the persistence of an imaginative capacity in its people — a creative instinct that has sustained the South throughout its history and that produced a major literature during the twentieth century. The southern myth was, of course, the construction of those members of the Southern Renaissance such as Allen Tate who, as Lewis P. Simpson noted, "had done a great deal of hard work at inheriting his inheritance" (*Man of Letters* 248–49). By the end of Naipaul's journey through the South, it is clear that this quality of the region — a collective awareness of the importance of the past and of tradition, however mythologized — is his central concern. The "work" of inheriting an inheritance has been Naipaul's vocation from youth on as well. In the same way that the South was a problem of conflicted emotions, divided loyalties, and sheer ambiguity for Tate, Faulkner, and others of the Southern Renascence, the British colonial system is Naipaul's disquieting inheritance, and in order to live with the enormously disturbing legacies of his

6. Naipaul's Turn in the American South

past, he has had to grapple with the painful aspects of both his childhood homeland of Trinidad and his adopted home in Britain. The importance of the South for Naipaul is that it serves as an example of a society in which a people appear to have come to terms with a cultural inheritance equally conflicted with his own.

With his friend Applewhite at the end of his journey, Naipaul engages in a reflection on this very matter of one's relation to a cultural inheritance. Certainly, it is an issue that occupies Applewhite's poetry, including his work in the volume *Ode to the Chinaberry Tree*, and, as Applewhite recounts in "A Trip with V.S. Naipaul," it was the unspoken motive underlying Naipaul's interest in Applewhite's relation to the eastern North Carolina tobacco district that was his childhood home and that remains the primary subject of his writing. What Naipaul probes in his contacts with Applewhite is a shared sense of longing for affiliation, but also a shared sense of separation. In Applewhite's admission of insecurity — shipwrecked like Tarzan in a tropical land, "separated from the cultural base of his ancestors' origins" (Applewhite 50) — Naipaul discovers an anguish identical to his own, and in Applewhite's poetic art he recognizes a method of dealing with this grief close to what he has employed in *A House for Mr. Biswas* and a number of other works. The conversation with Applewhite, the opportunity to stop at the Applewhite home still owned by the family though farmed by an employee, and especially the visit to the family cemetery kindle in Naipaul a shared appreciation of the writer's anguish in relation to a past that is fraught with disappointment, incompleteness, and shame. In his momentary fraternity with Applewhite, Naipaul gains solace in the company of another writer who, working within a culture as "inarticulate" and "haltingly self-conscious" as his own, "had attempted a language" (Applewhite 52) that would bring meaning and order to that subject. Like the graveyard which Applewhite and Naipaul hesitate to enter lest it be reduced from the level of myth to that of factuality, the inheritance that both writers pursue must be "possess[ed] by interpretation" (Applewhite 54).

For Naipaul, the recognition of the necessity of myth is the South's most endearing quality. This "reach[ing] after expressiveness and meaningful order" (Applewhite 49) in the midst of a world of increasing geopolitical chaos is, in fact, the crucial artistic undertaking of our time, and, at the end of his turn in the South, Naipaul finds confirmation of the value of his own artistic and moral quest. The continuing presence of a relationship to history and myth that Naipaul values in the South is not unlike what he has uncovered, or fashioned through interpretation, in his adopted home in Wiltshire, England. There, in the West of England where he has lived for decades in the shadow of Stonehenge, Naipaul's imagination has engaged layers of civilization reaching back to British prehistory. Like rural England, the South is a region in which there exists a complex awareness of relation to the past; at the same time, it is a region in which industrialization and urbanization are making steady inroads and in which a meaningful relationship to the past is accomplished more by art than in actuality. As Naipaul understands well enough, the meaningful order that many have sought in the mythic landscape of the South is a construction of the writer as well as an actual attribute of the region, and yet in the very impulse to construct myth, Naipaul uncovers a measure of deliverance. The southern fascination with myth and history mirrors Naipaul's own search for a meaningful relation to a troubled past.

- 7 -

The Fiction of Kent Haruf

In 1999, when Kent Haruf burst on the scene, so to speak, with his bestselling novel *Plainsong*, he was already fifty-six years old. At this point, Haruf had been writing fiction for well over thirty years and had published two previous novels, *The Tie That Binds* in 1984 and *Where You Once Belonged* in 1990. Although his early novels earned him a degree of critical recognition, neither was a popular success. Following graduation from Nebraska Wesleyan University and the Iowa Writer's Workshop, where he earned an MFA, most of Haruf's life had been spent working in agriculture, construction, and teaching. Only after the popular success of *Plainsong*, which was also filmed as a CBS television movie, was Haruf able to devote himself full-time to writing.

It seems fitting that Haruf, the son of a Methodist minister and one who has spent most of his life on the Great Plains, should achieve his first real success with a novel entitled *Plainsong*. His writing is, after all, both a "song" of the plains and a stylistic approximation of "plainsong," a variety of monophonic Christian vocal music expressive of the quiet devotion and devout faith of the denominations by which it is practiced. Haruf's writing is marked by an attitude of stillness and reflection devoted to the enduring relationship of human beings to a particular place, a stable code of ethics, and an unwavering faith in the goodness of life. This faith in what T. S. Eliot called the "permanent things" affords solace and defense against the chaotic force inherent in both nature and human society — a force of disorder that within our nation's symbology has always been connected with the western frontier.

Even today, the West, populated as one imagines by a raggedy band of misfits, cultists, survivalists, and hardened loners, remains the locus of America's outlaw mythology. Like the "American nomads" of whom Richard Grant writes in a book of the same name, Haruf depicts westerners who are engaged in a "process of retreat and withdrawal, from the damage within themselves and human relationships in general" (62). Unlike Grant's nomads, however, who include lost conquistadors, mountain men, cowboys, Indians, hoboes, and bull riders, among others, and all of whom seem to prefer their proud, uncompromising solitude to the less-than-ideal accommodation of everyday life, Haruf's rebellious spirits find themselves tamed, even amid the physical isolation of the great western plains, by the redemptive force of an enduring civilization. Unlike the many desperado figures in our popular culture (Clint Eastwood, Waylon Jennings, Thelma and Louise, and the rest), Haruf's drifters and rebels crave the protective shelter of those caring, generous souls, themselves often reclusive by nature, who discover their own redemption in acts of charity. Thus, in Haruf's fiction the western myth is humanized and assuaged, and the simplistic image of the outlaw hero prevalent in our popular culture is displaced by a more realistic image and underlying truth: that the goodness of heartland America and of America as a whole is grounded in traditional values and virtues that foster acceptance rather than isolation, serenity rather than violence, belief rather than doubt. As Jonathan Miles wrote (in an otherwise dismissive review), *Eventide* is "a life raft for people who felt they were drowning in the sour froth of pop cynicism" (E2).

The problem is, of course, that as a civilization we *have* been drowning in a sea of cynicism, and the consequences of this sneering distrust become ever more apparent, decade by decade. As Leszek Kołakowski has suggested, there exists "a close link between the dissolution of the sacred" and certain "spiritual phenomena" that contribute to the decline and perhaps "suicide" of Western culture. According to Kołakowski, these phenomena include "the love of the amorphous, the desire for homogeneity, the illusion that there are no limits to the perfectibility of which human society is capable, immanentist eschatologies, and the instrumental attitude toward life" ("Revenge of the Sacred" 69). The damaging effects of these phenomena manifest themselves throughout our culture, from extraordinary high divorce rates to the reduction of social commu-

7. The Fiction of Kent Haruf

nities to a humorless, legalistic exercise of correctness and to the cult-like appeal of radical ideologies. At the core of Kent Haruf's artistic sensibility, there exists just such an awareness of the waning of belief in the sacred. Like Kołakowski, Haruf records the dangerous appeal of the amorphous: the urge to flee from the burdens of responsibility, tradition, and constancy in search of greater personal freedom and choice. In novels that depict the need for commitment, charity, and most of all faith, Haruf points to the destructive implications of a humanistic philosophy that would elevate personal freedom and pleasure above all other values. With his profound reverence for life, Haruf opposes those forces of contemporary culture, from the deadening influence of state bureaucracies to the dulling materialism and standardization of consumer culture, that undermine the value of human life and the awareness of the sacred.

Given Haruf's pervasive sense of cultural damage, it is not surprising that his thematic intentions focus on two central matters: first, a compelling documentation of the decline of the sacred and, second, a register of the damage that this decline has caused. In his understanding of the concept of the sacred, however, Haruf is less interested in the influence of sectarian religious practices than he is in a deep-seated and universal religious sensibility that underlies the most important human affiliations, among them the relationships of parents and children, the response to nature, and the ever-present awareness of human mortality. Though much of contemporary behavior seems to proceed from the cynical assumption that existence is fundamentally irremediable and anarchic, the centrality of purposeful action grounded in faith has always stood at the center of Western identity. Within classical culture focused on the *vita activa*, there resided an unshakable confidence concerning the potentiality for human action. It is this faith, including a conviction regarding the existence of an afterlife, that has been generally dismissed with the rise of skepticism in contemporary culture, within which it is not action but various forms of constriction and relinquishment that have preoccupied philosophical speculation. In the view of modern theorists from Nietzsche to Heidegger and from Sartre to Foucault, existence is best understood in terms of absence and loss, and human action is more apt to be viewed as purposeless and indifferent than as good. Within the culture of suspicion that has arisen in the wake of this destructive theory, all assertions of purposeful action are greeted with distrust. Gradually, throughout the past century, an "age of decline" in which Czeslaw Milosz detects an ever greater materialism, nihilism, and "collapse of values" (*Land of Ulro* 227–28), the conception of human life as the *vita activa* has largely disappeared among intellectuals, and a culture of absence and opposition has taken hold.

Kent Haruf's novels constitute a sophisticated response to this mounting tide of defeatism. At the center of these fictional works is a focus on the classical–Christian faith in human existence as purposeful and good, and at the heart of this mythos is a recognition of the new beginning that enters the world with the birth of every child. A vivid example of this affirmation is the meeting of the elderly McPheron brothers and seventeen-year-old Victoria Roubideaux in the novel *Plainsong*. Harold and Raymond McPheron, lifelong bachelors sunk in a stagnant round of farm chores and a sterile, silent home-life, appear to be doomed by their loss of opportunity for purposeful action. As Harold says, "Think of us. Crotchety and ignorant. Lonesome. Independent. Set in all our ways. How you going to change now at this age of life?" (*Plainsong* 112). Reduced to a fruitless and reclusive condition, lacking beauty, joy, or the challenge of the unfamiliar, they are simply living out their lives and waiting for death. Yet *Plainsong* and *Eventide*, Haruf's two novels that focus on the relationship of the McPheron brothers and Victoria Roubideaux, depict the transformation of isolated, unproductive lives into a more hopeful condition of mutual responsibility. Their meeting with Victoria — indigent, bereft of emotional support, and uncertain where to turn after she becomes pregnant — rekindles hope because it allows them the opportunity to engage in purposeful action. After their meeting with Victoria, the McPherons are spurred to decisive action. As Raymond informs his brother of his decision to shelter the young woman, he delivers the news more as an ultimatum than a request: "Now, are you going to go in on this thing with me or not? Cause I'm going to do it anyhow, whatever." To which Harold replies, "I will. I'll agree. I shouldn't, but I will. I'll make up my mind to it" (*Plainsong* 113).

The spare, laconic expression of the McPherons suggests their moral

7. The Fiction of Kent Haruf

clarity and their determination not merely to reflect but to act on behalf of their beliefs. Unbeknownst to them, Victoria begins to share in this ethical perspective after she learns that she is pregnant. Following her visit to the Holt County Clinic, she stands in the street outside sensing that reality for her has become "hard-edged, definite, as if it were no longer merely a late fall afternoon in the hour before dusk, but instead as if it were the first moment of noon in the exact meridian of summer" (78). Her newfound sense of distinctness and lucidity are the result of the revelation that she is now almost solely responsible for the future well-being of a particular human being. As the McPherons realize, this responsibility "ain't going to be no goddamn Sunday school picnic" (*Plainsong* 113), but for Victoria it is in reality the great opportunity of her life. It is most certainly the first time in her unstable, loveless existence that she has entered into a permanent and total attachment to anyone or anything. As her pregnancy proceeds, Victoria's self-awareness and her appreciation of everything outside herself change. Even the dry, windswept, desolate landscape of Holt County seems transformed.

In terms of this thematic emphasis, the landscape of northeastern Colorado, in fact, plays a significant role in *Plainsong* and in all of Haruf's novels. The fictional Holt County, a mythic landscape that is at the same time more desolate and more plenteous of spirit and beauty than any actual setting that one could encounter, is the stuff of moral allegory. Although it may be based on an actual locale, that of northeastern Colorado, the region that Haruf depicts is more akin to that of John Bunyan: it is a desolate landscape with its own City of Destruction (Denver, that is), an imaginative locale in which the consequences of moral choice loom larger than any geographical feature. From what Haruf tells us of its early history in *The Tie That Binds*, Holt County is the place where a version of natural selection has taken place among settlers who have had to wrest a meager living from the dry, sandy soil, and those who have remained possess special qualities of determination, durability, and patience coupled with the virtues of humility and kindness. They are in this sense a "chosen people"—chosen not only by God but by the stark, winnowing effects of the American heartland. An Old Testament sensibility attaches easily to this culture and to Haruf's rendering of it, and especially pertinent is the biblical account of Exodus. The early settlers on the western frontier were leading their families out of slavery in the East, the land of Pharaohs in the guise of crippling taxes and governmental tyranny, to the homestead lands west of the Mississippi. Like the Promised Land beyond the River Jordan, western land held out the promise of freedom and new life.

Accordingly, the landscape described in *Plainsong* suggests an existence that is often cruel and unforgiving but that demands moral decisiveness and clarity. The night in early March when Raymond sets out for his ill-fated second "date" with Linda May, Haruf captures a sense of the special moral loveliness of the plains: "It was a Saturday night, the sky overhead clear of any cloud, the stars as clean and bright as if they were no more distant than the next barbed-wire fence post standing up above the narrow ditch running beside the narrow blacktop highway, everything all around him distinct and unhidden. He loved how it all looked, except that he would never have said it in that way. He might have said that this was just how it was supposed to look, out on the high plains at the end of winter, on a clear fresh night" (*Eventide* 206). The moral idealism of heartland America that Haruf evokes in this passage hearkens back to faith in America as a second Eden — a paradise not only because of its material abundance but also because of its spiritual richness. In this land settlers of modest means, or of none at all, could seek a life of dignity and purpose. In this noble endeavor, they brought with them the transforming knowledge of an inherited faith and ethical culture, and this inheritance would at least afford direction and hope, if not always success. In the West these settlers preserved and renewed the civilization that they brought with them from the East. From this perspective, America's role in world history was understood to be that of conservator of the ancient traditions of reverence for life that her earliest European settlers had brought with them. The sheer scale and rough splendor of the West were, after all, intricately connected with a national mythos of providential history that Russell Martin terms "spatial hope" (xviii). Even as life in the eastern cities seemed to close in upon one, even as the nation as a whole seemed at times to have lost its way, one could look to the West as a mythic setting of national virtue and strength.

7. The Fiction of Kent Haruf

This potent myth remains a significant factor in our nation's conception of its identity and of its relationship to the rest of the world.

Equally a part of this myth is the recognition of the paradox that the attractiveness of the frontier West as a last bastion of hope has necessarily contributed to that region's diminishment as those who flee the East in search of opportunity bring with them civilization's ills. Inevitably, hope must be qualified by evidence of the inherent corruption of human nature, an unregenerate feature of existence that trumps even frontier optimism. It was this same evidence of corruption in the Old World that impelled the Founders to establish an intricate system of checks and balances, a governmental system grounded on hope but also on the recognition of the inherent fallibility of human nature. Hannah Arendt credited the wisdom of American democracy when she noted that, following the gradual loss of conviction in religion and tradition throughout the post-medieval period, "the revolutions of the modern age appear like gigantic attempts to repair these foundations" ("What Is Authority?" 501). In Arendt's view, among all major efforts to restore conviction, only the American Revolution was successful in attending to the lapse of political order and reinstating a system that was both stable and compelling of belief. While Arendt outlined many challenges to the survival of American civilization, she never lost faith in the value of the Founders' vision of a liberal democracy governed within a constitutional framework of law.

It is not Haruf's intention, of course, to engage in a discussion of political theory within the context of his fiction, but, based on the manner in which he addresses similar concerns, it is clear that he shares Arendt's faith. One of the qualities that the McPheron brothers share with Tom Guthrie is an adamant refusal to surrender their rights as free citizens. In their refusal to do so — as when Tom stands up to the attempts of Russell Beckman and his family to usurp his proper authority as a teacher — Haruf's protagonists defend their democratic rights to move about and to congregate freely, to be recognized as equals under the law, and to "speak their piece." Clearly, however, Haruf fears that these rights are at risk within a society in which, as Kołakowski noted, the claims of homogeneity and the radical demands of free will appear to override traditional restraints of custom and belief.

As a result of the determination of at least some of its citizens to preserve their freedoms, Holt County might well be seen as a promised land of the sort upon which the Founders premised their efforts. In contrast with the pointless frenzy of postmodernist culture, Haruf's fictionalized world is a place of coherence and purposefulness: a place where roads are platted on a grid running straight north-south or east-west, and a place where an innate respect for order still resides in the human heart. The fictionalized Holt County possesses a deep simplicity—a quality that, as Mark McCloskey points out, "is equated with virtue" (617)—that acts as a counterbalance to the dominant culture of alienation embodied in the closest large city, Denver. This urban enchantress is the place to which many of the younger residents of Holt County flee from the seeming boredom of life on the plains and where they seek pleasure in activities that, like the coarse party to which Dwayne escorts Victoria during her pregnancy, tend toward the destruction of new life. In doing so, they are deserting a better place of clear values and active goodness for a dark underworld of moral confusion and self-contempt. In Haruf's imaginative world, those who flee from rural America to the city soon find themselves in dreary, isolating circumstances, surviving in characterless apartment buildings in which human beings are severed from nature and walled off from one another.

The contrast between the city and life on the McPheron ranch could not be any more striking. Here the brothers are immersed in the rich life of nature; here the weather plays a critical role in their efforts; and here birth and the nurturing of new life are the central activities. In his intricate descriptions of the McPheron cattle operation, Haruf details the processes of birthing, weaning, and milking, as well as separating out cattle for slaughter, a labor that is bounded by the elemental forces of nature. There is, for example, the powerful but disturbing scene in which Haruf recounts the autopsy of a beloved horse, Elko, as witnessed by her owners, two young boys. Yet in the way that Haruf describes the cattle and farming operations, there is the inescapable implication that the same order of necessity enfolds human affairs, and it is largely in these terms that the McPherons initially interpret Victoria's pregnancy. Though she is not a cow giving birth to a calf, Harold at first finds it difficult to

7. The Fiction of Kent Haruf

separate her condition from that of the larger order of nature within which he as a rancher has been immersed for seventy years. Clearly, he and Raymond do come to distinguish her condition from that of the farm animals with which they are more familiar, yet on the elemental level, at least, the pattern of human life, with the cycle of birth, growth, maturity, and death, is no different from what the brothers observe in their ranching operation, and it is this fact that human existence is bounded by necessity that gives rise to their discovery of life's precious opportunities for charity. Just as the brothers sometimes have to step in to assist in the birth of calves, they willingly assist Victoria in the months before and after the birth of her daughter. From their perspective, it is assumed that they will volunteer this assistance as a matter of course.

Out of this elemental condition emerges a culture of humanity and compassion, yet even as Haruf's novels depict acts of decency and kindness on the part of the McPherons and others, they suggest a paradoxical truth that the heartland's harsh and unforgiving environment should foster such nobility while the less demanding urban milieu represented by Denver seems a place of exploitation and degradation. Like William Blake in this respect, Haruf finds the urban scene filled with "Marks of weakness, marks of woe." Those who have known grief, ranchers like the McPherons who have themselves struggled and have witnessed the efforts and often the failures of others, have learned hard lessons of concern and self-restraint, while others like Vicky's boyfriend, Dwayne, fail to register the suffering of others, perhaps because they have never had to suffer themselves.

The reality of suffering and the need for responsible behavior are made apparent throughout Haruf's writing. In his first novel, *The Tie That Binds*, we are introduced to Edith Goodnough, a woman who practices self-denial and service to others every day of her life. Growing up in a hard-bitten agricultural economy before World War II, Edith finds that she must give up the great love of her life, John Roscoe, in order to care for her widowed father after he loses all but one of his fingers in a reaping machine accident. Unlike her younger brother, Lyman, who as his name suggests is essentially disingenuous and irresponsible, Edith is conscientious, perhaps to a fault. While Lyman spends the first two decades of his adulthood traveling aimlessly around the country, sending

Edith a packet of $20 bills every Christmas along with only a tersely worded postcard identifying the city in which is living, Edith forgoes love and the chance for independence in order to devote herself to the care of a disabled parent. When Lyman finally returns to Holt County, he and Edith live together for six "good years," "almost as if they were honeymooners" (*Tie* 166). For Edith, however, the good years end all too soon, as Lyman drifts into senility.

Edith Goodnough is not the only character in *The Tie That Binds* who experiences tragedy. Sanders Roscoe, the novel's first-person narrator, is a young man who must learn the hard lesson that life is ennobled only by facing up to the circumstances that one finds oneself in. In Sandy's case, this involves facing the consequences of his own indecisiveness toward the role of fatherhood. After he marries Mavis Pickett in 1963, he and Mavis lose their first baby in a car accident in which Lyman Goodnough is the driver. In 1969 Sandy and Mavis have another child, a daughter named Rena Pickett, who then becomes a frequent visitor at the Goodnough farm. There, in a moment of anger and confusion, the crazed Lyman attacks Rena and Edith after beating the family dog, Nancy. In the end Edith is unable to care for her increasingly dependent brother, and she decides to end Lyman's and her own life by setting fire to the farmhouse, a solution that is only forestalled when Mavis and Sandy hear Nancy barking where Edith has tied her up outside. Having rushed to the burning farmhouse, Sandy realizes that Edith wishes to die, and he attempts to prevent the fire crew from entering the house. The crew are able to restrain him and remove Edith and Lyman, but Lyman dies in the hospital that night. Then, at the age of eighty, Edith is charged with murder. At the end of the novel, it is the beauty of Edith's character that impresses Sandy, even as she faces prosecution for her brother's murder. As he says, she has spent her entire life "without her ever understanding how to say anything like a continuous yes to herself." She is "still in the ways that matter, just as fine and beautiful as she must have been in 1922" when she was dating John Roscoe (*Tie* 245–46). Haruf's handling of syntax in these and other passages seems a perfect reflection of both the narrator's countrified manner and, more to the point, the countryman's stubborn resistance to the easy cliché and thoughtless turn of phrase of his urban counterpart. The speaker's voice, like his nickname "Sandy," conveys a gritty resistance to the self-serving correctness of liberal culture, in lieu of which he speaks only heartfelt if sometimes awkward truths.

It is hardly coincidental that the prosecutor's decision to bring charges against Edith is prompted by the unwelcome prying of a glib young investigative reporter from one of the Denver papers. The media of our time, after all, trade in a cynical commence of lies and half-truths, peddled in the rapid-fire flux of distorted and contextless words and images. As James Bowman writes in *Honor: A History*, "news and entertainment have grown ever more indistinguishable in the last decade," a fact that Bowman sees as one consequence of the rise of "celebrity culture" in place of the old honor culture (317). As Bowman sees it, the rise of investigative journalism is a manifestation of contemporary culture's willingness to subject the private and in some cases trivial details of honorable public lives to a corrosive cynicism while, at the same time, excusing all manner of indiscretion and even criminal behavior on the part of celebrity entertainers. The public demands continual entertainment from its clownish celebrities, but it also delights in seeing serious and decent individuals brought down. The spectacle of an eighty-year-old matron on trial for murder is just the sort of story that melds news and entertainment. In contrast to this meretricious entertainment, Haruf's fiction labors through a narration that depicts generations of sacrifice and real consequence to construct an architecture of tales which function as moral fable, patiently placing present-day events in the coherent context of settled communities. The austere, inhospitable environment of the fictionalized Holt County represents a useful corrective to the current appetite for glib journalistic editorializing with its suggestion that, given the material abundance of American life, all things come easily as a matter of entitlement, and no fault attaches to any behavior, however mistaken. By contrast, Haruf's vision is more weighty and deliberate. As is reflected in the slow, resolute quality of his narration, every action must be weighed with care because all words and actions possess consequences beyond our knowing. Recognizing the consequential nature of our behavior, however, is the first step toward salvaging our imperfect lives.

In this respect, Haruf's fiction proceeds from a profound idealism since it implies the possibility of improving the world through the actions of those who take their responsibilities and limitations seriously. The kindness of strangers that so often intercedes to arrest the ugly normality of abuse or indifference proceeds from the recognition that suffering and impairment are real and that human resources are finite. The abandonment of a teenaged girl by her boyfriend after she becomes pregnant is, after all, what many have come to accept as the norm in contemporary society, yet in *Plainsong* Victoria Roubideaux is befriended, first by her high school teacher, Maggie Jones, and then by the McPheron brothers. It is a small miracle that such unlikely saviors would step in to aid the girl, although at the same time such saving is also a confirmation of life's absence: the fact that such unlikely miracles *have to be* deployed attests the prevailing callousness of modern society, which is thus redoubled in Haruf's telling. Our condition of loss is made to seem all the more inescapable by Haruf's reliance on quirky acts of charity in which a few noble strangers — several of them elderly persons who do not survive the stories they inhabit — step in to take the place of family structures that are found to be wanting. Within these relationships (for example, the relationship of the dying Ida Stearns to the two Guthrie boys — providing loving attention in the absence of a mother who has deserted them to live with her sister in Denver), such a large reliance on private acts of charity testifies to the collapse of the structures of order and belief that Arendt referred to as the "private realm."

For eons the private realm was ruled by the authority of the *pater familias*, a figure that decades of post–*Father Knows Best* ridicule has rendered laughable but that for millennia afforded private life a clear sense of boundaries and purpose equivalent in its way to the authority of tradition and religion within the public realm. From the perspective of contemporary culture, with its demands of maximum personal freedom and its arrogant rejection of all restraints on free will, paternal authority seems an unwelcome holdover from the past, yet, as Tennessee Williams understood, those who are dependent on the kindness of strangers rarely end well, and their dependence is a gauge of the collapse of normal institutions and authorities. The category of "normality," in any case, has long

7. The Fiction of Kent Haruf

ceased to exist outside the American heartland, and even here it seems much at risk. Haruf's disturbing accounts reveal a society in which the mutual care of husbands and wives, children and siblings, and teachers and pupils has been supplanted by the assumption that essential human needs can be serviced at will by any person or agency. From this abstract and bureaucratic perspective, all human affiliations are capable of easy replication and substitution. The problem is that once the state enters the private realm, human expectations, like the serviceable pies that the Holt café dishes up in predictable varieties of apple, cherry, and coconut cream, are reduced to the level of function and routine. Fortunately, in Haruf's fiction, in response to an increasingly abstract and bureaucratic culture, these old-fashioned virtues continue to be asserted.

A crucial element in this faith is the presence of *caritas*, an action of charity that Diana Postlethwaite mistakenly interprets as "fundamentally humanistic, this-worldly" (258). In fact, Haruf's novels are replete with miracles, redemptive acts that imply more than the kindness of strangers based on humanistic assumptions, for what is involved therein is an underlying faith in the sacredness of life. Among these saving relationships is that of D.J. Kephart, a forlorn, impoverished waif who lives with his grandfather, and Dena Wells, the daughter of a depressed, alcoholic woman separated from her husband. Their condition, unfortunately, makes D.J. and Dena representative figures of contemporary American children. It is a fact, after all, that today three quarters of American children live in households of transient, unwed, separated, or divorced parents who are often incapable or unwilling to care for their children. Yet, from their distressing condition of insecurity and neglect, D.J. and Dena flee to an abandoned neighborhood shed which they begin to furnish with discarded furniture, rugs, and other domestic objects of the sort that embody a sense of normality. The shed provides a refuge for them in the context of a harsh, brutal world, but by its very existence, it also serves as evidence of just how disturbed the social realm has become. In the section where Haruf describes the week of Christmas vacation during which D.J. and Dena huddle together under a thick blanket reading library books and drinking from the thermos of coffee that D.J. brings, the sense of the shed as a refuge is made explicit. Here is an oasis of happiness and security, as suggested by Haruf's comment that "what was happening in the houses they'd come from seemed, for that short time, of little importance" (*Eventide* 180).

The relationship of D.J. and Dena raises several important questions related to the problematic nature of purposeful action within a society that has largely dismissed the claims of authority and tradition. Why should Dena feel such need to preserve a stable family? Why, in the face of all that their culture shows them about the "normality" of dysfunction, should D.J. take responsibility for Dena, just as he does for his ailing grandfather? Even as their culture provides a safety net of welfare checks and "services," D.J. and Dena sense that it seems incapable of addressing the real source of damage. The neglect and abuse that they suffer is, more than anything, the product of a permissive, no-fault culture in which selfish indifference is excused rather than challenged.

The contrast between a morally engaged, even moralistic, heartland culture and the fallen world of modernity underlies the thematic structure of each of Haruf's novels. In his second novel, *Where You Once Belonged* (1990), Haruf sketched a moral landscape of particularly harsh contrasts: one in which virtue is rewarded — by life at least, if not by happiness — and the wages of sin are quite literally death. What Haruf is offering the reader in this and all his books, in fact, is a survival manual to an apostate culture in which there seems to be an absolute loss of consensus as to the first principles of life. While the general culture looks in vain for these precepts amid an inane and decadent popular culture or, equally hopeless, urges the individual to look within himself for moral truth, Haruf recognizes that a clear understanding of moral being can be derived only from traditional sources of instruction.

One of these sources is most certainly the inherited wisdom passed down within families, assuming that those families have not yet severed their contacts with the moral and religious body of knowledge that informed human life throughout the centuries of Judeo-Christianity. Haruf's writing is not devoted to religious teaching in a parochial sense: there is little if any of the overt Christian allegorizing that one finds, for example, in every story by Flannery O'Connor. Still, Haruf makes clear that the moral teachings passed down through families, communities, and traditional culture are essential to the continuance of life. In the absence of these teachings, human beings drift off into a false pursuit of self-fulfillment, seeking happiness in the very places where it is least likely to be found.

In *Where You Once Belonged*, a novel whose title itself points unmistakably to the theme of belonging and loss, two central characters are contrasted as representatives of traditional faith and moral apostasy. The novel's narrator, Pat Arbuckle, is a small-town newspaper publisher more than twenty years out of the University of Colorado. In his lifetime work of running the Holt *Mercury*, Arbuckle is continuing the vocation of his father. His childhood friend, Jack Burdette, is a typical high school sports star, idolized for his exploits on the football field but, in his case, incapable of making the adjustment to the more prosaic world of adult responsibilities. As we follow Jack's downward spiral — his emotionally abusive relation of eight years with Wanda Jo Evans, his impulsive marriage to Jessie Miller, and his misappropriation of funds at the Farmers' Co-op elevator, all of it culminating in his disappearance and return more than a decade later — we recognize that Jack's actions are grounded on no principles whatsoever other than self-gratification and ego. Unlike the plodding but deeply contemplative narrator of the story, Jack is a hard-drinking, brash, self-centered, and often violent man who leaves behind a trail of unhappiness for others.

Everything about Jack Burdette, in fact, suggests heedlessness and dissipation. The pinched, fallen quality of his world is suggested by Haruf's description of the Letitia Hotel, the place where Jack hangs out after leaving home early in life. The hotel, once among Holt's finest residences, has descended through the years from being a respectable address to a cheap boarding house. Jack's presence and his drunken antics while in residence add nothing to the hotel's reputation.

Like all of Haruf's novels, the explication of moral consequences in *Where You Once Belonged* hinges on the element of time: in order to comprehend the damage of a life like Jack Burdette's and the productiveness of Pat's steadfast virtue, it is necessary to trace events over a period of decades. Growing up in the small town of Holt, Colorado, in the 1950s and 1960s, Pat and Jack might not seem so very different. One could imagine that Pat, the more "literary" and studious, would indeed follow in the footsteps of his father as editor of the Holt *Mercury* or even pursue a journalistic career in the larger world of Denver, or beyond. Likewise, one could see the popular and athletic Jack Burdette going on to play football at the University of Colorado, as he briefly does, and returning to Holt to pursue a successful career with a local business. The crucial difference between Pat and Jack becomes apparent only over a period of many years. Pat makes his way in the world of journalism and at the same time settles into a stable, if not entirely successful, first marriage; he then stumbles into a far more affectionate relationship, ironically, a relationship with Jack Burdette's former wife.

In the case of Jack, the decades expose the consequences of a deeply flawed character. Before his disappearance from town at the end of 1976, Jack has worked in a desultory manner at the Farmers' Co-op, dated but refused to marry the emotionally vulnerable Wanda Jo, and spent his time drinking, fighting, and arguing. As Arch Withers, the man who trained Jack for his elevator job, asserts, Jack doesn't care about anyone but himself. Eventually, the moral contrast between Pat and Jack is made manifest in their physical appearance. When he eventually returns to Holt, by now in his mid-forties, Jack is overweight, his face discolored and puffy, his movements "slow and ponderous" (158). Having lived a life of dissipation in California, a figurative Sodom and Gomorrah where "[t]hey got things ... you never even heard of" (158), Jack appears disgustingly disheveled, and the contrast is heightened by the presence of the healthy and vigorous Pat.

Like a pebble tossed in the water, the damaging consequences of Jack's behavior spread out across the town of Holt. Charlie Soames, the elderly co-worker with whom Jack plots to embezzle $150,000, suffers humiliation and ostracism and eventually commits suicide. Jessie Burdette, similarly ostracized after her husband absconds with the funds belonging to the Co-op shareholders, suffers financially and emotionally but refuses all forms of state welfare. In part because of this, and because of her determination to maintain her self-respect in spite of Jack's crime, Jessie eventually regains the respect of the townsfolk. In particular, her bravery and goodness attract the attention of Pat Arbuckle, who has been

7. The Fiction of Kent Haruf

divorced from his wife, Nora, following the death of their daughter Toni in an automobile accident. It is while Pat is dating and essentially living with Jessie that Jack suddenly returns from California determined to reclaim his wife and two sons, Thomas John ("T.J.") and Robert ("Bobby").

One would hope that Pat's goodness and perseverance would be rewarded with a long period of happiness in the company of Jessie and her two sons. At the same time, one might wish Jack's lifetime of bad faith to culminate in an appropriate punishment. While certainly Pat and Jack may be said to have been "rewarded" throughout their lives with a good measure of joy and misery, respectively, the novel's conclusion does not suggest that virtue and vice always find their proper reward, at least not in the short run. In the novel's highly disturbing ending, after Jack is released from jail on the basis of the statute of limitations, he appears at Jessie's house, ties up Pat, and forcibly abducts Jessie and the boys. Praying that his new family are still alive, Pat says: "I want to believe that much and I hope for more" (176).

The novel's ending, however morally incongruous, serves to enlarge our sense of Pat's moral stature. His response to the abduction, with Burdette still not found three months after the event, is to persist in hoping for the best. Pat's chief moral quality, and perhaps that of all of Haruf's protagonists, is his enduring faith in the goodness of life. Despite the deterministic environment in which he and all human beings exist, populated as it is by faithless and selfish creatures such as Jack Burdette, Pat retains his faith and works to contribute positively to his community. With his constant faith, even in the face of what may be another tragic loss in his life, Pat is one of Haruf's truly heroic figures.

Despite the cases of moral indifference that Haruf narrates, there remains a ray of sunshine in his world, although this ray of hope derives largely from the personal engagement of a small remnant who stand outside the mainstream of contemporary liberal culture. As the general society grows more and more disaffected, convinced of the futility of any action, it is only the resolve of a few individuals that holds things together. From their remote farm seventeen miles south of the small town of Holt, Colorado, the McPherons are engaged in an effort to preserve a heritage of traditional values: those bedrock values of honesty, loyalty, humility, and hard work that are central to Haruf's writing. This vision relies on the belief that America is indeed the last best hope of the world—"a shining city on a hill," to cite Ronald Reagan's improvement on John Winthrop's phrase in *A Model of Christian Charity*. In this vision of our civilization, America is a land in which there still exists the possibility of independence and liberty for all; it is a land in which the innate goodness of mankind has not been corrupted by the necessity of subservience and mendacity imposed by a caste system or by ideological tyranny; above all, it is a land in which an ideal of productive action still governs the lives of at least a saving remnant. Yet the miraculous opportunities that Winthrop and Reagan cited have always been shadowed by an immense burden: in the words of Governor Winthrop, that of remaining steadfast in "this work that we have undertaken" so that God does not "withdraw His present help from us" and we shall not "be made a story and a byword through the world." To a large extent, whether America succeeds or fails in this labor depends on its faith in the possibility of purposeful action, whether of an entrepreneurial or political or philanthropic sort. The lesson of virtue that Haruf's fiction teaches involves a restoration of America's faith in itself and in its ability to shoulder new responsibilities. Ultimately, Haruf is simply asking whether we, as a society, care enough to nurture new life, and whether we care enough to continue living ourselves.

Epilogue

The Dialect of the Tribe

Tribalism is the strongest force at work in the world today. — Vine Victor Deloria, Jr. (1969)

When Vine Victor Deloria wrote these words in 1969, he must have felt that America was indeed at the start of some grand transformation into a new tribal mode of consciousness. The radical changes that had taken place in the course of the 1960s had unleashed a heady sense of personal freedom and a false faith in the perfectibility of human society. Among his contemporaries, Deloria must have perceived a new self-assurance based on the conviction that they alone, having shed the benighted prejudice of all previous generations, possessed a near perfect wisdom; they alone had freed themselves from the moral restrictions of the past. Like the unfeeling but seemingly benevolent computer HAL aboard the ultramodern spaceship hurtling its way through space in the 1969 film *2001: A Space Odyssey*, they were a generation that had progressed beyond the conventional boundaries of inherited custom and restraint. They were a new tribe of human beings, out to explore a new consciousness to which traditional rules and patterns of thought seemed utterly irrelevant. This flight from the past, however, is in reality not a progression toward some unimaginably sublime future; it is, as the philosopher Max Picard understood, a regression to the tribal condition: "What the Flight wants is this: to be primal, original, creative, as God is." At the heart of tribalism in its modern sense is the unleashing of a prideful and unbounded ego asserting itself in competition with the divine and, as a consequence, rejecting the conception of the universe as God's sacred creation.

Epilogue

Unfortunately, much of our culture, and not just our literature and film, now accommodates itself to the tribal condition. All aspects of society, from education to the workplace to religious services, have become more "user friendly" and consumer-centric. The electronic media, for most contemporary consumers the successor to the book and magazine culture that once decisively influenced general consciousness, feature one dreary representation of hopeless materialism after another, including four separate versions of the television series *CSI* featuring slow-motion reenactment of carnage and graphic presentations of post-mortem autopsies, a narrative format now emulated by dozens of other series. For its part, ever-popular reality television involves nothing more than switching on a video camera and pointing it at contestants who are presumed to be effortlessly interesting just by being themselves. On the web, popular websites feature videos of young people opening packages so that viewers can vicariously enjoy the sensation of opening a continual stream of gifts. Blogs devoted to self-revelation and self-display are ubiquitous.

Yet accompanying this mindless narcissism comes another, even less benign feature of the tribal culture. The focus on self-gratification necessitates the rejection, often the violent rejection, of any force that would restrain pleasure. The result is a callous and cynical selfishness abetted by a convenient faith in unlimited personal freedom. Within this belief system, all behavior that would limit an individual's activities is deemed intolerant and repressive, while those forces that would promote further permissiveness are seen as praiseworthy. The imposition of standards, common values, and established forms of order are considered repressive; the loosening of authority, the reduction of standards to momentary impulses and whims, and the democratization of resources are positives. It is a development that Hannah Arendt foresaw over fifty years ago in an essay entitled "What Is Authority?" Here, Arendt clarified a crucial change in sensibility taking place in the late twentieth century. As she described it, the decline in shared belief in classical–Christian civilization "is tantamount to the loss of the groundwork of the world, which indeed since then has begun to shift, to change and transform itself with ever-increasing rapidity from one sphere into another" (465).

The relentless rejection of authority, however, points toward a condition of social primitivism that involves anarchy, violence, and demoralization. As Arendt recognized, a large number of consequences, many of them seemingly contradictory and chaotic, derive from this rejection. Lacking the authority of established institutions, customary belief, and inherited traditions, the public continually searches for sources of authority, not only in the revolutionary spirit that Arendt identified but also in the apolitical realm of fads, fashions, and private realities. But when one abandons the faith of one's fathers, substituting a pseudo-religion assumed to have arisen during the comparatively recent past within a particular geographical locale that happens to be one's own, one is on dangerous ground. How much more dangerous, mindless in fact, are the claims of countless contemporary practitioners of self-liberating, self-healing, and self-creative spiritual movements. What all of these pseudo-religions have in common is the grandiose promise of unrestrained individualism and unbounded personal freedom. Yet none of these simple-minded theorists, from New Age spiritualists to radical libertarians, seems to have considered the dangers of jettisoning modes of rationality that have served human beings for thousands of years. Stripped of complex means of conceiving of their relationship to nature, society, and divinity, human beings can never develop beyond the stage of self-absorbed adolescents blithely unacquainted with the wishes or needs of others and intent on gratifying their own desires.

What, one may ask, is the reaction of the narcissist when his belief in boundless self-gratification runs up against the claim of others intent on claiming *their* boundless self-gratification? In the idiom of our times, this conflict results in the need to "push back," a familiar situation within a culture populated by self-seeking narcissists in which each ego operates in raw competition with every other. Thus we have the familiar theme of reality television: the single winner, reigning bachelor, sole survivor, biggest loser (that is, *winner* of the weight *losing* contest). It represents a view of life that endlessly awards prizes to self-satisfied egoists on the basis of little or no accomplishment.

But what is the response of those who do not win? Inevitably, despite the ubiquitous fantasy served up by reality television, most human beings will at some point in life end up losing, as all will at the end. Despite the fantasy in which many viewers seem so firmly entrenched, every person will eventually face setbacks at work, conflicts in marriage, and, yes, even that cruelest of assaults on the ego, the reality of aging and mortality. In most cases, however, they will face setbacks long before they reach the daunting challenges of middle age. How does the narcissistic ego react to the news that it is expected to submit to authority at work and to subject itself to a routine or schedule? What happens when the narcissistic ego faces disappointment in a romantic relationship? What is the response of the self-absorbed ego to social rejection by one's peers, not just vicariously being "voted off the island" along with one's favorite reality star but actually being rejected and ostracized in real life? What happens when the unbounded ego, convinced of its sacred right to unfettered power and freedom, finds itself countermanded by actual limitations and responsibilities?

Some indication of what happens is suggested by the violent reaction of Dylan Klebold and Eric Harris to their reported snubbing by other students at Columbine High School. Reportedly, the actions of Klebold and Harris were the result of two angry young men who wished to retaliate against students who, they felt, had intentionally harmed them. From their own point of view, rooted in a private reality of violent role-playing, Klebold and Harris appear to have been possessed by a frightening absolutism of self that would sweep from the earth those whom they considered to be false and hypocritical according to their idiosyncratic and malign standards.

There is, of course, a sad irony in the fact that two young nihilists especially sought to eliminate those among their peers whom they identified with the very faith that might have saved them: students who belonged to a Christian youth group. They were right only in this one respect: the dominant secular humanist culture of our times — that diseased culture that in its acute phase one must label "tribal" — offers nothing to redeem life from a pointless round of acquisition and consumption. Their own murderous rage against the system was both the product and evidence of this fact. In its pure form, humanism cannot provide a rationale for life, especially in the case of the needful, emotionally confused adolescent. Klebold and Harris were guilty of callous brutality of an unspeakable kind which nothing can excuse or extenuate, but the spiritual wasteland in which they grew up and in which they chose to imprison themselves created an environment perfectly geared to endless human damage. Violence is the predictable, if not inevitable, result.

Klebold and Harris were apparently so twisted, so separated from the face of God, that they sought innocence and goodness as their targets, yet the really frightening aspect of their behavior is that these alienated young men were in many respects representative of large numbers of their peers. They were exceptional only in that they actually resorted to the bloody vengefulness that others fantasize every day via violent video games and rock lyrics. In this sense, Columbine was not a freakish and inexplicable explosion of adolescent angst: it was the manifestation of what two intelligent if highly disturbed young men believed that their culture expected of them. In their intimidating ankle-length dusters, armed with a fearsome arsenal of weapons and explosives, and motivated by a consuming fascination with death, Klebold and Harris were hardly less morbid than the general culture in which they were immersed. Like any number of alienated adolescents, they were at the same time emotionally damaged outcasts and smug, self-confident narcissists, and their narcissism supported the idea that they in particular had been "chosen" as avenging angels set against the injustice of the world. (The haunting image of Cho Seung-hui, the Virginia Tech killer, made up for the camera in what, under other circumstances, might seem a childish cowboy or ninja costume as he posed wielding pistols in each hand — only real ones, in this case — is further evidence of the narcissistic core at work in such killings, and in youth culture generally.)

It is not just the millennial generation, however, that we have to worry about. Long ago, Mick Jagger, now so mainstream as to appear as a spokesman for a major financial services company, had mimicked the tribalistic, self-pitying plaint of a depressed adolescent focused on darkness, death, and the black heart within himself. It is true that Jagger's adolescent persona only wished to paint the world black, not annihilate it, but that astringent, Warhol-like aesthetic of dark minimalism and psychic antagonism was a harbinger of things to come. Now Jagger's message is not only mimed in every twisted adolescent rock and hip-hop

Epilogue

performance but staged, filmed, televised, and acted upon as well. Reportedly, both Klebold and Harris were immersed in a nihilistic subculture that included video games such as Doom and films such as *The Basketball Diaries*, *Natural Born Killers*, and *The Matrix*. Afterward, in an even more bizarre turn of events, the Columbine massacre was recycled back into this same subculture by performers like Marilyn Manson, Alice Cooper, Eminem, and Ill Bill, each citing the massacre in their performances, and always, it seems, in apparent sympathy with the murderers. A video game entitled Super Columbine Massacre RPG!, which put players in the role of Klebold and Harris, even appeared on the market.

Clearly, the pervasive force of the narcissistic ego is a key element of contemporary culture, and the central fact about the narcissist is, of course, that he is incapable of taking an interest in anything outside his private world. From an educational point of view, this sort of individual is one who, as the exculpatory saying goes, learns quite well when he is "interested in the subject": the reason being that what he is interested in is himself or those few aspects of the curriculum that he has adopted as proxies of the self. The difficulty with this, aside from the inherent unhealthiness of narcissistic isolation itself, is that the inability to comprehend objective reality forecloses intellectual, emotional, and spiritual development, thus leaving the individual intellectually and emotionally unprepared for life, though bloated in terms of self-will. As, in this way, the public comes to possess less and less knowledge of actual reality, decisions and choices are made on the basis of easily grasped popular mythologies and fashions. As the public loses connection with the complex civilization inherited from the past, it comes to live in a continuous present filled with questionable mental reflexes and unconsidered "truths," and such ignorance leads to less informed choices.

Ultimately, however, it is not really possible to speak of "choices" in the case of a public that is largely ignorant of its own past since it is impossible to choose among alternatives unless one has been tutored in the complex nature of these alternatives. A large segment of the American public is now so poorly informed that it cannot identify what event is celebrated on Easter or what occurrence is commemorated on the Fourth of July. Nor can a large segment of the American public name the vice president of the United States or locate France on a world map. Yet these same individuals can mouth the lyrics of each of Beyoncé's hit songs and provide a detailed run-down of each of the teams in the National Football League playoffs. The problem is that Beyoncé and the Bears offer little insight into what direction foreign policy should take or how domestic programs should be funded and administered, yet it is these same voters who, in the final analysis, are called upon to decide. The perennial difficulty of democracies, that those entrusted with the vote are necessarily of average intelligence and education, has been exacerbated in our decadent, self-indulgent age of educational "pass/pass" and lifetime intellectual complacency.

Our tribal culture has discredited learning as an end in itself, and in its place has prioritized materialism, physical gratification, and above all else personal will. Tribalism in this sense implies the crude reduction of daily life to grasping responses of desire and self-indulgence. As David Gelernter wrote of the "huge divide in social character" that separates our time from that of even the comparatively recent past of the 1930s, "the continual practice of proper behavior on an endless succession of trivial, meaningless occasions" (218) does shape character and contributes to success in those endeavors and emergencies that await every human being at some point in life. But this "practice of proper behavior"—the very words would draw hoots of derision from the *Saturday Night Live* crowd—is something long vanished, as unfamiliar to most children today as bedtime prayer. In its place is an unremitting pursuit of self-development and self-gratification, and it is this, the willful self, that lies at the center of our new-found tribal condition. Detached from normal responsibilities and restrictions, the self in the narcissistic condition is especially subject to the great evil of boredom, and, as the French poet Charles Baudelaire so clearly understood, the "cure" for boredom is violence, perversion, and escapism.

Indeed, the poet and critic Czeslaw Milosz wrote that we live in an age that may be *too* affluent, *too* clever, *too* well-informed: a complacent age in which an overabundance of narrow historical knowledge and readily available search results have displaced a coherent sense of cultural identity based on the central core of broader mythic belief that once served to restrain tribalistic tendencies. Within classical–Christian civilization there were indeed limits as to what was even thinkable. Violence toward one's parents, betrayal of country, abuse of children, and desecration of churches were actions that, on the rare occasions when they did occur, were met with universal condemnation. Within the traditional order of the past, arrogance of power, whether in terms of the flaunting of physical, political, or economic force, has always been recognized as the evil that it is. Our great national strength has always derived from the fact that there has existed a core of universally acknowledged values and institutions, but this is becoming less and less the case. We are slipping away from the core values of honesty, loyalty, honor, and faith — all of these values of self-control and private devotion that were the legacy of the Judeo-Christian tradition. Never before has there existed so much confusion about our national purpose as there is today; never before have we been so distant from our founding ethos as now. The danger is that this loss of faith will soon translate into a tangible condition of Balkanization manifested not only in the fierce political rhetoric of the culture wars, wars largely of words, but in more overt forms of conflict. Our preeminence as a nation is at risk because we have lost the purposeful cohesiveness based on common values that has always been the major source of our strength.

As I have demonstrated in an earlier chapter in this book, Kent Haruf seems to find particularly disturbing the fact that one of the institutions most at bay is that of the nuclear family. Certainly, the ideal of the two-parent family, once universally embraced in Anglo-American culture, has lost much credibility, but this is not, as many would imagine, merely the result of vague pressures on the modern family. It has lost credibility as a result of a deliberate attack by leftists, feminists, psychotherapists, and anarchists who wrongly suppose that children can be reared by the collective nurturing of the state. As Roger Scruton has written, the traditional conception of the family, mocked by Marx and Engels in the nineteenth century, has come under greatest pressure in the past three decades as "part of a great cultural shift from the affirmation to the repudiation of inherited values" (*West and the Rest* 70). The dismissive treatment of the nuclear family pervades academic discourse and

The Dialect of the Tribe

now plays continually in the popular media, in which it is nearly impossible to encounter a two-parent family in which the father is not depicted merely as a peripheral presence, or worse, a malign one. The concept of absent fathers or of part-time father-figures as personified by anonymous men drifting in and out of households now dominates the media and has been normalized within our culture. Unfortunately, the absence of fathers and the loss of a supportive family life that results from that absence have everything to do with the decline of America into a tribal society.

Above all else, the condition of tribalism entails an inability to think as an individual. Elias Canetti, among the most astute analysts of crowd behavior, described the dangerous pleasure that human beings derive from merging with the crowd. With its sense of blessed equality and relief from "the burdens of distance," collective behavior promises an explosive though illusory relief from routine anxieties: "It is for the sake of this blessed moment, when no-one is greater or better than another, that people become a crowd" (*Crowds and Power* 18).The astounding absence of reasoned discussion in the national media — indeed, the contempt with which such discourse is met throughout the popular media — should be especially troubling to anyone who values traditional Western civilization. Rational discussion, it should be stressed, is never the product of the sort of group activity that takes place on the various talk shows or social media web sites. Original thinking is the product of individual effort, not that of groups. Within classical–Christian civilization, the very definition of humanity entailed the ability to think and discuss in terms of ideals, reasoned choice, self-restraint, and faith; it involved the capacity to invest one's energies, even to the long-term disadvantage to oneself, in the future of one's family, community, and country or city-state. The briefest survey of today's popular broadcast and Internet media is enough to confirm that these attributes do not underpin contemporary consciousness, at least not as it is represented in the media. Instead, we are served up an endless diet of offensive and degrading violence, teasing sexuality, inane sentimentality, and pointless reality programming. One can only assume that this media wasteland mirrors the mental vacuity of its viewers.

Epilogue

Especially apparent in contemporary discourse, as V.S. Naipaul clearly recognizes in his critique of Third World revolutionaries and of the fraudulent admiration which they elicit from liberals in the West, is the loss of the ability to make distinctions of value and scale. In his classic novel *A Bend in the River*, Naipaul dramatizes the naïve adulation on the part of European intellectuals for African liberationist leaders who are, in reality, little more than thuggish despots. Drawing on his experience of teaching in Uganda, Naipaul dissected with painstaking clarity the bad faith of liberals who readily substituted empathy for reason.

In contemporary culture, it is not difficult to find examples of this kind of irrationality. The death of a single human being (or, for that matter, of an animal or a plant), if portrayed in terms pathetic enough, is transmuted into a tragedy of global proportions. The death of the brain-damaged woman Terri Shiavo, tragic as it and as all such deaths are, did not merit months of media coverage or a special session of Congress. Nor did the abuses at the Abu Ghraib prison in Iraq, as distasteful as they were, warrant months of continuous media coverage, especially in contrast with the enemy's ceaseless bombings, kidnappings, and beheadings — actions that actually did constitute war crimes. In all of this, the public has lost the ability to discriminate matters of scale and degree. Having been tutored to respond unthinkingly to media manipulation and sensationalism, the American public seems now incapable of distinguishing what is truly evil from what may symbolize evil or may be made to appear evil — or what may actually *be* evil but evil to a lesser extent. Dante's schema for the Inferno, one recalls, featured an intricate design involving degrees of evil based on the seven deadly sins and their subdivisions, each with its distinctive shades of criminal intent and a sliding scale of punishment. Educated in the civilization of Christianity and the Greek and Roman classics of philosophy, law, and rhetoric, Dante recorded precise moral distinctions that were universally shared by his contemporaries. How much less civilized are our own contemporaries, among whom even the worst crimes are excused as the product of environment or "culture," while non-crimes such as the utterance of seemingly outdated opinions are made out to be monstrous. Every newly reformed addict is paraded on the television talk shows for our admiration, while truly noble sacrifice, lifetimes of effort by deeply earnest, compassionate individuals, escapes comment. Those who violently resist arrest are portrayed as victims of "excessive force," while those heroes who risk their lives to protect their fellow citizens are deemed abusive, charged under civil and criminal codes, demonized by the media, and in some cases hauled off to prison in place of the criminals.

With the rise of tribalism, we are every day at greater risk, but it is not only the blatant violence of a Columbine-style attack that puts us in jeopardy. In a culture of excessive tolerance, moral strictures of any kind are perceived as an unfair attempt to restrict personal choice. Immediately, the moral authority of the precept is challenged on the basis that, within a democratic culture, each individual is entitled to an opinion of equal weight, and, within a culture in which traditional authority has been repudiated, moral knowledge is viewed as nothing more than opinion.

As Berlin points out in *The Roots of Romanticism*, this dismissal of authority had a long chain of development within romantic thinking beginning with Kantian and Hegelian conceptions of the moral will and evolving into various forms of utilitarianism, anarchism, and radical libertarianism, as well as into extreme forms of nationalist and racialist thinking. Philosophical anarchism, which goes beyond relativism to the point that it rejects all stable and purposeful conceptions of reality, undermines the role of reason in organizing or administering society. In place of reason, the anarchist believes that the unfettered impulse of society's masses, expressing itself spontaneously and "naturally," will lead to a true and fulfilling outcome. The career of James Agee, whose ethical moorings were the subject of one chapter in this book, reveals the damage of anarchism both to the writer as an individual and to his work. Despite the enormous advantages of education, upbringing, and opportunity that he enjoyed, Agee chose to embark on a literary career in which he championed nihilism and defeatism. Constantly attempting to undermine American capitalism and bourgeois society, Agee was left at the end with nothing but an early death resulting from his self-indulgent and self-destructive behavior. His literary career, which produced only two completed books aside from an early book of poetry, suffered to an equal degree.

Epilogue

Agee was, if anything, a romantic idealist seduced by radical visions of liberation and perfectibility, and in this respect he was merely the late product of a long tradition of romantic social thought. As in Agee's case, there has been throughout Western culture a striking effect of the late-Romantic ethos on our culture's ability to adhere to an ethically coherent belief system. For one thing, a radically new usage of language is implied. All manner of imprecision, ambiguity, and slippage in the meaning of words seemed to be overlooked and even encouraged. Words are abstracted from reality; phrases, shouted often enough, become unchallengeable mantras. The fundamental laws of logic are ignored; coherence and organization are abandoned, along with all sense of self-critical standards of presentation. Substituting for the conventional elements of rhetoric that have formed the basis of educated discussion for millennia, we now submit to the power of the electronic image. Most of the images upon which responses are based emanate from a media that is by no means innocent of bias, and the very pace of images flashed on the screen and passively absorbed affords no opportunity for scrutiny or debate. The photograph of a suffering individual, such as that of the many Hurricane Katrina "victims" awaiting rescue, can influence national priorities more decisively than any number of carefully researched books and articles. In the case of Katrina, the notion of victim attached itself almost immediately to those who were adversely affected by the storm, and it soon took on an indiscriminate, emotive, irrefutable sort of authority. Even the gangs of looters who gleefully gutted the city of New Orleans were portrayed as victims: they were looting out of anger at a failed system; they were looting out of frustration; they "had to" loot to survive; they were "mostly" stealing food, even when images repeatedly showed them hauling off widescreen televisions and cases of liquor. Anyone so callous as to challenge the "truth" that looters were victims rather than victimizers deserved an electronic lynching, and that is exactly what they got. When former first lady Barbara Bush pointed out that most of the Katrina "refugees," as they were labeled, were better off in the Astrodome than they had been before the storm, her remark was reported with a disapproving sneer.

When national policy is driven by such images as that of the Katrina

The Dialect of the Tribe

damage, it can hardly be coherent or rational. As Alfred Hitchcock implied with his ominous treatments of morally ambiguous mid-century America, an antagonist culture has emerged in which the public, egged on by an opportunistic news media, responds with reflexive distrust to those institutions and leaders whose authority was taken for granted in the past. For a long time now, at least since the national ordeal of Watergate, there has been a tendency for the public to second-guess authority of all kinds, and certainly the media has not been loath to pander to and encourage this conspiracy theory mentality. In such a tribal condition, the immediate impact of events is more important than any amount of patient analysis. Policy is reduced to an endless and futile effort to control image and spin — and to counter the opportunistic attacks of the opposite party — while the nation as a whole is continuously weakened in relation to more ordered and coherent societies. In such a context, thought comes to seem a dangerous impediment, and principled action is practically unthinkable. We descend into the condition of an electronic mob of the sort that demands immediate gratification and instantly seeks out scapegoats when its wishes are not gratified. In the end, the interactive space becomes the arena in which society enacts its blood sport, sacrificing those individuals who appear to be out of step with whatever social attitudes are deemed correct at the moment. Those who "just don't get it," to quote Bill Clinton in a 1992 presidential debate with George H.W. Bush, deserve only scorn. In these electronic gladiatorial contests, politics is conducted within a blood-lust atmosphere in which new victims are served up almost daily. Opponents are ambushed with abusive labels based on the basis of speculation or fabrication. The rules, precedents, and traditions of civil debate are cast aside as the mob is carried forward by the demagoguery of emotive images and inflated, bifurcated rhetoric.

It is important to understand the emotional lever that underlies this sort of discourse. It is the mob's fascination with change for its own sake and with the sense of its own power. One of the ugly consequences of this primitive motive, anticipated centuries ago in the philosophical writing of Herder (itself influenced by that of Rousseau, Leibniz, and Hamann, among others), is the weakening of formal institutions, whether these be political, social, or religious in nature, in favor of a growing attachment to one's "tribe." "For [Herder], as for Nietzsche, the state is the coldest of all cold monsters," wrote Isaiah Berlin in his magisterial study, *Vico and Herder: Two Studies in the History of Ideas*. "Nothing in the whole of human history is more hateful to him than Churches and priests who are instruments of political power; as for the state ... it robs men of themselves" (162). In place of established political parties or legal institutions such as state-sanctioned marriage, Herder would have us pursue those forms of self-realization that derive from one's local affiliations and communal sources of identity. Shared language, sense of place, common history, even climate appear to Herder to be decisive. Rather than relying on formal institutions or inherited traditions, elements of civilization that transcend the particularities of time and place, Herder based his philosophy on an intense empathy with specific individual cultures existing at a single time and place. It was within local culture itself, and especially within those regional and folk cultures in which human beings lived closer to their "natural" condition, seemingly untainted by artifice or coercion, that one discovered the most meaningful, authentic expression of humanity.

Through his many Romantic and post–Romantic followers, including early twentieth-century anarchists such as Emma Goldman and, a generation later, James Agee, Herder has had an enormous influence on modern conceptions of social relations. Within a complex, erratic, and sometimes incongruous history whose major figures include Hegel, Marx, Nietzsche, Carlyle, Tolstoy, Heidegger, Sartre, and Foucault, among others, utopian conceptions of liberation, perfectibility, authenticity, engagement, community, and selfhood have permeated modern thinking to the point that, for large segments of cosmopolitan populations, they have become reified terms grounding rationality itself. Indeed, from within post–Romantic rationality, it is impossible to perceive the artificiality of such conceptions of edenic perfection, and it is precisely within this rationality that the thinking of most contemporary Americans and Europeans can be located. In this sense, adherents of tribalism have not consciously *chosen* a tribal condition — they are incapable of choosing because they are immersed in a form of rationality that is the product of Romanticism's pervasive influence on consciousness itself.

The Dialect of the Tribe

While the intellectual origins of tribalism can be traced back as far as Rousseau, it is the manifestation of this mode of consciousness that I have studied in this book. One aspect of the new consciousness is a widespread cynicism regarding those institutions and individuals who are connected with order and authority. Seen through the prism of the unbounded ego, public affairs is now conceived in a bizarrely immature and personalized way. The public responds to the business of heads of state as if those leaders were celebrities from the tabloid press trading the intimate details of their private lives for publicity. One need only examine the irreverent sarcasms of British and American political satire on such shows as *Spitting Image* and *Saturday Night Live*, with their amusing political impersonators, to understand how the media has undermined public trust in its leaders. Respect for the office of president or prime minister, as for all figures of authority, is a crucial element in maintaining cultural cohesion and social order, and in order to maintain this respect a certain amount of imaginative distance needs to be preserved. Unfortunately, in addition to the sardonic humor of late night television, the public's ceaseless taste for reality has unleashed all manner of investigative reporting, Internet leaks, and sensationalized news coverage, in all of which there exists a cynical assumption of self-interest, misgovernance, and even conspiracy on the part of those in positions of authority. It is no wonder that the public is incapable of focusing in a serious way on public issues. Matters of public policy, even those that involve the very survival of our civilization, can't compete with the adolescent fantasy that politics is a den of iniquity and that only the virtuous public — with the assistance of the noble, disinterested press — sees it for what it is. Because of the suspicion of authority that now exists, as Shelby Steele pointed out in a *Wall Street Journal* op-ed of 2 May 2006, "Our leaders face a double bind. If they do what is truly necessary to solve a problem — win a war, fix immigration — they lose legitimacy." If they do nothing, as is more often the case today, they retain the public's affection, at least for the moment, but betray their oath of office. The more resolute and decisive their action, the less credible they appear within a culture of universal suspicion.

What happens to a society in which a majority of the populace reflexively distrusts the judgment of its elected representatives and rejects the authority of its central institutions? Lacking respect for authority, this society reverts to direct democracy: that is, the reduction of decision-making to opinion polls or the sort of town-hall meetings that have become de rigueur — for demonstration purposes, at least — in recent presidential campaigns. Direct democracy carries with it many negative consequences, one of which is the stifling of reasoned debate amid the aura of conformity that all opinion polls construct. There is, after all, a naïve acceptance of the objective validity of public opinion as reported in the media and an unwillingness on the part of the individual to depart from it. At the same time, the judgments of knowledgeable individuals are rendered suspect, in part because they are automatically perceived as elitists who set themselves above the crowd.

The tribal characteristics of opinion polling become increasingly apparent as it becomes possible to cite instantaneous polls that reflect the immediate effects of visual stimuli within minutes of their appearance. With polls registering public reaction to visual stimuli, and with conformity of opinion reinforced by the release of instantaneous polling results, we have entered the Orwellian realm in which the electronic screen endlessly confirms, alters, shapes, and recycles public opinion. As it turns out, however, this opinion-shaping power is not controlled by a centralized authority but by the anarchic process of postmodern media itself. In this way, we are enslaved by an inhuman, unreflective process, not the tyranny of Big Brother but one that compromises individuality even more completely. At least in Orwell's fictional world it was possible to conceive of the existence of rebels such as Winston Smith at odds with the state. Among the electronic tribe, rebellion is hardly possible because it is squelched by the irresistible pressure toward conformity that mass opinion exerts. In the twilight state of consciousness, drugged by a seductive but mind-dulling succession of striking images and opinion polls that imply a "correct" consensus, the postmodern viewer can hardly be expected to articulate objections to the ceaseless, rapid-fire flow of "information" and the mass pressure to conform.

The danger of this sort of media tribalism is that the public may become an uncontrollable mass that shifts its position wildly, attacking its leaders one moment and praising them the next, supporting or opposing foreign policy on a whim and paralyzing the ability of those government leaders who wish to act in a deliberate manner. One of the results of this suspicion is the resort to mass opinion as evidenced through the popularity of the web log. Those left-wing sites that not only attacked conservatives in recent elections but who also assaulted liberals whom they deemed not liberal enough are nothing more than a virtual lynch mob: a gang in which the loudest, most blatant and irresponsible voices carry the greatest weight, and in this mob setting whatever gets attention — the sensationalistic, flashy, and crude — gains credence. Lacking the careful deliberation of actual policy formation, the political culture in which we live points to the sort of extremism that weakens our national resolve and influence. Ironically, that segment of the public that frequents the radical blogosphere — those who are alienated from established institutions and have rejected forms of traditional political discourse that would include the study of serious books, journals, and newspapers — somehow believe themselves to be better informed than the rest of society. They imagine that they are "in on the secret" of a vast conspiracy (right-wing or otherwise) involving an abuse of power, a cover-up, or an injustice. The danger of this childish penchant for conspiracy theory is that it is based upon the conviction that a single individual or small group possesses the ability to know the truth in all its complexity more surely than does the rest of mankind. Such self-assurance quickly descends into social primitivism: lacking checks or benchmarks of any kind, the self's criteria for knowing the world is reduced to the savage grunt of sympathy or the incoherent groan of revulsion.

In this tribal condition, having rejected the authority of its leaders and institutions, the public finds opinion balkanized among different ideological points of view, each unwilling to compromise with the other. Yet in this state of self-absorption, members of the public are not acting or thinking as individuals, however much they may see themselves as nobly refusing to conform to the demands of authority. Rather, they have become mere ciphers of strong opinion makers, each of them more demagogic than the next. Thought has been foreclosed; no real diversity of thinking is permitted, particularly in those instances in which "diversity" per se is invoked as the motive of action. Thought is constricted by intimidation, and agreement is enforced, not sought by means of persuasion and argument. It is this censorship of human thought and feeling that most clearly defines the divisive politics into which we are sinking and that connects it with the totalitarian politics of the past.

In a society of interest groups at war with one another, it is inevitable that individuals will become cynical and demoralized rather than see themselves as part of a great common enterprise. They are no longer proud citizens of the world's greatest democracy but disaffected and self-interested cynics, resentful of any restriction of their personal freedom and unwilling to sacrifice for the common good. In such an environment, politics of whatever extreme persuasion descends to the moral equivalent of road rage. The rage that a driver feels when he is cut off on the roadway is simply an index of his conviction of autonomy and self-importance: what is at stake is not just a few seconds of driving time but the fact that, by forcing him to acknowledge another's existence, another driver has, quite literally, put a brake upon his ego. The political rage of isolated interest groups is no different: having identified oneself with a particular interest group, one has declared one's right to the free play of ego. As one "becomes" a gay, a feminist, or an environmental activist, rather than a person who happens to be homosexual, female, or a person who appreciates nature, one begins to exhibit the grandiose posture of self-importance that we have witnessed so often in contemporary public life. Seeing oneself as a victimized member of an identity group, the condition that all minority groups automatically claim for their constituents, immediately confers the stature of martyrdom. One is no longer one among many, a fallible, irresolute, misguided, average human being: once granted the status of the victimized interest group, one is forceful, unique, godlike, unchallengeable.

Yet moral principles can never really function within a society so utterly unhinged and divisive as this analysis suggests. As Peter Hitchens writes in *The Abolition of Britain*, those who "cease to believe in their national myths, and cease to know or respect their history ... seek tribal sensations by being part of a supposed 'generation'" or become easily manipulated fanatics of one sort of another (46). In the long run, reality,

The Dialect of the Tribe

the reality of the changeless conditions of human mortality, vulnerability, longing, and spiritual need, returns to punish those who abandon its constraints. The fantasy world on offer, whether from pandering politicians, marketing agencies, or overindulgent parents, proves disastrous once the debts are called in and one enters the actual realm of experience. At that point there are no supportive parents or teachers or genial media counselors to save us.

Evidence of America's mounting cultural confusion is readily available. Suspicion of our "giant corporations" is a frequent refrain of the political left, as it was, certainly, for James Agee, whose political essays and film reviews — as well as his influential book *Let Us Now Praise Famous Men*—featured an endless number of attacks on the very companies that supply many of our material necessities and create our most rewarding jobs. The public, unfortunately, has little conception of how much is at risk with the loss of faith in the conception of labor that once contributed so much to meaningful existence. The left's notion of seizing and redistributing corporate profits (while miraculously retaining the jobs and prosperity that those same corporations produce) is simply adolescent fantasy worthy of the Clement Attlees and Julius Nyereres of the world. Fantastic it may be, but it is far from harmless. Anyone who has lived inside the demoralized, unproductive, hopeless conditions of a communist state knows to what depths the egalitarian fantasies of socialism will lead. They lead to harsh winters with little food, decades of frustrated poverty, and lifetimes of untreated illness culminating in early death. Unnumbered lives were sacrificed to the mindless idol of communism in the last century, and now the American left wishes to revive this monstrous ideology on our own shores.

Agee was not by any means the only writer of his generation to be seduced by the appeal of liberation. In his case, the instinct for rebellion led him more toward anarchism and libertarianism than toward collectivism, though Agee was both an anarchist and a politically engaged anticapitalist at the same time. Like many radicals of his time and since, Agee repudiated what he considered a deathly bourgeois society in which the virtues of perseverance, thrift, judgment, and self-restraint played a central role. In the world that Agee fantasized, one could live in the absence of a fixed address, a long-term employer, a shared religious faith, or a commitment to marriage. Like so many on the left, Agee seemed oblivious to the fact that human nature requires stability and faith in order to persevere in the difficult tasks of life. The anarchic freedom that Agee promoted, and that Dostoevsky understood to be so destructive, has led to horrific consequences in the real world. Anyone who does not understand what this means has failed to study the history of the past century, especially those murderous decades in which the promises of the left in Europe, Asia, Africa, and Latin America were soon followed by political oppression on an unprecedented scale.

Unlike the virtual world in which one traipses through a fairy land of unlimited freedom in which any thought, word, or act is possible, the actual world entails inescapable consequences. It is not just that as a nation we have become more cynical, more smug, and more selfish: we have, I believe, begun to lose contact with our real nature as human beings; we have begun to separate ourselves from the realm of necessity that is our true home. The morass of glib abstraction, reflexive emotion, and mindless image that reigns in the popular media is a deathly influence, and one that will paralyze the will and confuse our instincts for survival. Ultimately, it will reduce America to the faithless sneer of self-loathing and cynicism, a condition from which no nation recovers without passing through the inferno of impoverishment and defeat.

In an essay entitled "The Constitution and the Antagonist World," Russell Kirk stressed that the written constitutions of great nations are worthless unless supported by "the unwritten constitution, the web of custom and convention [that] affirms an enduring moral order of obligation and personal responsibility" (470). It is precisely this "unwritten constitution" that is at risk today as American culture and Western civilization in general slip ever further toward the tribal condition of unthinking conformity and reflexive response. In the unmoored, ever shifting sympathies of postmodern tribalism, the mass of men, egged on by an unreliable media and demagogic leaders, lurch from one sacred enthusiasm to another. As digital technology makes possible instant communication and instant interaction among viewers, media, and opinion makers, the possibility of reflection and reasoned argument diminish.

The entropic force of tribal consciousness itself takes over, with unpredictable and extreme consequences. What is most precious, that unwritten constitution of custom and convention, is utterly forgotten. In the ensuing confusion, individuals endure the anguish of random and disordered lives. For society at large, there is the specter of enormous waste and widespread demoralization. We slip from the civilized state of selflessness and decency into the tribal realm of brutish vulgarity and combative self-interestedness. Yet, though it may seem too late to restore the high ideals of service, aspiration, humility, and self-respect that characterized classical–Christian civilization, we can hope, as Kirk himself did, that the "conservative yearning" will reassert itself and that these ideals will find their way into the hearts of a rising generation. Then perhaps, by some great effort and sacrifice, we can claw our way back to the civilized condition of free men and women that conservative writers have forever sought.

Works Cited

Agee, James. *A Death in the Family*. In *James Agee: Let Us Now Praise Famous Men, A Death in the Family, and Shorter Fiction*. Ed. Michael Sragow. New York: Library of America, 2005. 465–739.

―――. *James Agee Rediscovered: The Journals of Let Us Now Praise Famous Men and Other New Manuscripts*. Ed. Michael A. Lofaro and Hugh Davis. Knoxville: University of Tennessee Press, 2005.

―――. *Letters of James Agee to Father Flye*. New York: Ballantine, 1971.

Agee, James, and Walker Evans. *Let Us Now Praise Famous Men*. In *James Agee: Let Us Now Praise Famous Men, A Death in the Family, and Shorter Fiction*. Ed. Michael Sragow. New York: Library of America, 2005. 1–399.

Applewhite, James. "A Trip with V.S. Naipaul." *Raritan* 10.1 (1990): 48–54.

Arendt, Hannah. *The Human Condition*. Chicago: University of Chicago Press, 1958.

―――. "What Is Authority?" In *The Portable Hannah Arendt*. Ed. Peter Baehr. New York: Penguin, 2003. 91–142.

Barson, Alfred T. *A Way of Seeing: A Critical Study of James Agee*. Amherst: University of Massachusetts Press, 1972.

Berlin, Isaiah. *Freedom and Its Betrayal: Six Enemies of Human Liberty*. Ed. Henry Hardy. Princeton: Princeton University Press, 2002.

―――. *The Roots of Romanticism*. Ed. Henry Hardy. Princeton: Princeton University Press, 2003.

―――. *Vico and Herder: Two Studies in the History of Ideas*. New York: Viking, 1976.

Bhabha, Homi K. *The Location of Culture*. London: Routledge, 1994.

Bloom, Allan. *The Closing of the American Mind*. New York: Touchstone, 1988.

Bowman, James. *Honor: A History*. New York: Encounter Books, 2006.

Bronowski, J., and Bruce Mazlish. *The Western Intellectual Tradition: From Leonardo to Hegel*. 1960. New York: Harper Torchbooks, 1975.

Burke, Edmund. *Reflections on the Revolution in France*. In *The Portable Edmund Burke*. Ed. Isaac Kraminick. New York: Penguin, 1999. 416–73.

Works Cited

Canetti, Elias. *Crowds and Power*. Trans. Carol Stewart. New York: Farrar Straus and Giroux, 1984.

――――. *The Torch in My Ear*. Trans. Joachim Neugroschel. New York: Farrar Straus and Giroux, 1992.

Chenetier, Marc. "Introduction." In *Letters of Vachel Lindsay*. Ed. Marc Chenetier. New York: Burt Franklin, 1979.

Coetzee, J. M. "The Razor's Edge." *New York Review of Books* (1 November 2001): 8–10.

――――. *Waiting for the Barbarians*. New York: Penguin, 1982.

Coles, Robert. *Flannery O'Connor's South*. Baton Rouge: Louisiana State University Press, 1980.

Dostoevsky, Fyodor. *The Brothers Karamazov*. Trans. Andrew R. MacAndrew. New York: Bantam, 1981.

――――. *The Demons*. Trans. Richard Pevear and Larisssa Volokhonsky. New York: Knopf, 2000.

――――. *Selected Letters of Fyodor Dostoyevsky*. Ed. Joseph Frank and David I. Goldstein. Trans. Andrew R. MacAndrew. New Brunswick, NJ, and London: Rutgers University Press, 1986.

Eagleton, Terry. "A Mind So Fine: The Contradictions of V.S. Naipaul." *Harper's* 307 (Sept. 2003): 79–85.

Eliot, T.S. "Tradition and the Individual Talent." In *20th Century Literary Criticism: A Reader*. Ed. David Lodge. New York: Longman, 1972. 71–76.

Evans, M. Stanton. *Blacklisted by History: The Untold Story of Senator Joe McCarthy and His Fight against America's Enemies*. New York: Crown Forum, 2007.

Faulkner, William. *Go Down, Moses*. New York: Modern Library, 1955.

――――. *Light in August*. The Corrected Text. New York: Vintage International, 1990.

Frank, Joseph. *Dostoevsky: The Stir of Liberation, 1860–1865*. Princeton: Princeton University Press, 1986.

――――. *Dostoevsky: The Mantle of the Prophet, 1871–1881*. Princeton: Princeton University Press, 2002.

――――. *Dostoevsky: The Miraculous Years, 1865–1871*. Princeton: Princeton University Press, 1995.

――――. *Dostoevsky: The Years of Ordeal, 1850–1859*. Princeton: Princeton University Press, 1987.

French, Patrick. *The World Is What It Is: The Authorized Biography of V.S. Naipaul*. New York: Knopf, 2008.

Gelernter, David. *1939: The Lost World of the Fair*. New York: Free Press, 1995.

Golding, William. "Nobel Lecture 1983." In *A Moving Target*. New York: Farrar Straus Giroux, 1983. 203–214.

Gooch, Brad. *Flannery: A Life of Flannery O'Connor*. New York: Little, Brown, 2009.

Works Cited

Grant, Richard. *American Nomads: Travels with Lost Conquistadors, Mountain Men, Cowboys, Indians, Hoboes, and Bullriders.* New York: Grove Press, 2003.

Graves, Robert. *Goodbye to All That: An Autobiography.* Rev. 2nd ed. New York: Anchor, 1957.

Griffiths, Paul J. "The Center Does Not Hold." *Commonweal* 132.3 (11 Feb. 2005): 21–23.

Hacker, P.M.S. *Wittgenstein.* London: Routledge, 1999.

Harpham, Geoffrey Galt. *On the Grotesque: Strategies of Contradiction in Art and Literature.* Princeton: Princeton University Press, 1982.

Harris, Mark. "Introduction." In *Selected Poems of Vachel Lindsay.* Ed. Mark Harris. New York: MacMillan, 1963. vii–xxii.

Haruf, Kent. *Eventide.* New York: Knopf, 2004.

———. *Plainsong.* New York: Vintage, 1999.

———. *The Tie That Binds.* New York: Vintage, 1984.

———. *Where You Once Belonged.* 1990. New York: Vintage, 2000.

Hayek, F.A. *The Road to Serfdom.* Fiftieth Anniversary Edition. Chicago: University of Chicago Press, 1994.

Himmelfarb, Gertrude. *One Nation, Two Cultures.* New York: Knopf, 1999.

———. *The Roads to Modernity: The British, French, and American Enlightenments.* New York: Knopf, 2004.

Hitchens, Peter. *The Abolition of Britain: From Winston Churchill to Princess Diana.* New York: Encounter Books, 2000.

Hubben, William. *Dostoevsky, Kierkegaard, Nietzsche, and Kafka.* 1952. New York: Touchstone, 1997.

Hummer, T.R. "Laughed Off: Canon, Kharackter, and the Dismissal of Vachel Lindsay." *Kenyon Review* 17.2 (1995): 56–96.

Hutchisson, James M. *Poe.* Jackson: University Press of Mississippi, 2005.

Jackson, Robert Louis, ed. *Dostoevsky: New Perspectives.* Englewood Cliffs, NJ: Prentice-Hall, 1984.

Jacobs, Robert D. *Poe: Journalist and Critic.* Lexington: University Press of Kentucky, 1969.

Johnson, Paul. *Intellectuals.* New York: Harper & Row, 1988.

Kirk, Russell. *The Essential Russell Kirk: Selected Essays.* Ed. George A. Panichas. Wilmington, DE: ISI Books, 2007.

Kołakowski, Leszek. "Looking for the Barbarians." In *Modernity on Endless Trial.* Chicago: University of Chicago Press, 1990. 14–31.

———. *Metaphysical Horror.* Rev. ed. Ed. Agnieszka Kołakowska. Chicago: University of Chicago Press, 2001.

———. "The Revenge of the Sacred in Secular Culture." *Modernity on Endless Trial.* Chicago: University of Chicago Press, 1990. 63–74.

Works Cited

———. "Revolution — A Beautiful Sickness." In *Modernity on Endless Trial*. Chicago: University of Chicago Press, 1990. 215–24.
Kristol, Irving. *Neoconservatism: The Autobiography of an Idea*. New York: Free Press, 1995.
Lasch, Christopher. *The Culture of Narcissism: American Life in an Age of Diminishing Expectations*. 1977. New York: Norton, 1991.
Lawrence, D. H. "The Spirit of Place." In *20th Century Literary Criticism: A Reader*. Ed. David Lodge. London: Longman, 1972. 122–27.
Lindsay, Vachel. *A Handy Guide for Beggars*. New York: Macmillan, 1916.
———. *Letters of Vachel Lindsay*. Ed. Marc Chenetier. New York: Burt Franklin, 1979.
———. *The Poetry of Vachel Lindsay: Complete and with Lindsay's Drawings*. 2 vols. Ed. Dennis Camp. Peoria, IL: Spoon River Poetry Press, 1984.
———. "Whitman." *The New Republic* 5 December 1923: 3–5.
Livermore, Gordon. "Stepan Verkhovensky and the Shaping Dialectic of Dostoevsky's *Devils*. In *Dostoevsky: New Perspectives*. Ed. Robert Louis Jackson. Englewood Cliffs, NJ: Prentice-Hall, 1984. 176–92.
Lofaro, Michael A., and Davis, Hugh. *James Agee Rediscovered: The Journals for Let Us Now Praise Famous Men and Other New Manuscripts*. Knoxville: University of Tennessee Press, 2005.
Lytle, Andrew. "Fiction and the Essence of Things: Stephen Crane's 'The Open Boat.'" In *Southerners and Europeans: Essays in a Time of Disorder*. Baton Rouge: Louisiana State University Press, 1988.
———. "The Subject of Southern Fiction." In *Southerners and Europeans: Essays in a Time of Disorder*. Baton Rouge: Louisiana State University Press, 1988.
Martin, Russell. "Introduction." In *New Writers of the Purple Sage: An Anthology of Contemporary Western Writing*. New York: Penguin, 1992. xiii–xxiii.
McCloskey, Mark. "*Plainsong*." In *Magill's Literary Annual 2000*. Pasadena, CA: Salem Press, 2000.
Mead, Walter B. "'I Know More Than I Can Tell': The Insights of Michael Polanyi." *Modern Age* 49.3 (2007): 298–307.
Meyers, Jeffrey. "V.S. Naipaul and Paul Theroux." *PN Review* 26.3 (1999): 37–47.
Miles, Jonathan. "*Eventide*: Where the Dust Motes Glow." *New York Times* Book Section (May 23, 2004): E2.
Milosz, Czeslaw. *The Land of Ulro*. Trans. Louis Iribarne. New York: Farrar, Straus, Giroux, 1981. 227–28.
———. *Selected Poems, 1931–2004*. New York: HarperCollins, 2006.
Minogue, Kenneth. *Alien Powers: The Pure Theory of Ideology*. New York: St. Martin's, 1985.
———. *Politics: A Very Short Introduction*. New York: Oxford University Press, 2000.

Works Cited

Monk, Ray. *Ludwig Wittgenstein: The Duty of Genius*. New York: The Free Press, 1990.

Naipaul, V.S. "Conrad's Darkness." In *Critical Perspectives on V.S. Naipaul*. Ed. Robert D. Hamner. Washington, DC: Three Continents Press, 1977. 54–65.

———. "The Documentary Heresy." In *Critical Perspectives on V.S. Naipaul*. Ed. Robert D. Hamner, Robert. Washington, DC: Three Continents Press, 1977. 23–25.

———. *The Enigma of Arrival*. New York: Vintage, 1988.

———. *Literary Occasions: Essays*. Introduced and edited by Pankaj Mishra. New York: Knopf, 2003.

———. *A Turn in the South*. New York: Knopf, 1989.

Novak, Michael. *The Spirit of Democratic Capitalism*. Lanham, MD: Madison Books, 1991.

O'Connor, Flannery. *Collected Works*. Ed. Sally Fitzgerald. New York: Library of America, 1988.

———. *The Habit of Being*. Ed. Sally Fitzgerald. 1979. New York: Noonday Press, 1988.

Orwell, George. *My Country Right or Left, 1940–1943*. Volume 2 of *The Collected Essays, Journalism and Letters of George Orwell*. Ed. Sonia Orwell and Ian Angus. New York and London: Harcourt Brace Jovanovich, 1968.

Panichas, George A. *Restoring the Meaning of Conservatism: Writings from* Modern Age. Wilmington, DE: ISI Books, 2008.

Podhoretz, Norman. *The Bloody Crossroads: Where Literature and Politics Meet*. New York: Simon and Schuster, 1986.

Poe, Edgar Allan. *The Fall of the House of Usher and Other Writings*. Ed. David Galloway. New York: Penguin, 1986.

———. *Poetry and Tales*. Ed. Patrick F. Quinn. New York: Library of America, 1984.

Postlethwaite, Diana. "A Healing Melody: Kent Haruf's Unadorned Yet Elegant Novel Makes Extraordinary Music Out of the Ordinary Rhythms of Daily Life in a Small Colorado Town." *The World and I* 15.2 (Feb. 2000): 258.

Rampersad, Arnold. "V.S. Naipaul: Turning in the South." *Raritan* 10.1 (1990): 24–47.

Reiman, Donald H., and Powers, Sharon B. *Shelley's Poetry and Prose: Authoritative Texts and Criticism*. New York: Norton, 1977.

Ruggles, Eleanor. *The West-Going Heart: A Life of Vachel Lindsay*. New York: Norton, 1959.

Said, Edward. "Expectations of Inferiority." *New Statesman* 102, no. 2639 (16 October 1981): 21.

Scruton, Roger. *Gentle Regrets: Thoughts from a Life*. London: Continuum, 2005.

Works Cited

———. *The West and the Rest: Globalization and the Terrorist Threat.* Wilmington, DE: ISI Books, 2002.
Silverman, Kenneth. *Edgar A. Poe: Mournful and Never-Ending Remembrance.* New York: HarperPerennial, 1992.
Simpson, Lewis P. "The Antebellum South as a Symbol of Mind." *Southern Literary Journal* 12.2 (1980): 125–37.
———. *The Dispossessed Garden: Pastoral and History in Southern Literature.* Athens: University of Georgia Press, 1975.
———. *The Fable of the Southern Writer.* Baton Rouge: Louisiana State University Press, 1994.
———. *The Man of Letters in New England and the South: Essays on the History of the Literary Vocation in America.* Baton Rouge: Louisiana State University Press, 1973.
Smith, Steven B. *Spinoza's Book of Life: Freedom and Redemption in the* Ethics. New Haven and London: Yale University Press, 2003.
Sorell, Tom. *Descartes.* Oxford: Oxford University Press, 1987.
Stallman, Robert Wooster. "The New Criticism and the Southern Critics." *A Southern Vanguard: The John Peale Bishop Memorial Volume.* Ed. Allen Tate. New York: Prentice-Hall, 1947. 28–51.
Sutcliffe, F.E. "Introduction." *Discourse on Method and the Meditations.* Trans. F.E. Sutcliffe. Harmondsworth, England: Penguin, 1968. 7–24.
Turner, Frederick Jackson. *The Frontier in American History.* 1920. n.p.: Bibliobazaar, 2008.
Wilson, Charles Reagan, and William Ferris. *Encyclopedia of Southern Culture.* Chapel Hill: University of North Carolina Press, 1989.
Wittgenstein, Ludwig. *On Certainty.* Ed. G.E.M. Anscombe and G.H. von Wright. Trans. Denis Paul and G.E.M. Anscombe. New York: Harper Torchbooks, 1972.
———. *Philosophical Investigations,* 2nd ed. Ed. G.E.M. Anscombe and R. Rhees. Trans. G.E.M. Anscombe. Oxford: Blackwell, 1958.
Wood, Michael. "Is That All There Is?" *The Nation* 279.22 (27 Dec. 2004): 29.
Yardley, Jonathan. "Review of *Half a Life,* by V.S. Naipaul." *Washington Post Book World* 21 October 2001: 2.
Yarmolinsky, Avrahm. *Dostoevsky: Works and Days.* New York: Funk & Wagnalls, 1971.
Zenkovsky, V.V. "Dostoevsky's Religious and Philosophical Views." In *Dostoevsky: A Collection of Critical Essays.* Ed. René Wellek. Englewood Cliffs, NJ: Prentice-Hall, 1962. 130–45.

Index

Addams, Jane 81
Agee, James 2, 27, 89–112, 183, 184, 186, 191, 192; *A Death in the Family* 89, 97, 100; *Let Us Now Praise Famous Men* (with Walker Evans) 89, 99, 101, 102, 103, 104, 105, 106, 107, 108, 109, 191; *Letters to Father Flye* 91, 92, 95, 110
agrarianism 13, 58, 77, 86, 138, 145
"Alexander Campbell" (Lindsay) 69
alienation 89, 90, 91, 126, 144, 162, 177
anarchism 109, 175, 180, 183, 186, 191, 192
antagonist culture 29, 30, 185
Applewhite, James 142, 152, 153
Arendt, Hannah 129, 161, 166, 174, 175
Armstrong, A.J. 70

Beats 128
Berlin, Isaiah 31, 94, 183, 186; *The Roots of Romanticism* 94; *Vico and Herder: Two Studies in the History of Ideas* 186
Blake, William 92, 102, 103, 163
Bloom, Allan 11, 12
Bowman, James 23, 165
Brecht, Bertolt 17
"The Bronco That Would Not Be Broken" (Lindsay) 80
The Brothers Karamazov (Dostoyevsky) 91, 94, 96, 109, 110, 111
"Bryan, Bryan, Bryan, Bryan" (Lindsay) 67, 76
Bunyan, John 13, 159
Burke, Edmund 21, 22
Bush, George W. 118

Calvinism 26, 63, 64
Campbell, Will 142
Canetti, Elias 9, 10, 181
chastity 57, 63

Chenetier, Marc 71
chivalry 57, 59
civil rights 114–118
classical–Christian civilization 2, 6, 8, 15, 16, 20, 22, 29, 31, 78, 84, 158, 174, 180, 181, 193
Coetzee, J.M. 136
cogito 33, 34, 37, 44, 46, 47, 50
Coles, Robert 114, 115, 119; *Flannery O'Connor's South* 114
Columbine massacre 30, 176, 177, 178, 183
communism 49, 82, 116, 127
"Concerning Edgar Allan Poe" (Lindsay) 54
"The Congo: A Study of the Negro Race" (Lindsay) 53, 54, 65, 82, 83, 87
Conner, Elizabeth 86
Constitution of the United States 21, 22
cultural reformation 55
culture of repudiation 29, 92

Dante (Durante degli Alighieri) 182
Davis, Hugh 90
A Death in the Family (Agee) 89, 97, 100
Deloria, Vine Victor, Jr. 173
Descartes, René 33–40, 45, 46, 50
Dostoevsky, Fyodor 2, 27, 89–112, 192; *The Brothers Karamazov* 91, 94, 96, 109, 110, 111; *The Idiot* 93, 112; *The Possessed* 89, 90, 93, 94, 97–99, 108, 110
DuBois, W.E.B. 83

Eastman, Max 82
"Eldorado" (Poe) 65
"Eleonora" (Poe) 62
Eliot, T.S. 5, 29, 155
The Enigma of Arrival (Naipaul) 145, 152
Eureka (Poe) 35–38, 44, 48, 50, 67, 68

201

Index

Evans, M. Stanton 14
Eventide (Haruf) 156, 158, 160, 168

"Factory Windows Are Always Broken" (Lindsay) 66
"The Fall of the House of Usher" (Poe) 45–47
family life 119, 168, 171, 181
fascism 131
Faulkner, William 7, 8, 17, 30, 146
Flannery O'Connor's South (Coles) 114
Fletcher, John Gould 52, 53
Flye, Father James Harold 90, 92, 96, 100
"For Annie" (Poe) 62, 65, 66
"The Forest-Ranger's Courtship" (Lindsay) 86
Foucault, Michael 109, 157, 186
Frank, Joseph 91, 93, 94, 98, 99, 100, 103, 106, 110, 112
Freudianism 113

Gelernter, David 179
"General William Booth Enters into Heaven" (Lindsay) 83
Giannone, Richard 114, 127
Ginsberg, Allen 128
Gnosticism 68
"The Gold-Bug" (Poe) 47
Goldberg, Jonah 129
The Golden Book of Springfield (Lindsay) 54
Goldwater, Barry 117
Gooch, Brad 116, 122
Gordon, Caroline 125
"Gospel of Beauty" (Lindsay) 75
Grant, Richard 156
Graves, Robert 87
Grimshaw, James A. 114
Guerrillas 150

The Habit of Being (O'Connor) 11, 113, 119, 120, 128, 135, 146
Hacker, P.M.S. 36
A Handy Guide for Beggars (Lindsay) 70
Haruf, Kent 2, 27, 28, 155–72, 180; *Eventide* 156, 158, 160, 168; *Plainsong* 155, 158, 159, 160, 166; *The Tie That Binds* 155, 159, 163, 164; *Where You Once Belonged* 155, 168, 169, 170–71
Hawkes, John 120, 121
Hayek, F.A. 13

heartland 8, 10, 53, 67, 71, 72, 76–79, 85, 86, 142, 156, 159, 160, 163, 167, 168
Hegel, Georg Wilhelm Friedrich 42, 49, 66, 186
Herder, Johann Gottfried 185, 186
Hester, Betty 120, 127, 128
Himmelfarb, Gertrude 9, 10, 11, 21, 71
Hitchcock, Alfred 19, 25 185
Hitchens, Peter 190
Hitler, Adolf 106, 107
Hobson, Fred 142; *Tell About the South* 142
Holocaust 107
"Hop-Frog" (Poe) 43, 57
A House for Mr. Biswas (Naipaul) 153
Hubben, William 111, 112
Hummer, T.R. 52
Hurricane Katrina 184
Hutchisson, James M. 53, 55, 64, 66, 67

"I Like Nancy Boyd" (Lindsay) 86
The Idiot (Dostoyevsky) 93, 112
I'll Take My Stand 137
"Incense" (Lindsay) 84

James Agee Rediscovered (Lofaro and Davis) 90, 92, 98, 107
Joyce, James 7
Judeo-Christian tradition 16, 19, 115, 118, 168, 180

"Kansas" (Lindsay) 74
Kennedy, John F. 116–17
Kirk, Russell 12, 111, 112, 114, 118, 119, 192, 193
Kolakowski, Leszek 35, 39, 43, 44, 50, 93, 98, 156, 157, 161
Kristol, Irving 19

Land of Ulro (Milosz) 158
"Landor's Cottage" (Poe) 65, 66
Lasch, Christopher 47
Lawrence, D.H. 5
Lee, Maryat 117, 119, 128
Let Us Now Praise Famous Men (Agee with Walker Evans) 89, 99, 101, 102, 103, 104, 105, 106, 107, 108, 109, 191
Letters to Father Flye (Agee) 91, 92, 95, 110
"Ligeia" (Poe) 62
Lindsay, Vachel 1, 26, 27, 51–88; "Alexander Campbell" 69; "The Bronco

202

Index

That Would Not Be Broken" 80; "Bryan, Bryan, Bryan, Bryan" 67, 76; "Concerning Edgar Allan Poe" 54; "The Congo: A Study of the Negro Race" 53, 54, 65, 82, 83, 87; "Factory Windows Are Always Broken" 66; "The Forest-Ranger's Courtship" 86; "General William Booth Enters into Heaven" 83; *The Golden Book of Springfield* 54; "Gospel of Beauty" 75; *A Handy Guide for Beggars* 70; "I Like Nancy Boyd" 86; "Incense" 84; "Kansas" 74; "Litany of the Heroes" 78; "The Wizard in the Street" 54
"Litany of the Heroes" (Lindsay) 78
Literary Occasions (Naipaul) 146, 148
Lofaro, Michael A. 90; *James Agee Rediscovered* (and Davis) 90, 92, 98, 107
"Longfellow War" 66
Lowell, Amy 87
Lowell, Robert 116, 119
Lytle, Andrew 58, 138; "The Subject of Southern Fiction" 58

male chivalry 56, 63
"The Man of the Crowd" (Poe) 40
Marxism 14, 49, 82, 130
"The Masque of the Red Death" (Poe) 47, 64
McCarthy, Mary 120
McCloskey, Mark 162
Mead, Walter B. 38
Mertz, Paul E. 102
Meyers, Jeffrey 146
Miles, Jonathan 156
Milosz, Czeslaw 46, 158, 179; *Land of Ulro* 158
Milton, John 59, 86; *Paradise Lost* 59
Minogue, Kenneth 16, 29, 39
Monroe, Harriet 54, 56
moral relativism 107, 108, 135, 183
Murdoch, Iris 128

Naipaul, V.S. 2, 13, 15, 19, 22, 29, 129, 136–54, 182; *The Enigma of Arrival* 145, 152; *A House for Mr. Biswas* 153; *Literary Occasions* 146, 148; *A Turn in the South* 136–54
Nashville Fugitives 151
New Deal 117
New Springfield 65, 69, 73
Nietzsche, Friedrich 111, 112, 157, 186

nihilism 89, 90, 95, 97, 110, 158, 176, 178, 183
Novak, Michael 2, 16; *The Spirit of Democratic Capitalism* 2, 16
nuclear family 16, 30, 44, 180

O'Connor, Flannery 1, 11, 13, 22, 113–35, 146, 168; *The Habit of Being* 11, 113, 119, 120, 128, 135, 146; *The Violent Bear It Away* 120–26, 128, 134
Orwell, George 18, 188

Panichas, George A. 4, 19
Paradise Lost (Milton) 59
Patterson, Edward H.N. 67
Pickford, Mary 59
Plainsong (Haruf) 155, 158, 159, 160, 166
Poe, Edgar Allan 1, 10, 12, 13, 22–26, 33–72, 76; "Eldorado" 65; "Eleonora" 62; *Eureka* 35–38, 44, 48, 50, 67, 68; "The Fall of the House of Usher" 45–47; "For Annie" 62, 65, 66; "The Gold-Bug" 47; "Hop-Frog" 43, 57; "Landor's Cottage" 65, 66; "Ligeia" 62; "Longfellow War" 66; "The Man of the Crowd" 40; "The Masque of the Red Death" 47, 64; "The Purloined Letter" 36, 41, 42, 43, 56; "Ulalume" 61, 70; "William Wilson" 34, 35
Polanyi, Michael 38
The Possessed (Dostoyevsky) 89, 90, 93, 94, 97–99, 108, 110
Postlethwaite, Diana 167
Pound, Ezra 53
Powderhead 130, 132–34
Puritanism 20, 28
"The Purloined Letter" (Poe) 36, 41, 42, 43, 56

race relations 82, 107, 140, 149, 150
Rampersad, Arnold 151
Reagan, Ronald 74, 118, 172
reformed Protestantism 8, 26, 28, 52, 58–60, 63, 64, 68, 74, 75, 80, 84
refuge 8, 11, 14, 17, 18, 23, 48, 57, 167
religious faith 18, 25, 28, 30, 79, 90–94, 96, 103, 110, 114, 115, 119, 120, 126, 127, 135, 141, 142, 157
Roe v. Wade 127
Roosevelt, Franklin D. 106, 107, 117
The Roots of Romanticism (Berlin) 94
Rossiter, Clinton 20

Index

Rousseau, Jean-Jacques 187
Ruggles, Eleanor 52, 53, 56, 68, 71, 82
rural culture 23, 73, 162

Scruton, Roger 18, 29, 180
secular humanism 121, 125, 126, 135, 176
Sessions, William 113
Silverman, Kenneth 56, 63, 64
Simms, William Gilmore 55
Simpson, Lewis P. 3, 48, 152
Smith, Steven B. 39
Sorell, Tom 35
The Spirit of Democratic Capitalism (Novak) 2, 16
Steele, Shelby 187
The Stylus 66
"The Subject of Southern Fiction" (Lytle) 58
suicide 95, 108, 170
Sutcliffe, F.E. 38

Tate, Allen 138, 146, 152
Tell About the South (Hobson) 142
tenant families 99, 101–09, 112
The Tie That Binds (Haruf) 155, 159, 163, 164
tramping 60, 69, 70, 74, 79
tribalism 31, 129, 173–81, 185–93
A Turn in the South (Naipaul) 136–54
Turner, Frederick Jackson 8

"Ulalume" (Poe) 61, 70
universal civilization 15, 144
Up from Slavery (Washington) 139, 150
urban-industrial culture 65, 67, 71, 73, 76, 78, 79, 86, 144, 145, 163

Vico and Herder: Two Studies in the History of Ideas (Berlin) 186
The Violent Bear It Away (O'Connor) 120–26, 128, 134

Washington, Booker T. 139, 150
Welty, Eudora 11
Where You Once Belonged (Haruf) 155, 168, 169, 170–71
"William Wilson" (Poe) 34, 35
Wills, Elizabeth Mann 58, 59, 60, 70
Wilson, Woodrow 81
Wittgenstein, Ludwig 18, 35, 36, 38, 40, 41, 46, 50
"The Wizard in the Street" (Lindsay) 54
Wood, Michael 145
World War II 107

Yaddo artists' colony 116
Yarmolinsky, Avram 110, 111

Zenkovsky, V.V. 92, 109